I0662569

Mary Hunt's

Debt-Proof Living

Mary Hunt's
Debt-Proof Living

MARY HUNT

BROADMAN
&HOLMAN
PUBLISHERS

Nashville, Tennessee

0-8054-2078-9

Published by Broadman & Holman Publishers, Nashville, Tennessee
Editorial Team: Vicki Crumpton, Janis Whipple, Kim Overcash
Typesetting: PerfecType

Unless otherwise stated all Scripture citation is from the NIV, the
Holy Bible, New International Version, copyright © 1973, 1978,
1984 by International Bible Society.

Disclaimer: The intent of this book is to provide accurate and author-
itative information about the subject matter covered. It is published
with the understanding that the publisher and author are not
engaged in rendering legal, accounting, or other professional services. If legal advice or other professional advice, including financial,
is required, the service of a competent professional should be sought.

For Harold
and all the joys that money cannot buy

Table of Contents

Introduction

The economy is booming. Unemployment is down. The stock market is up. Yet Americans are deeper in debt than ever before. What is wrong with this picture?

The consumer credit industry wants us to believe consumer debt is necessary to bridge the gap between our pitiful incomes and the lifestyles we deserve. Lines of credit have become the socially acceptable means of survival in this gotta-have-it-now world. Everywhere we turn we're told that no matter our income we deserve to be several levels higher.

That is wrong. We don't need more credit or more stuff. What we need is the courage to think for ourselves, the maturity to tailor our lifestyles to fit within our incomes, and the willingness to find contentment where we are and with what we have.

We need the courage to understand that money is not for spending. It is for managing first and then for spending. We need to grow up and see money not as power or prestige but as protection—God's provision for our physical needs.

Contrary to financial pressures and stress we might feel from time to time, the problem is not that we don't have enough money. The problem is we don't know how to manage what we do have. We see money as a qualifier. It is a down payment on what we want. It is the lever we use to lift ourselves to economic privileges we have not earned.

For most of the past decade I have devoted my life to learning about money and personal finance. I was not, however, born with the passion I now possess.

At first, it was a matter of survival. It took twelve years for me to plunge my family into the pit of financial despair.

Trapped. It appeared there was no way out. But appearances are not always what they seem. Slowly but surely we began to fight, scratch, and work our way out.

In 1992 we'd been working on our horrendous mountain of debt for nearly ten years and had about $12,000 of debt remaining. I desperately wanted to find an additional source of income so we could make those final payments, close the chapter on that part of our lives, and move on.

About that time I had a wild idea. What if I created some kind of forum so that I could help others help themselves and help myself in the process? It seemed plausible and a way I might be able to speed the payback process. I had nothing to lose by trying, so I went for it.

My number one reason for starting a newsletter was not a secret: I was in it for the money. I came clean in the first issue of *Cheapskate Monthly.* I told everyone who would listen that for pocket change I would provide them with information and motivation to get out of debt just as my family was doing. We would take the journey together.

I am smarter now than I was then because—to my utter amazement—teaching teaches the teacher. That fact came as a big surprise. Naively, I thought I knew it all—at least enough to fill the few issues of the newsletter I planned to produce.

I was wrong: I never dreamed I could become so passionate about a subject I had heretofore considered hopelessly boring.

I did raise the funds we needed to reach our goal—and in a relatively short period.

By my original design it was time to move on. But I'd developed such a bond with so many readers that my new passion transcended my original plan. I was hooked, and pulling the plug on the newsletter was not an option. It didn't cross my mind.

I also noticed that something weird was going on. My new knowledge was intoxicating; I couldn't get enough. I was driven to learn more and more. Every week I'd receive stacks of letters from readers. Some were filled with questions; others were cries for help. Some were testimonials about how this person or that couple was understanding for the first time ever the principles and specific steps to take charge of their finances and become effective money managers.

The more I wrote, the more I developed a burning desire to know more. As I learned, I watched with astonishment as my family's personal financial picture began to improve—significantly. As I taught my readers to anticipate the unexpected, we became better prepared. As I waded into the waters of beginning investing, our portfolio took an amazing growth spurt. I could hardly believe the confidence I felt in the knowledge I was gaining.

Often I would step back and look at myself through eyes of astonishment. "Look at you! What an unlikely development for someone who was so financially ignorant, so downtrodden by debt, and so unwilling to change." I liked what I saw. My husband liked it too.

Since then, *Cheapskate Monthly* has been in continuous publication, I have written lots of books, and I've spoken to many thousands of people.

I have cheered and teared as countless numbers of readers announced their victory over debt. I have also agonized watching some of them return to the lifestyles that got them into the mess in the first place.

There is no doubt in my mind that getting out of debt is the important first step in gaining control of personal finances. But then what?

The only way to stay out of debt and keep moving toward a secure financial future is to adopt a new way of living. That means giving up old ways of thinking, changing attitudes, and rejecting the notion that we are entitled to more than we can afford even when the credit industry says we are more than qualified.

Let me warn you right up front: I am seriously opinionated on this matter of money, credit, and consumer debt. I refuse to pull punches or take the soft approach. I lived far too many years in financial bondage to see that condition as tolerable. I paid back more than $100,000 in unsecured debt and lived to tell about it. I've been there. I know what it takes. I know the temptations and challenges that hit us every day. It has occurred to me that there might be more than one way to do things, but I'm not ready to concede that just yet.

I am the first to admit that the countless offers of entitlement and promises of happiness that wash up in our mailboxes and splash against our television screens day after day are more than just enticing. They are downright seductive. And I know the pain and personal devastation of cashing in on those promises only to find that having it now and paying for it later is not the path to contentment and peace of mind. It is the way to self-centeredness and defeat.

I have written this book to present my case, in the most powerful way I know, that it is possible to live a rich, fulfilling life without consumer debt.

One of the most gratifying aspects of what I do is to have readers tell me I've changed the direction of their lives. If that has been so for even one person, I am blessed, because I know my passion has found purpose. In that, I have found unspeakable fulfillment.

## Part One

Debt-Proof Living in Theory

In the same way you would insist on a sturdy, well-built foundation on which to build your dream house, you need a strong foundation on which to build your financial life. In part 1, we are going to create that solid foundation using sound yet simple financial principles that will stand the test of time.

Don't be surprised if at first you find some of this information overwhelming. There's a lot to learn and a lot to do even if your finances are in pretty good condition. You won't be able to do everything at once, so relax and learn all you can. Take it one step at a time, and you will find that you can begin immediately to improve your personal financial picture.

I am confident you will find a sense of enjoyment and personal satisfaction as you get your debts and spending under control, as you learn specific strategies and let go of the hit-and-miss method of money management. Everything will not change overnight, but as you take the first steps and then commit to steady progress, you will be well on your way to achieving the financial security you desire.

## Chapter One

Debt-Proof Living Philosophy

MOVING FROM DEBT RECOVERY TO DEBT PREVENTION

*Knowledge is the difference between really living and just
existing. Existing is instinctual; living is the exercise of
certain learned skills, attitudes and abilities that you
have acquired and honed to a sharp and focused edge.*

Phillip C. McGraw

Getting out of debt is like getting through boot camp. It's a lot of
hard work, and some days you want to quit. But when graduation
day arrives, memories of pain and trouble pale in the light of the
pride and accomplishment you feel. You made it! You didn't quit.

Like graduation, becoming debt free is not the end—it's the
beginning of a whole new adventure. To drop out at graduation and go back to your old way of living would be to turn your
back on everything for which you have been preparing. It
would be to close the door on your dreams of financial ease. In
some way, it would diminish the importance of what you
accomplished. Who would be so foolish as to do the difficult
work and then not stick around to enjoy the reward?

Not long ago I heard from someone who dropped out. In
her letter, Bonnie described how she and her husband had

gotten into quite a debt mess during the early years of their marriage. It took them three years to unload $18,000 of credit card debt, but they did it! They were debt free. And they assumed they were finished. That is when they dropped out.

Bonnie and her husband bought a home and soon welcomed their first child. Of course, they needed all kinds of things for this new chapter in their lives. The baby needed a new crib; they needed a new sofa. It all seemed so logical and necessary.

Apparently, they needed many other things too, because by the time Bonnie wrote, they were in debt again—this time they owed more than $26,000. Bonnie described how she and her husband make good money, live fast-paced lives, have no savings, and spend thousands each year eating out. Every nickel that comes in goes out to keep the bills at bay.

I could feel Bonnie's panic as I read her closing paragraph: "We did it once. We know we can do it again. But how do we avoid falling back into the cycle of debt the next time? There must be some way for us to cure ourselves of this disease once and for all. I'm afraid that if we become debt free this time, the way we think about money might lead us right back into debt again . . . and again . . . and again. How can we win over debt for a lifetime? Help!"

I must have stared at that letter for a full hour as a million thoughts raced through my mind. Over and over, I kept coming back to the simple truth that getting out of debt is only the first step. That is how you get to the starting point. Staying out of debt and moving forward to financial independence—that's the bigger challenge. And that's where the big rewards await.

I thought about the thousands of people I have met and communicated with over the years who have made it to the starting line. Are they progressing, or did they, like Bonnie, mistake the starting line for the finish line? How many of them grabbed the prize and went back to their old ways of living and thinking, putting the lessons they learned in "boot camp" far away from their daily lives? Did they go through this, hoping that they wouldn't have to think about money anymore?

Bonnie's letter brought to mind my own situation and how I repaid a boatload of debt; how the temptation to fall back into the old ways of incurring debt becomes less intense and certainly manageable, but never really goes away. What keeps me from going back? How can I encourage people not to stop but to move on to the next level and beyond? Is it possible to win over debt for a lifetime?

I startled myself when I jumped to my feet and answered Bonnie as if she were sitting across the desk. Yes, it is possible, and no, I will never go back! You have to get to the starting line, establish your long-term goal of reaching financial freedom, define that goal in terms of steps, and then change gears from debt recovery to debt prevention. You have to think specifically, not generally, about how you're going to get there and then rejoice because each step from now on will be one of progress, not repair.

I continued pontificating, in the privacy of my office, on this matter of maintenance—a way of living I would soon call *debt-proof living*. It was a defining moment as I described to myself what a debt-proof life looks like: You spend less than you earn; you give, save, and invest confidently and consistently; your financial decisions are purposeful; you turn away from impulsive behavior; you shun unsecured debt; you borrow cautiously; you anticipate the unexpected; you scrutinize your purchases; and you reach for your goals by following a specific plan.

Depending on where you live, you may recall with clarity the year of El Niño. That's what the media called that curious climate condition of 1998. El Niño made weathermen from coast to coast giddy with all kinds of unusual weather to report.

In California where I live, El Niño washed sections of the beach out to sea and took a few homes along for the ride. It was amazing to watch as certain other structures were pounded relentlessly but remained intact. Was El Niño selectively cruel, targeting some homes and for no apparent reason sparing others? No, he slammed the entire area with equal force and showed no mercy. What made the difference was how the homes were constructed. Those tied to bedrock weathered the storms just fine; those built on shifting sand did not.

Before El Niño's visit, my untrained eye could not predict which homes would survive such an ordeal. Foundations aren't exactly out there for everyone to see. Often it was the more showy, ostentatious homes that flunked the test. They looked good, but they could not remain standing when things got rough.

In the same way that Laguna Beach homeowners are well advised to make sure their homes are tied to something immovable, the way you manage your money must be tied to unchanging truths and principles. If your financial behaviors are based on shallow thoughts and fickle feelings, the storms of life will wipe you out. And there will be storms—I guarantee it.

Bonnie and her husband were washed out to the sea of debt because they did not tie themselves to a solid foundation of unchanging truth. Once they saw that the initial problem was fixed, they tossed aside the principles that had served them so well in getting out of debt. They handled debt recovery well but failed to kick into debt-prevention mode. They got to the starting line, and then they quit.

Truth be told, you may not have a clue as to what you believe about money and its role in your life. Or you might firmly believe things that are not true. No matter what you've done or believed in the past about money and how to take care of it, now is the time to tie yourself to a foundation that will not change, one that will withstand the storms of life.

PRINCIPLES FOR DEBT-PROOF LIVING

YOU MUST NEVER KEEP IT ALL

The first thing you must do when money flows into your life is give some of it away.

YOU MUST NEVER SPEND IT ALL

Always pay yourself before anyone else. Always. Not only must you set aside a portion of all the money that you earn, but you have to put that money to work for you. Merely saving is not enough.

THERE ARE ONLY FIVE THINGS YOU CAN DO WITH MONEY

Give it, save it, invest it, lend it, and spend it. Notice where spending comes in that lineup: last. Spending should never be the first thing you do with your money. The proper management of money is specific and orderly. If we short-circuit the system by spending it first, we create fiscal disorder and, finally, financial chaos.

GOD IS THE SOURCE

Your employer, your spouse, your investments, your trust account, your parents, or any other entity is not the source of your money. God—who gave you the talents, intelligence, and ability to think and work—is the source. Your responsibility is to be a good steward of all that you receive. Employers, investments, spouses, and parents are only the conduits in the delivery system. Grabbing onto this truth will bring a sense of peace and calm to your life. No longer will you fear a drop in the stock market or the plunging of real estate values. No longer will you lie awake worrying about losing your job. The way your money is delivered may change radically and frequently, but the source never changes. It is the same yesterday, today, and forever.

WHAT YOU RECEIVE IS WHAT YOU DESERVE

God promises to supply all your needs. He says if you delight yourself in him he will also give you your desires. He is not ignorant of your needs or your desires. He never falls asleep on the job or misses a due date. All he asks is that you obey his laws and trust his word. Those who do, and go on to demonstrate they can be trusted with more, are blessed beyond what they deserve or what they could possibly imagine.

PAY CASH

Plastic—ATM cards, debit cards, and credit cards—are all stand-ins for money. They are not the real thing; they are just representatives—and often poor ones—when they enable debt. Paying cash requires making some lifestyle changes and sacrifices, but it will keep you from drowning in a sea of red ink on your journey to financial freedom. Paying cash keeps you focused. Paying cash promotes contentment because it adds meaning and value to the things you do buy. Paying cash lets you own things, not merely acquire them. Paying cash adds meaning and value to the thing purchased. Paying cash makes spending difficult and uncomfortable. And that is exactly the way it should be.

NO DEBT NO MATTER WHAT

Unsecured debt is like cancer. At first it is not life-threatening because it involves only a cell or two. But it never stays tiny. It begins to grow and then it takes over. It becomes the master; you become its slave. Never believe that a little debt, manageable as it may seem, is OK. It is not. Neither is a little cancer.

DEVELOP A STRATEGY

Without a plan for getting there, reaching your goal of financial freedom will remain a dream. A plan turns a dream into a goal. Having a plan liberates you from depending on willpower. Willpower is unreliable emotional fuel. When you have it, it can get you going at breakneck speed; but once the emotion is gone, you fizzle. You should not rely on willpower. A written plan stands firm whether you're on an emotional roller coaster or an even keel.

MORE MONEY IS NOT THE ANSWER

I used to believe that if I had more money, everything would be fine. Then we'd get a raise, and we'd have more money—but it wasn't enough. That money became the down payment—the qualifier—to get whatever it was that cost more money than we actually had. And that made things worse because we turned more money into more debt.

Not long ago I heard from Lynn, and sadly, her story illustrates this point perfectly:

> I am thirty years old and have worked since I was fifteen. I married straight out of high school. I have always been good at selling any product I represented, and that is where my nightmare begins.
>
> While working at my first "real" job in a bank, a customer recruited me to become a copier salesperson. I was hesitant until he showed me his commission

check for that month. I got really excited about my potential to make good money too. So I resigned my position and started selling office products.

My first commission check was $1,500; the next one was even better. After a couple of months I began to see just how much I could make, so I leased a new BMW for myself and a fully loaded Nissan Pathfinder for my husband. I needed many other things as well to demonstrate to people just how successful I was. I began incurring debt, all the while thinking *I'll just pay it off with my next commission check.*

As the months went by, meeting my quota became more difficult. I worried about where I would find my next customer. The stress became unbearable, so I quit that job after three years. But that didn't stop the car payments and the unsecured debts that were breathing down our necks.

Lynn's letter went on for many more pages to describe how the situation worsened. She closed by announcing their plans to file for bankruptcy.

Let's go back and see where this train started to derail. I believe it happened the day Lynn impressed herself with her newfound wealth and failed to see that first $1,500 commission check as $1,500 cash. She wrongly viewed it as a harbinger of things to come. To her it *represented* a life of luxury, where she could have anything she wanted and where money would be no object. She assumed the checks would continue to roll in and, of course, in ever-greater amounts.

Sure enough, one more did roll in. Now a nebulous representation became a guarantee on the future. Until she acted on her false assumptions, we can accuse her only of stupid *thinking.* She *acted* stupidly and to her future detriment, however, when she used her current income to qualify for those fancy leased cars and, as she put it, many things to "demonstrate" her success. Perhaps she attended just one too many "Fake It Till You Make It!" motivational sales seminars.

Lynn's situation is a perfect example of why, for most people who carry revolving consumer debt, more money will never be enough. More money only creates more debt! Then the stress and unrelenting nature of more debt requires more money, and a vicious cycle—where more money is never enough—establishes itself.

IT IS NOT HOW MUCH MONEY YOU MAKE BUT WHAT YOU DO WITH IT THAT MATTERS

I have a feeling you learned sufficiently from Lynn's mistakes to be way ahead of me on this simple truth. It is possible that had she and her husband made a pledge to live by simple, sound, financial values, they would have enjoyed a nice lifestyle. They were making decent money. They just didn't know, or didn't care, how to take care of it.

Imagine two identical families. Same income, same expenses—everything exactly the same. The only difference: the Smiths are into instant gratification while the Joneses prefer delayed gratification.

The Smiths act on their desires as they come up. They buy now and agree to pay later. They carry revolving consumer debt equal to that of the average American family, which means they pay around $1,200 a year *in interest* on their revolving, unsecured debts.

The Joneses have no unsecured debt. If they don't have the money to pay for the things they want, they wait until they do. Because they do not send $1,200 a year ($100 each month) to the consumer credit industry to cover interest the way the

Smiths must, they funnel it into an investment account that earns an average 10 percent a year.

At the end of ten years, the Smiths have stuff, but $0 invested. The Joneses, on the other hand, have the same things (remember these families do everything alike) and a tidy nest egg of $20,925.90.

No matter how many times I consider these facts, I am no less amazed. The fictional Smiths and Joneses live the same. They buy the exact same things; they make the exact same amount of money. They are mirror images. The only difference is the timing of their spending. The Smiths spend first and *pay* interest later. The Joneses save first and *earn* interest later.

PAY IN FULL NOW OR PAY TWICE LATER

In my "pre-days," when I was dumber than dirt about debt and personal finance, I assumed that if I found something on sale, I could *not* afford not to purchase it. Because I was always strapped for cash, I found the situation absolute justification to use a credit card to make the purchase. Little did I know—or care—that by the time I made all the minimum payments, racked up all kinds of interest, and eventually paid for those sale items, I had paid twice or three times (depending on the interest rate) the sale price. But worse, because it took so long to pay something off, chances were very high that I didn't even have the stuff any longer.

LIVING WITHOUT DEBT IS TANTAMOUNT TO A TAX-FREE INCREASE

If the Smiths, as described above, were to see the value of paying off their debts rapidly and living without unsecured debts, they would immediately have an additional $100 in *their* pocket, not in the credit card company's coffers—dollars on which taxes have already been paid.

REASONS TO DEBT-PROOF YOUR LIFE

TO PROTECT YOUR MARRIAGE

Whether you are married now or hope to be one day, you need to understand just how devastating debt can be on the relationships you hold most dear. Experts report that half of all new marriages fail, and as many as 80 percent of all divorces are the direct result of financial trouble. Debt is a major symptom of pending financial trouble. Divorce is expensive, but more than that, it is devastating for all parties, especially the children. If strengthening your marriage were the only reason to debt-proof your life, it would be reason enough.

TO SURVIVE LEAN TIMES

If you have a load of debt, even the slightest shift in your economic picture can plunge you into financial despair. Debt represents a very heavy load and makes the journey nearly unbearable. It offers few, if any, options. If you are debt free, you are traveling light. Living without debt offers alternatives to help you survive times of challenge and struggle.

TO REDUCE YOUR STRESS

Financial stress comes in many forms: worry, sleeplessness, communication breakdown, depression, and anxiety. The medical community reminds us that stress takes a terrible toll on our health. We are less immune to disease and illness. Our bodies bear the consequences of the heavy loads our minds must carry when we place our lives in financial jeopardy. Debt-proof living can turn stress into joy, peace of mind, and rest.

TO PROTECT YOUR FUTURE

Revolving debt forces you to transfer your future wealth to your creditors' bank accounts. Debt-proof living is an insurance policy for your future income. It builds a protective shield that creditors cannot penetrate. One woman I spoke with recently brought this truth home to me in a poignant way. Only months before our encounter, her mother died leaving her a sizable inheritance. How comforted she should have felt knowing she was so important to her mother that she purposely blessed her daughter in this way. Although the mother would never know, this woman had run up such significant debt that it was going to take every single penny of her inheritance to bring her current and back into favor with her creditors. Through tears, she finally understood what it means to transfer your future wealth to your creditors.

TO TEACH YOUR CHILDREN

If your kids read magazines, go to school, watch television, listen to the radio, know what a fast-food restaurant is, or have ever been inside a store or supermarket, they already know something about entitlement and instant gratification. Right under your nose they are developing into world-class consumers. They may be well on their way to becoming future debtors of America too. If you do nothing to intervene, statistics indicate your kids are headed for a life that will be severely and negatively impacted by consumer debt. By debt-proofing your life, you will affect your children's lives as well because families reproduce themselves. Kids learn through observation and imitation, and when all the smoke clears, they usually turn out like their parents.

TO EXPERIENCE FULLY GOD'S CARE AND PROVISION

By letting go of debt and depending on God to keep his promises to supply all our needs, we open our lives to his power. If you are always running ahead taking care of everything with a credit card, you may never know how God intended to care for you.

THREE PERSONAL MONEY MANAGEMENT STYLES

The way I see this whole matter of personal money management, there are three basic management styles or ways of life.

First are those people (the majority of Americans, by the way) who are what I call revolvers. They carry credit card balances from one month to the next. They owe far more than they can pay; they spend more than they earn. They are forever juggling finances, trying to keep their heads above water. Revolvers enjoy the idea of a cashless society. They are every consumer credit marketing department's dream customer because they fit a predictable profile and contribute to the huge profit margins of the credit card companies.

The next group is composed of those who live paycheck to paycheck and spend every dime they make. They are the daredevils. They flirt with credit cards, debit cards, and ATM cards, finding it more convenient to swipe than carry cash. These folks usually pay their credit card balance in full every month, but just barely—and often with nothing left over. Now and then they might revolve for two or three months to get the account back to paid status (the holidays are always a struggle), but for the most part they stay even.

The third group is the smallest and is made up of people whom I lovingly refer to as debt-proof livers (a term I don't say aloud for obvious reasons—maybe DPLs would be a better designation). They embrace the debt-proof lifestyle because they do not live on credit nor do they flirt with credit cards. They live according to a specific plan. What they do with their money is by design. They give, they save, they invest, they live beneath their means. They expect the unexpected, they are prepared, they live exuberantly and with confidence because they can smile at the future.

Before we continue discussing these money management styles, I should explain something about myself—something that affects how I write and communicate.

I'm not very good with abstract thinking or technical concepts. I have to be able to "see" to understand. I have to see pictures, illustrations, and color. If these cannot be tangible, they must at least be visible in my mind's eye.

Murky concepts and boring data do not stimulate my imagination. They bounce off my mind as if they were made of rubber.

That is why I love word pictures, those visual images created with words alone. For me, a word picture is an incredibly powerful tool that turns an abstract thought into a clear concept, complete with shape and dimension.

I have learned to attach visual images—word pictures—to difficult concepts and boring data as a way to bring that information to life. When it penetrates my mind, I can process and digest it. Drawing and then observing word pictures is the only way I know to transform dull and tedious concepts into clear and useful information.

As a person with the attention span of a gnat, I depend on word pictures not only when I write but also when I read or listen. Visual images hold my attention and colorize my thoughts. Word pictures keep me awake and focused. And if they make me laugh, all the better.

As a little girl, I loved to listen to the stories Jesus told that are recorded in the Bible. My dad told me that those parables are earthly stories with heavenly meanings. They are word pictures Jesus used to teach new concepts in terms his followers could understand.

I recall how the parables of the woman with the lost coin and the shepherd with ninety-nine sheep gave shape and meaning to adult-sized concepts. Today I can see those word pictures exactly the way I saw them when I was five. They are masterpieces hung forever in the gallery of my mind.

With that in mind, let me throw on a smock and beret, grab my palette and canvas, and paint for you some word pictures to illustrate the three types of money managers.

DEBT-RIDDEN DEXTER

You probably tried walking up the down escalator when you were a kid. It can be quite a challenge, but even so, it is fun—for a while. That's exactly what Dexter is doing. Can you see him? A full-grown man attempting to reach the next floor but doing it completely the wrong way.

When he first started this crazy way of getting ahead, he could keep in sync with the speed of the escalator. It would move one step down; Dexter would take one step up. Down, up. Down, up.

But look at what's going on now. He's trying to do this up-the-down-escalator action while carrying baggage—heavy baggage and lots of it. He has two gigantic suitcases, one in each hand, a bulging briefcase jammed under one arm, and another very large box under the other arm. He has a heavy bag slung over one shoulder that is making things even more difficult. He can't see his feet for all the gear, most of which he keeps dropping. In his attempts to recover, he finds himself back at the bottom, hat askew, shirt torn, and shoes flying. Finally he gets everything back under control and begins the challenging climb all over again.

It is quite frustrating to watch him. *Can't this guy see what he's doing wrong?* It is obvious to the spectators what changes he needs to make to get where he needs to go, but he's so wrapped up in his predicament, he hasn't the time or the inclination to listen. He is determined to do this his way.

The perspiration pours from him whenever he attempts to take the moving stairs three at a time. Lenders, disguised as concerned onlookers, offer a helping hand. He always reaches out to accept their "help," and it does relieve his burden—but only temporarily. They make it look as if they are helping to carry his heavy load, but the truth is, they are making poor Dexter's bags heavier.

He can forget about making any progress. Actually, he's forever losing momentum. Remaining upright becomes his impossible dream. He's an exhausted, beat-up, pitiful sight. Even the slightest misstep sends him crashing to the bottom.

Dexter is debt-ridden, and he is not enjoying life as he might if he didn't have all this heavy baggage. Sadly, he will soon find himself defeated, flat on his back in the basement.

PAYCHECK-TO-PAYCHECK PENELOPE

Penny is walking as well—on a treadmill. Things are different for her. Unlike Dexter, she has no heavy baggage, just her purse and a small bag. She stands upright, maintains a perfectly timed stride, and appears to be doing a really great job at walking. It *looks* as if she is going somewhere, but of course she is not making progress. She is expending all kinds of energy but is getting nowhere. Because it takes so much effort to stay in exactly the same place, one wonders how long she'll be able to keep it up.

Penny spends what she earns. Month after month she keeps up. She faithfully pays her credit card balances, makes the rent on time, even drives an above-average leased automobile. *So what if I don't save and have nothing in reserve,* she reasons. *At least I'm not in debt.*

From time to time, Penny slips up for any number of reasons. For example, it usually takes her three months to pay the holiday bills. When something unexpected hits, like car repairs or a new roof, of course she has no choice but to spread the payments over time. That's when she loses her rhythm and nearly falls off the edge. But she has those handrails, and she hangs on. It isn't critical. She recovers quickly and then does double time to get back to that old position—back in sync—knowing she can't take a rest. She can't slow down or change a thing.

Penny gets a raise now and then, and that allows her to increase her speed slightly. Sometimes she even runs a while. But then, because of higher prices, an added expense, or something unexpected, she settles back into her rut. She lives paycheck to paycheck, spending all that she earns. Nothing left over. Always walking, never progressing.

DEBT-PROOF PETER

Look at Peter. He's walking at a brisk pace, sport jacket flung over one shoulder, head held high, smiling at everyone he sees. Not far ahead is a beautiful thing: a moving side-walk—one of those people-sized conveyor belts.

He steps onto the moving sidewalk. Without changing his brisk pace and normal stride, he's almost flying. The air is rushing through his hair. He even feels taller.

Peter's regular steps on the morning sidewalk now become the equivalent of three or more of his unaided strides. How cool is that? He just keeps walking. Without increased effort on his part, he is nearly propelled to his destination—and in record time.

If he chooses to slow down, or even stop for a rest, that's OK. He just moves to the right so others can pass on the left. He doesn't lose momentum. He doesn't slip back or lose ground. Even though he stops walking, he continues to enjoy a pleasant ride. He has a choice: to walk briskly or to slow down and enjoy the journey. Either way, he still makes progress toward his destination.

Peter is a perfect picture of someone living a debt-proof life. He finds meaning in the journey, not the destination. Because he carries no debt—choosing instead to put the money he isn't sending to creditors to work for his future—his money works for him and produces offspring that also work for him. His momentum is turbocharged, without increased effort on his part or the need for additional energy. He doesn't stumble and fall, and he's not obsessed with money. He's enjoying life.

How you travel through life is completely your decision. You can choose to go the wrong way on a one-way escalator carrying such a heavy load that you cannot even see where you are going; you can get stuck on a treadmill living paycheck to paycheck; or you can choose to travel on a moving sidewalk that will take you where you want to go.

I'm pleading with you to make a decision right now to build a strong financial foundation into which you will drill deeply and drop the pilings for your life. Learn the principles so well that you could repeat them in your sleep. Hang onto them for dear life when your emotions go wild, when temptations overwhelm. Depend on them when everything in you wants to quit and go to that place that exists only in your imagination—where money is no object and you can spend with reckless abandon.

I can promise that the foundation built on debt-proof living principles will stand up under all kinds of circumstances. When the challenges come—and they will—your foundation will hold and you will make it through.

Debt-proof living is not a righteous call to deprivation. It is not defined by austerity, poverty, guilt, and fear. It is not about extremes, bizarre behavior, misery, hoarding, or finding a way to recycle dryer lint.

Debt-proof living is a lifestyle where you spend less than you earn; you give, save, and invest confidently and consistently; your financial decisions are purposeful; you turn away from compulsive behavior; you shun unsecured debt; you borrow cautiously; you anticipate the unexpected; you scrutinize your purchases; and you reach for your goals by following a specific plan.

Debt-proof living is about generosity, gratitude, and obedience. It is about sound choices and effective decisions. To debt-proof your life means to know exactly what to do with your money and have the freedom to earn and spend it when and how you choose. Debt-proof living is a way of life—a financially disciplined lifestyle that produces peace and joy. Debt-proof living is your invitation to a rich and abundant life.

Chapter Two

Intelligent Borrowing or Stupid Debt

ALL DEBTS ARE NOT CREATED EQUAL

The only thing worse than investing in things that depreciate is paying interest on money invested in things that depreciate.

Blaine Harris

Not all debts are created equal, nor is every type of loan hazardous to your wealth.

There is a world of difference between a home mortgage and a revolving credit card balance. Both are liabilities for which the borrower is legally responsible. The first I call *intelligent borrowing;* the latter is *stupid debt.*

Those who are living debt free and are debt-proofing their lives would sooner poke toothpicks under their fingernails than live in the grip of stupid debt. They participate only in intelligent borrowing, if at all.

INTELLIGENT BORROWING

Intelligent borrowing means that some level of safety and limited risk for both the lender and the borrower is built into the transaction. Here is what intelligent borrowing looks like:

1. The borrower has a safety valve—a legally and morally sound alternative to get out of the obligation.

2. The debt is secured. The lender holds something that is at least as valuable as the amount of the loan, something known as collateral. Think of collateral as a security deposit for the lender.

3. The loan is for something that has a reasonable life expectancy of more than three years as opposed to something that will be down the drain before the bill arrives.

4. The loan is for something that will increase in value, unlike a couple of movie tickets and dinner in a fancy restaurant or great new outfit.

5. The interest rate is reasonable.

The best example of intelligent borrowing is a real estate loan or home mortgage. Let's see how it measures up to each of the intelligent borrowing characteristics:

1. Is there a safety valve or escape route? Yes, there is a way of escape for both the borrower and the lender. If you, the borrower, find you just can't handle those high payments or you want out for any other reason at all, you can sell the house and pay the lender from the proceeds of the sale. Because the loan becomes an asset for the lender, he can sell his position.

2. Is the debt collateralized? Yes. With a mortgage, the real estate is the collateral—the lender's security. The lender has a legal lien on the property until the mortgage is paid in full, and that gives him a legal position in the transaction. If you as the borrower do not hold up your end of the bargain to which you agreed, the lender may take the property as payment for the outstanding loan.

3. Does the purchase have a reasonable life expectancy of more than three years? Yes, of course. This is true not only for the structure itself but also for the land on which it sits. Buying a home is a long-term investment.
4. Will it increase in value over time? Yes. Real estate is always considered an appreciating asset even though specific values may decline during economic cycles. As a general rule, real estate always gains in value over time.
5. Is the interest rate relatively reasonable? Yes. In nearly all situations, mortgage rates are lower than other types of consumer loans, usually by as much as two-thirds.

STUPID DEBT

Take every aspect of the intelligent borrowing scenario above and think just the opposite. Now you understand stupid debt.

This is the kind of debt you agree to, often impulsively, when your desire is in high gear and your brain is in neutral. It is so easy—much too easy.

While there are many ways to rack up a pile of debt, credit cards are by far the most popular. Almost anyone these days—even high school students—can get a credit card. There's no qualifying process to speak of, no long applications to fill out or references to submit. Students don't even need a job or a cosigner.

Someone with a credit card and available credit limit can in effect take out very expensive loans on a whim and at nearly every place, including cyberspace. You simply make your decision, swipe the magic plastic, sign your name, and presto!—you've made a very long commitment to stupid debt. Painless?

Sure, it is in the beginning. But not for long, my friend. Not for long.

Let's say you use your credit card to acquire the very latest computer, complete with scanner, fax modem, jumbo monitor, DVD player, turbocharged CD Rom, and—the best part—a free printer. It's on sale (which to many naïve consumers is a clear sign of providential entitlement) and you want it right now. Why should your lack of cash prevent you from making this really good deal? (Remember the free printer.) You have plenty of room on your account to cover it.

As you haul that baby to the car, the last thing on your mind is how you will actually pay for it. You didn't consider for one second how this new debt will affect your current payment structure. It can't be that bad, you reason, because you got approved. And you get a *free printer!*

Let's see how this purchase measures up against the criteria for intelligent borrowing:

1. Does the borrower have a way out at any time? No. If you don't pay as agreed, the credit card company won't come after the computer—they'll come after you. Unless you can sell the computer for what you paid for it (fat chance), you have no way out.

2. Is the debt collateralized? No. The credit card company is holding nothing of value to fulfill this debt if you are unable to pay. But they've got a tight grip on you. They don't want that computer or anything else you buy with a credit card, for that matter. This loan is unsecured.

3. Does this purchase have a life expectancy of at least three years? No matter how you cut it, a three-year-old computer is not exactly cutting-edge technology. By its third birthday it has little monetary value even though it may still compute. In fact, that paragraph I wrote

only moments ago listing the features of this machine is already out-of-date. Just think about that for a minute!

4. Will it appreciate in value? From the minute you walk out of the store, a computer is in the fast lane to obsolescence. It's depreciating with every click of the mouse.

5. Is the interest rate reasonable? No. As of this writing, the average credit card annual interest rate is 17.8 percent, while a thirty-year fixed-rate mortgage is 6.79 percent per year.

The computer purchase fails the intelligent borrowing test miserably by getting a "no" response to all five questions. Paying for a computer over time cannot qualify as intelligent borrowing, and if paid for with a credit card or other form of consumer credit, it would qualify as a stupid debt.

ANATOMY OF A STUPID DEBT

Let's say this computer deal we're analyzing has a price tag of $2,000. The credit card terms are typical: 17.8 percent interest with minimum monthly payments of 3 percent of the outstanding balance. I just plugged those figures into my Minimum Payment Credit-Card Interest Calculator[1] and—hold onto your floppy disk—it will take 13 years and 9 months to pay the total price tag of $3,759, including interest. Did you get that? Thirteen years to pay nearly twice the purchase price for a computer that will be functionally obsolete in much less than half the time. There's no other way to characterize such a transaction than pretty stupid.

What will make things even worse is if, after two or three years, you decide to upgrade to a new computer even though you still have ten years to pay on the first one. Nevertheless, if the credit is available, it is quite easy to add another purchase (like a new computer) to the growing load of debt.

In no time at all, the forever revolving credit card balance is not seen for what it really is (a very high-priced loan on a lot of stuff you might not even own anymore) but rather as a normal part of life—like the rent, phone bill, and cost of food. In fact, I could show you high school personal finance curriculum that suggests keeping consumer debt at a manageable level, not to exceed 20 percent of income. I find that somewhat outrageous.

BEYOND STUPID

While the computer example is remarkably illogical, other kinds of stupid debt make the computer scenario appear somewhat reasonable. Turning restaurant meals, travel, groceries, utility bills, movie tickets, vacations, gifts, gasoline, and school clothes into debt and then choosing to pay for them with minimum monthly payments over many years and at rates that effectively double the original costs brings new meaning to the term *stupid.*

Spending money you don't have yet to pay for things you don't have anymore is anything but intelligent. Nevertheless, that is exactly what millions of people in the country are doing every day, every month, year after year after year.

SEMI-INTELLIGENT OR SEMI-STUPID DEBT

There are times when debt cannot be so easily delineated between intelligent and stupid. Sometimes it starts out intelligently and then turns stupid.

As you know, a home mortgage qualifies as intelligent borrowing because it limits risk for both the borrower and lender and is fully collateralized—at least it's supposed to be that way.

The homeowner can borrow only up to a certain limit, so the lender has reasonable assurance that the property has a current market value more than the outstanding loan.

HOME EQUITY LOANS

A home equity loan, curiously known in the industry as HEL, is typically a second mortgage that positions itself in such a way to allow the homeowner access to the equity (that margin between what is owed and what the property is worth). Equity is the borrower's asset—and a precious asset at that.

A HEL opens a large line of credit for you, pledging your equity as the collateral. You can borrow against it whenever you want. Technically it is a secured debt because of the collateral feature. And the borrower's safety valve remains because the home can be sold to satisfy both of the debts. But it can be very risky—and that is when it can cross over into stupid territory. There are five ways the stupid factor can sneak into an otherwise intelligent mortgage situation:

1. If you borrow against your equity to clean up your credit card debt and then run up your credit cards all over again, that leaves you with twice the debt—the equity line and the credit cards. Not smart.

2. Some people treat a home equity loan as a permanent debt to be paid off when the house is sold. They might have felt a greater urgency to pay off the debts if they were in the form of credit card balances.

3. The convenience of having your home's equity available at your fingertips can be a formidable temptation. Knowing the money is readily available, you are more likely to fritter it away on something, like a well-deserved family vacation, instead of saving the money

first as you might have if you did not have such easy access to your precious equity.

4. If you are unable to keep current on both of your mortgages, either of the lenders can foreclose.

5. Sometimes the home equity loan and first mortgage together actually exceed the current market value of the property. There are lenders these days who offer to finance not only the full value of the home, but more than the property is worth. These 125-percent loans put the borrower in a tenuous position—the monthly payments are severe, but selling the property ceases to be a way out because more is owed than it would bring at sale (see chap. 15).

Even taking into consideration the fact that the interest on the home equity loan may be deductible from your taxable income, the risks involved with this potentially stupid debt can be weighty.

The equity in your home is an appreciating asset, for many people their only appreciating asset. If you leave it alone, it will grow as the property becomes more valuable and as you pay down the mortgage. That contributes to the intelligence factor of your home's mortgage. To muddy those waters with a HEL opens the door to stupid debt.

AUTOMOBILE LOANS

A car loan can contain elements of intelligent borrowing provided you make a large down payment and select a model that historically retains high resale value. An automobile loan is a secured debt; if you get into some kind of trouble, you can sell the car to repay the debt. Cars do not appreciate, however, so not all of the intelligent borrowing criteria apply.

A car loan can slide over to the stupid debt area if you put little or nothing down and stretch the payments past three years. It won't take long for you to be "upside down" in the loan, meaning you owe more than the car is worth. Borrowing a car for a long period of time, also known as leasing, is in most situations anything but intelligent. Getting caught on the leasing treadmill can be a very expensive proposition (see chap. 16).

STUDENT LOANS

If ever there was a gray area in this matter of intelligent borrowing versus stupid debt, it has to be the troublesome student loan.

Some argue that a student loan qualifies as intelligent borrowing because the resultant education will appreciate over time and will more than pay for itself in future income. Nevertheless, that is making some bold assumptions: first, that you will actually finish school; second, that you will be well suited for the field in which you are getting your degree; and third, that the field will welcome you. I find it just short of amazing that 85 percent of college graduates do not end up working in their major field of study. (But then I recall the decisions I made at that tender age, and I understand fully.)

Whether student loans fall into the category of semi-intelligent or semi-stupid has a lot to do with one's individual circumstances (see chap. 21).

RECOGNIZE THE SIGN OF DEBT

It is not difficult to recognize the difference between intelligent borrowing and stupid debt:

- Intelligent borrowing requires plenty of time and makes you think. You can do stupid debt in your sleep.
- You are not likely to get in over your head with intelligent borrowing. Stupid debt can dump you into the deep end of the ocean before next Tuesday.

- Intelligent borrowing requires a lot of research and thinking. The last thing stupid debt wants is for you to analyze anything—just sign here!

As a person desiring to debt-proof your life, your mission is to rid your life and your future of all stupid debt, to borrow money only when it cannot be avoided, and then to do so as intelligently as possible.

The trouble with debt can be likened to the proverbial frog in the pot of boiling water. If you try to pop him in once the water is boiling, he'll jump out. But if you start him out in cold water and slowly raise the temperature, he'll just sit there and cook to death.

People are like that frog when it comes to stupid debt. We wouldn't jump into the boiling water by purchasing something really big and expensive, like a car or boat, with a credit card, but months and years of consistent spending for smaller purchases while paying only the minimum payment each month allows the temperature to rise ever so slowly. Before we know it, we've reached the boiling point.

Stupid debt doesn't usually start out stupid. In the beginning it is simply a matter of convenience. You pay the entire balance during the grace period. Then one month the balance is a little larger than can be easily paid, so you pay half and plan to pay the balance next month. But then something comes up and it appears to make sense to let it roll over into the next month. Soon you're hooked with a balance too large to pay in full in a single month, and you're on your way. The water started boiling and you were completely unaware.

So why is debt such a problem?

1. *Debt promotes discontentment.* When you're charging things with money you don't have, you are not content with your income. You cannot be patient. You cannot

wait. You have to have it right now! But when you acquire things too easily without pride of ownership, it is easy to become dissatisfied quickly.

2. *Debt makes arrogant presumptions about the future.* By agreeing to have things now and becoming legally obligated to pay for them later, you make bold presumptions about what the future will hold in terms of money, ability, and health. What makes you believe that although you don't have the money now you will have it later? But worse, you also promise that you will be willing to turn over money you don't have yet to pay for things you may not have anymore. What makes you think you will be all that thrilled about spending money you've not yet earned for stuff you probably won't even remember? That's an arrogant attitude and an irresponsible presumption on the future.

3. *Debt requires you to transfer your future wealth to your creditors.* If given the choice of sending monthly support checks to the wealthy credit card industry or sending those same checks to build your own future, would you really choose the former? Probably not. However, when you agree to stupid debt, that is exactly what you've done. Your choice has been made, and there is no way out but to make full repayment, no matter how difficult or unreasonable that will be.

4. *Debt limits your options—and heavy loads of debt eliminate them altogether.* Debt keeps people tied to jobs and careers they hate. It forces moms who would rather be home with their kids to work outside the home. It can even give Mr. Right second thoughts about taking on a prospective bride because of her heavy, debt-ridden baggage.

5. *Debt steals your freedom and makes you a slave.* When
    you are under a load of stupid debt, you are in
    bondage. You have no way out but to work off your
    sentence. King Solomon, the wisest man ever to have
    lived, summed it up this way: "The rich rule over the
    poor, and the borrower is the servant to the lender"
    (Prov. 22:7).

One last thing on this subject. From here on out I am going
to omit the word *stupid* before the word *debt*. I'm sure I've
made my point by now. Just understand that whenever you
read *debt* in this book, it refers to stupid debt. Intelligent borrowing will be referred to as such and should not be construed
to mean the same thing as debt.

＞

---

1. This, and a few dozen other calculators, reside in the members area at
   www.debtproofliving.com.

## Chapter Three

A Plan to Debt-Proof Your Life

WITHOUT A PLAN, YOU'RE DREAMING

*We make our plans, and then our plans
turn around and make us.*

F. W. Boreham

Without a plan, a goal is only a dream. If your goal to achieve financial freedom is not attached to a specific plan, I can safely say you will never reach it because you will not know

- how to start,
- what to do, or
- when you've reached your goal.

A *dream* showcases the end result but completely skips the details. A *plan,* on the other hand, defines the goal, lays out the steps to reach the goal, and expresses the goal in terms that are measurable. A plan eliminates confusion because you have the directions right there in black and white.

For example, in the language of dreams, your desire to improve your health might be expressed as "I want to get into shape." In the language of achievable goals, you would first define what it means to get into shape and then outline the steps required to reach that goal. Such a statement might be, "I intend to run two miles a day for the next six weeks so I will be in good physical condition to participate in a 5K race six weeks from Saturday." Now your desire is no longer a dream because it is clearly defined and you have outlined the steps required to achieve it. The progress and outcome are measurable. Getting into shape has become a goal attached to a plan.

Maybe you've had the desire to "get control of your finances" or "get out of debt" long before you picked up this book. Well, have you done it? If not, the problem might be that you have never had a realistic plan. All you have had is a dream.

Let's take that desire and develop it into a goal. Goal statement: *I intend to achieve financial freedom and win over debt for a lifetime by consistently giving, saving, and never spending more money than I earn. I will know I've reached my goal when I have no unsecured debt; I have a $10,000 Contingency Fund; my Freedom Account is funded one year in advance; and I am consistently giving away 10 percent, saving 10 percent, and then living on 80 percent of my income.* (These terms will be explained fully in later chapters.)

Notice that the goal is clearly defined *(to achieve financial freedom and win over debt for a lifetime)*, the steps to reach the goal are specific *(by consistently giving, saving, and never spending more money than I earn)*, and there is a statement that defines how to recognize that you have reached your goal *(I have no unsecured debt; I have a $10,000 Contingency Fund; my Freedom Account is funded one year in advance; and I am giving away 10 percent, saving 10 percent, and then living on 80 percent of my income)*.

Now your dream of getting control of your finances has become a goal because it has three elements:

1. The goal is clearly defined.
2. The steps to reach the goal are clearly stated.
3. The goal has a measurable outcome.

Years ago I read something that stuck in my mind: You wouldn't dream of eating an entire salami in one sitting. But if you eat just one slice a day, in time you will eat the entire thing.

You must think of your goal of reaching financial freedom as the salami of a lifetime. You're going to get the job done just one slice at a time.

THE DEBT-PROOF LIVING FORMULA

The only reason I made it through college chemistry is because I could memorize formulas. I never did, and possibly never will, understand what I memorized. What I learned from the experience is that it doesn't always matter if you understand the details. As long as you get the formula right, you can count on the results.

Fortunately, the debt-proof living formula is much simpler and infinitely more easy to understand than anything having to do with chemistry. I am concerned, however, that at first glance you might see the formula as an impossible undertaking and conclude it would make a much better long distance telephone access code. Yet if used faithfully, this formula will allow you to obtain something far more valuable than a discounted phone rate: you will access financial freedom. The formula is 10-10-80. If you make a commitment to apply this formula to the management of your money, it will forever change your life.

Here's how the formula works: For every dollar that flows into your life you give away 10 percent, save 10 percent, and live on 80 percent. For every dollar you receive, ten cents is to give away, ten cents is yours to save for the future, and eighty cents is for creating the most abundant life possible.

I know what you're thinking: *Only if I win the lottery!* (You are so funny.) I understand your reaction. I know 10-10-80 is radical; it's unconventional and just short of un-American. But that's it, regardless, and I hope you'll stick with me long enough to let me explain.

I know something about being in *terrible*—and I do mean terrible—financial trouble. For more years than I like to admit, I spent not only 100 percent of every dollar I could get my hands on, but far more. Of course the only way I could do that was to spend money that didn't belong to me.

I thought I had a pretty good thing going. I didn't give, I didn't save, and I could spend lots more than we made.

To accomplish it, I tried every form of juggling, manipulation, trick, tactic, scheme, and loophole in the book. My method was the fast track to a horrible financial pit of despair. While it sounds like quite a feat to live well on someone else's money, it's anything but glamorous. I am here to report that without a doubt there's only one form of money management that results in joy, peace of mind, contentment, and financial ease: 10-10-80.

I do not know why this formula works. I have some clues, but when it comes right down to it, I accept this formula on faith. I believe it has much to do with balance. When I give to others first and then care enough about myself, my family, and my future to say that some is ours to keep, my insatiable desires are "hushed up." Giving and saving first allow me to see things differently. Amazingly my vision changes, and that lets me be more satisfied with what I have. Then I have more patience to wait until I have saved the money needed for a desired purchase. I am less prone to acting impulsively.

The gratification I used to receive from outrageous spending I now find when I give and when I save. It is, however, a little bit different. The rush I got from spending lasted about as long as it took me to get to the car—and it was quickly replaced by anxiety, guilt, and fear. But the gratification I receive from giving and saving goes on and on and on. Each time I give some of my money away and save some for the future, I make more than a deposit in the bank—I make a deposit into my emotional and eternal bank. That produces something satisfying that words cannot adequately describe.

GIVE AWAY 10 PERCENT

I'm fully prepared for your arguments for why giving away your money—any percentage at all—is not something you would even consider. I understand. I've heard every reason you could possibly imagine. And I listen carefully, remembering how many years I felt the same way. I intended to become a giver someday, and when that day came I would do it flamboyantly. I would give thousands of dollars at a time, not paltry sums. I had big plans, and I was going to do it my way . . . someday. So go ahead; make your list of all the reasons you absolutely cannot give away any of your income.

Now I will counter by saying that nothing you've listed holds water. Feel the way you will, but nothing you can say will change the fact that if you fail to open your life to the power of giving, you will never find the financial freedom and success you long to achieve and for which you were created to enjoy.

What Giving Does

Here is what giving does for me and will do for you:

Giving proves the condition of my heart. The very act of giving is an expression of gratitude. It is a tangible way I can say thank-you for everything I have and for every way I have been blessed. Without gratitude operating in my life, more will never be enough, and nothing will bring satisfaction.

Giving connects me to the world. We live in a materialistic society. We have so much. Giving opens my eyes to the big picture. It allows me to see the world through eyes of compassion. I see how vast the need, how short the time, and how unimportant my stuff is by comparison. When I connect to the world, I allow my heart to be broken. It is in that brokenness that my pride and arrogance can be washed away. Then I become contented with what I have, and that makes me more useful.

Giving connects me with God. It opens my eyes to who I am. When I take a step of faith and give back to God the first and the best part of my income, it makes statements about my past, my present, and my future:

- My past: I am grateful for everything in my life that has brought me to this place.
- My present: God is number one in my life.
- My future: I trust God to keep his word and meet my needs.

Giving teaches my brain that I have more than enough. When you give, you are telling yourself that you are beyond scarcity. It is affirmation that someone greater than yourself is in control. When I acknowledge that I have more than enough, I affirm that all of my needs have been supplied and that I am grateful.

Giving exposes my finances to God's supernatural intervention. Given the choice to appropriate or reject that kind of power in my life leaves no question. If you truly believe that God is in control of your life, it is a very foolish thing not to trust him in that regard.

Since I made the decision back in 1982 to become a purposeful giver, I have paid back more than $100,000 in unsecured debt. I have found unbelievable passion in a career I never could have imagined, using talents I did not know I had.

Has giving changed and blessed my life? You be the judge.

How to Give

"How do I give?" may seem like an elementary question, but it is one I am asked often and one I understand completely.

First, let me clarify that I am talking about giving away 10 percent of your *money*. I often receive letters from people telling me they give their time and their skills but not their money because they cannot afford it. I can only assume they are trying to convince me that the first two are substitutes for the last. I agree that we should be good stewards of everything, not only our money, but you will be missing the boat if you do not include your money—the most precious commodity of all. It takes faith and courage to give away what is most precious. That's why it is so meaningful and so powerful.

One of the easiest ways to get started with consistent giving is to treat it like a regular bill. Decide the exact amount you are going to give right off the top of the money you receive. Make up envelopes and payment coupons and put them in the front of your Bills-to-be-Paid folder. Now when you do your regular bill paying, make that your first payment.

If you have never been a giver, facing the 10 percent hurdle might be daunting, to say the least. Please don't let the number appear so large that you convince yourself to give nothing. If you don't have the faith to start with 10 percent, start some other place, like 2 percent. Then move to 3 percent. Ask God to increase your faith and your ability to trust in this area. Remember, more than anything else, God is concerned about the condition of your heart.

Where to Give

As you begin to consider all the needs in the world around you, I have a feeling something or someone is going to come to mind. What are the issues about which you are passionate? Do you attend a church where your soul is fed? That would be a good place to start. Think about your own community. What needs have you heard about that tugged at one of your heart-strings? That tugging just might be God's prodding. I cannot tell you where to give. That must be a personal decision and one I believe you will make easily once you start thinking about it.

Once you've made your decision about where to give, do it with no strings attached. Just give the money away. Write the check or deliver the cash. Giving in its purest form is done with a heart that says I wish it were more, and I expect nothing in return.

SAVE 10 PERCENT

Pay yourself first! This concept is not new, but I'll never forget the first time I really understood what it meant. I read it in a fascinating little book called *The Richest Man in Babylon,* written by George Clason and first published in 1926.

Say to yourself, "A part of all I earn is mine to keep." Say it in the morning when you first arise. Say it at noon. Say it at night. Say it each hour of every day. Say it to yourself until the words stand out like letters of fire across the sky. Impress yourself with the idea. Fill yourself with the thought. Then take whatever portion seems wise. Let it be not less than one-tenth and lay it by. Arrange your other expenditures to do this if necessary. But lay by that portion first. Soon you will realize what a rich feeling it is to own a treasure upon which you alone have claim. As it grows it will stimulate you. A new joy of life will thrill you. Greater efforts will come to you to earn more. For of your increased earnings, will not the same percentage be also yours to keep?[1]

During my worst years when I was spending with reckless abandon, I would have told you with all sincerity that we didn't have enough to save. Ironically, even though I was spending as if there would be no tomorrow, I would have considered it conceited and self-serving to keep any money for myself. If that is your reaction, I want to encourage you to let it go.

Understanding that a part of all you earn is yours to keep is a reasonable way you can acknowledge your worth, prepare for the unexpected, more quickly repair the damage that debt has done in your life, and go on to build a retirement nest egg. It is simply the right thing to do.

I strongly suggest that you need to begin saving 10 percent of your net (take-home) income regardless if you participate in an employer-sponsored savings plan like a 401(k). This is the ideal and the premise on which this book is based. If for some reason you simply cannot do that, adjust your savings accordingly, with the goal of getting it to 10 percent as quickly as possible.

Your Savings Agenda

Savings Level 1: Contingency Fund. No matter your situation, if you are deeply in debt or not, you must have a Contingency Fund. Every household needs one. This is liquid cash, meaning that in 24 to 72 hours you could get your hands on money you have earmarked for specific emergencies. Without a Contingency Fund you will spin your wheels trying

to get out of debt because every time something unexpected
comes up, you'll feel you have no choice but to run for the
credit cards. A Contingency Fund creates margin and allows
you to step away from the edge.

The amount you need in your Contingency Fund is ultimately your call. I do, however, have some strong suggestions
that I will share in chapter 6.

Your attitude about your Contingency Fund will either
make or break it. If you see it as a pool of money to be used at
will for anything that suits your fancy at the moment, you will
have completely missed the purpose of a Contingency Fund. If
and when the funds are used for the purpose for which they
have been set aside, they must be quickly replaced.
Maintaining a Contingency Fund provides much-needed space
between you and the financial edge.

Savings Level 2: Boost your Freedom Account. Unless
you've skipped ahead in this book or are part of my
Cheapskate Monthly family, you have no idea what I'm talking about. Not to worry. You're going to learn everything there
is to know about your Freedom Account in chapter 8. As you
build your Contingency Fund, you will also make regular contributions to your Freedom Account. Once you finish Savings
Level 1 and your Contingency Fund is in place, your 10 percent savings should then go straight into your Freedom
Account as an additional monthly contribution until the subaccounts you have established are fully funded for one year in
advance.

*Savings Level 3: Turbocharge your Rapid Debt-Repayment
Plan.* If you are still working on an RDRP (see chap. 7) when
you reach Savings Level 3, your 10 percent savings should now
go to speed the process of getting debt free. If you are debt
free, move right on to Savings Level 4.

By contributing your 10 percent savings each month to your RDRP, you will cut the time it takes to get to debt-free status by months, perhaps years. Your creditors will be amazed at how this former debtor turned over some kind of a new leaf—and to your utter amazement, they will begin doing all kinds of things to make sure you go back to your old ways. Yet to their attempts you will have the amazing courage to say: "Not a chance, Lance!"

Prepaying the principal on any loan is the way to reach the coveted *zero balance* in record time.

Every month, you pay interest on each and every dollar of the outstanding principal. You also pay it again next month on every dollar you allow to revolve. Each dollar you can remove from that column by prepaying it is a dollar you will never pay interest on again.

Once you are debt free (and you will write to tell me about it so I can celebrate too, right?) it's time to move on without missing a beat to . . .

Savings Level 4: It's time to begin building wealth for yourself, your family—your future! By now you have your Contingency Fund in place, your Freedom Account is funded for a minimum of one year hence, and you are debt free. It's time to party!

You are beginning to taste the fruits of financial freedom, and they are spelled o-p-t-i-o-n-s. You have choices to make as to the method and order of building your nest egg:

- Your savings can begin to build a down payment on a house if that is something you desire.
- Your savings can be used to prepay the principal on your mortgage. You are going to learn just how beneficial this choice can be in chapter 14.
- With your 10 percent savings you can begin building a serious investment portfolio.

- You can create a unique allocation of your savings so
  that you are both prepaying your mortgage and building that investment portfolio.

I believe one of the sweetest rewards I've enjoyed as a
result of living debt free is this matter of options. When we
were in that horrible pit of financial despair, it felt as if we
were in bondage. We were prisoners without choices. Our
creditors lived our lives for us; they were the ones who made
our financial decisions.

With each step we took toward financial freedom, we got
options in return. Soon you too will experience just how life-
freeing that can be.

Faithful Employees

Think of the 10 percent you pay to yourself as your
"employee." As you work your way through Savings Levels 1,
2, and 3, think of this employee as working hard on your
behalf to prepare and repair.

When you reach Savings Level 4, something wonderful
begins. Your employee is exposed to the miracle of compounding interest, and the reproduction process begins.
Soon you have another employee. Then three, four, five,
eight, ten. Your employees work hard, day and night—
whether you are thinking about them or not. They never
complain, take a day off, or call in sick. They just keep going
and going and going.

The 10 percent you pay yourself is the way you create
income for your future. It represents options and is an excellent cure for insomnia.

Soon a retirement nest egg will be a necessary part of life,
rather than an option for only the very wealthy. Company
pensions are fast disappearing, and with massive corporate

downsizing, job security has evaporated. Gone are the days when you could expect to work forty-five years with the same corporation and leave with your gold watch and a retirement income that would allow you to continue the lifestyle you had enjoyed. Even dependence on Social Security is at best uncertain. You need to choose to provide for your future now.

THE 80 PERCENT SOLUTION

Debt-proof living depends more on your spending habits than the size of your paycheck. It is going to be challenging to adjust your living expenses so that, including your debt repayment and current bills, you are spending no more than 80 percent of your net income. But it will get easier with time. The dollars being sent to creditors every month will become discretionary income once you reach debt-free status. The more you practice restraint in your spending, the easier it will become because, simply put, you're going to get better at it.

If you, like the majority of your fellow Americans, live on something closer to 110 percent of your income (seeing that in print does send shivers up your spine, doesn't it?), a drastic idea like living on 80 percent might cause you to give up right now. But remember, you didn't get where you are overnight, so to expect an instantaneous reversal would be unrealistic.

Nonetheless, now is the time to start. You can choose to turn around so that you are headed in the right direction, and every step will be one of progress.

Reducing your living expenses so they fit within 80 percent of your income requires scrutinizing every expense and then finding the best way to reduce it. By reducing everything a little bit, you may be able to avoid eliminating any spending categories. This is going to require creativity and discipline.

Frugality

Frugality has taken a lot of heat in the past few years. It has become quite a buzzword among economic extremists. As a result, many people have come to view frugality with disdain, assuming it demands a lifestyle based on dumpster diving and recycling dryer lint. Believe me, that's not it.

As it relates to debt-proof living, frugality is doing whatever it takes to keep your living expenses within 80 percent of your net income.

Frugality is not about stuffing everyone into the same mold so we all spend the same amount of money on things like food or housing. Frugality is about restraint, discipline, finding the best value, and not being wasteful. It's about making choices and understanding that if you say yes to one thing you may need to say no to something else.

Because I live frugally doesn't mean I don't spend money. It means I spend money thoughtfully and with a sense of discipline and purpose. As my life is blessed and my income increases, 80 percent of my net income increases as well. It's a beautiful thing.

Since the first issue of *Cheapskate Monthly* was published in January 1992, I have devoted my life to this matter of helping people learn to live within their means (which you now understand means 80 percent of your net income), and to do so with dignity and joy. There are many things you can do to reduce your expenses and bring your lifestyle in line with your income.

Your Starting Point

Most people (which does mean nearly everyone, so don't feel like the Lone Ranger) have no idea where their money goes or even how they spend it. This is partly due to human nature.

We trick ourselves by expressing our income in grandiose gross annual terms while we talk about our expenses as daily dribbles. For example, Sharon spends $3 a day for caffe latte and has an annual salary of $50,000. *And why not,* she reasons. Anyone who makes $50,000 a year certainly can afford a lousy $3 caffe latte every morning.

The truth is, she takes home something close to $2,500 (after taxes) a month and spends $90 of it on latte. My point: $3 is not to $50,000 what $90 is to $2,500. We think of our income and expenses in unrealistic terms.

Do you know where every penny of your paycheck goes? Sure, you probably know the big things like the mortgage payment, maybe the utilities. But what about the $200 ATM withdrawals you often make? Where does that money go? How much are you spending on groceries and other food to feed your family? How much do you spend in a month on something as benign as a newspaper? Gasoline? Auto maintenance? Movie tickets? Video games? Gifts? Clothing?

If your employer made a new rule that your paycheck next month would be equal to only the amount of this month's check that you could document with a list and receipts, how close could you come to getting a full paycheck next month? One thing is for certain: You'd be motivated to find out where all the money goes!

I believe I can safely say that money is leaking out of your life. It might be only a dollar here and fifty cents there, but it is going on day in and day out. Like a dripping faucet, it doesn't seem like much when it is only one drop at a time, but stick a bucket under there and look again in the morning. You will be amazed at how that tiny leak can accumulate into something significant.

You will never reduce your expenses effectively and consistently until you find out where you are. You need to know where your money goes. Only then will you be able to take the steps necessary to get it in line with 80 percent of your net income.

Leak Detection

I recommend keeping a Daily Spending Record. It's simple; it's effective. It will show you specifically where money is leaking out of your life.

Write down all your expenditures every day for a month. Make no effort to change your spending habits. You are making a snapshot of the way you live now, so attempting to alter it will defeat that purpose.

Keep it simple. Three-by-five-inch cards make the best Daily Spending Records. If you have a spouse, both of you should start out the day with a fresh card. Date it. As you go through the day, simply write down "what" and "how much" every time you spend money. No cheating, no forgetting. This is not a test. This is simply to find out where the money is going. You cannot be selective—you must be brutally honest. Just write it down one day at a time. Write down the cash you spend, the checks you write, the credit purchases you make. I really do mean everything—even those things you may think are too trivial to track.

At the end of each day, put the day's record in a drawer until you've accumulated one week's worth of spending records.

If there are two of you, you should have fourteen cards by the end of the first week. If you are single or you are doing this on your own for now, you'll have seven. Spread them out and take a look. See any patterns? Anything surprising? Without making a federal case about it, see if you can combine all of this information into one list—a Weekly Spending Record. If you buy coffee every day, add it up and make one entry on your Weekly Spending Record: Coffee—followed by the total amount. Did you go to the market? Add up all grocery expenditures and enter as one item: Groceries—followed by the total amount. Do the same for food eaten outside the home (restaurants, diners, fast food). Add up all the amounts and enter as one item: Outside food—followed by the total amount.

Your job is complete when your Weekly Spending Record totals the same amount as all your Daily Spending Records combined.

Repeat this Daily-Record-into-Weekly-Record for another three weeks. When you have four Weekly Spending Records (it doesn't matter if that's a full month or not), repeat the process, turning them into a Monthly Spending Record.

Something amazing is happening here. If you have been brutally honest, you begin to see the leaks. It is possible that you spent more money than you made the month in which you kept records. If so (and I have to believe you didn't rob a bank), the way you did that was to pay for things with credit. That has to stop, and now that you can see the monthly effect, it's going to be a lot easier to put on the brakes.

I have had people write and tell me that this simple exercise of recording all expenditures was like turning on a floodlight in a dark cave. Wow, what that light reveals.

Spending Plan

I don't do budgets for the same reason I don't wear straitjackets. To me a budget is another way to spell *deprivation*. It's a mold that doesn't fit me, like trying to see out of someone else's prescription eyeglasses.

A Spending Plan born from a desire to create a more reasonable Spending Record is something altogether different from a budget. A Spending Plan is something you create for *your* life that is uniquely based on *your* desires and responsibilities. It's a means for you—or if you're married, you and your spouse—to decide what you want to spend money on in advance rather than when caught up in the moment. Too often, opportunities come up, and out of a sense of urgency we make decisions that we later regret. If you and your spouse get a clear plan for how much you need to spend each month in each category of your life, you will not only save money, you will also save yourselves a lot of arguments.

Get out your Monthly Spending Record. As unlovely as it might be, you need to spend some time studying it. In which areas are you really out of whack? What can you do next month to change that entry? "Cook at home more often" is a typical response because grocery and food expenses often come out as big-time expenditures. Once you see how much you spend, you are open to learning ways to slash your food costs. What about the utilities? Is there any way to get that long-distance telephone bill down to something reasonable? There are hundreds if not thousands of ways to realistically reduce your expenses, and now that you've seen how out of control they are, you are going to be much more open to learning about how to tame them.

Before the next month begins, you need to write a Monthly Spending Plan. Simply take what happened last month, and project what's going to happen next month. If you spent $90 on caffe lattes, determine what you plan to spend next month on that item. If $90 is out of line, but $20 is palatable, write that down as your planned spending in that category. If you spent $400 on groceries, would it be reasonable to think you could reduce that to $350 next month? $300? Write that number down as the amount you plan to spend. Go through each category, projecting what you could do if you were more aware. Add it up. The total on your Monthly Spending Plan should not exceed 80 percent of your monthly net income. If it's out of balance, keep adjusting and planning how you can get those numbers in line.

From now on, everything you spend should be done in the new light of incurring no debt, finding the best value, and keeping your commitment to debt-proof your life.

The average paycheck-to-paycheck kind of person has a huge misconception about the way millionaires live and think. Most assume that millionaires spend whatever they like, have whatever they want, and never think or worry about money.

Not so! Statistics prove that self-made millionaires got that way by budgeting and controlling expenses. What's more, they maintain that status in the same way.

The next time you observe someone living in a flashy, "wealthy" way and you find yourself envying what looks like a carefree lifestyle, remember: chances are great that the person is deeply in debt, and what you see is just a phony front.

Truly wealthy people live understated lives. They are as normal as the folks next door.

So let's give three cheers for planned spending and controlling expenses—behaviors that promise a huge payoff in joy and peace of mind.

---

1. George Clason, *The Richest Man in Babylon,* (Penguin: New York, 1955), 19.

## Chapter Four

Money Is Not for Spending

IT IS FOR MANAGING FIRST AND THEN FOR SPENDING

You are worth what you saved,
not the millions you made.

John Boyle O'Reilly

It took me a long time to understand fully this profound truth: Money is not for spending. It is for managing first and then for spending. It takes courage to believe that, but when you do, it will profoundly change the way you think about and then take care of your money.

When money flows into your life, you are responsible for its performance. You are the composer, the concertmaster, and the conductor. You direct that money according to the score you have written. First you give, then you save, then you plan and strategize. All the steps are in place, and you confidently know exactly what to do. Every move is made by choice; nothing is left to chance.

Once you have made the allocations according to your Debt-Proof Living Plan, you know exactly how to spend your money. Some of it will flow right back out of your life. Some will be saved for the long term. Some of it will be appropriated to pay for your day-to-day living expenses, and so on. The point is, when you receive the money, you hold it with confidence while you intelligently direct it into all of the appropriate places according to your predetermined plan.

Once you grasp this concept, it is easy to see the foolishness of receiving money and immediately spending it.

THE NEED FOR DIRECTION

Without specific direction, trying to hold onto money is like trying to hold a handful of water: no matter how hard you try or how tightly you grip, the water leaks away. That's what happens to money if you do not consciously direct it to a specific purpose. That's what I mean when I say money is not for spending; it is for managing first. Managing allows you to respond intelligently, not just emotionally. When you spend first, the emotions take over and the results are, at best, unpredictable.

Money that is not directed will disappear. That's just a fact of life that most of us have proven many times over, much to our humiliation.

In your lifetime you will exercise discretion over millions of dollars. Let's say you and your mate are twenty-five, and your family income is the U.S. median, last reported to be about $38,000. If you both work until you're sixty-five, even if you never get a raise, you're going to bring in over $1.6 million. If your salary goes up just 3 percent a year, you'll earn over $3 million. If you land a promotion, you'll rake in even more. Clearly, having enough money is not the problem. The challenge is to hang onto more of what we have by directing it specifically and carefully.

Everything in the Debt-Proof Living Plan will help you learn to give sound and reasoned direction to all of the money that will flow through your fingers in your lifetime.

THE NEED FOR REDIRECTION

Let's say that you are aggressively accumulating your Contingency Fund at a rate of $300 a month. You reach your $10,000 goal. Unless you immediately redirect that $300 to another specific purpose next month, it will disappear. If you leave it to languish in your checking account, it will be absorbed into your daily living. If you redirect it, however, you are looking at $3,600 a year for some other specific purpose as you direct it.

Another example: You get a pay raise that translates into $43 more in your paycheck each week. Unless you specifically direct those additional funds, you will soon not even notice the raise because it will be mysteriously absorbed into your day-to-day living. I'm not suggesting that an annual increase of $2,236 net ($43 X 52 weeks) is insignificant. Not at all. But when received in weekly increments of $43, it can easily evaporate—five bucks here, fifteen there, and before you know what hit you, you're broke again. On the other hand, if you diligently and consciously direct that raise to protect it from the mysterious evaporation thing—each week you give away $4.30, add $4.30 to your savings plan and then appropriate the remaining $34.40 to some specific and meaningful purpose—a year from now there will be no mystery. You will know exactly where that raise went.

In my seriously pensive moments (thank goodness they don't hit me too often) I wonder how differently things might have been had I learned earlier in my life that money is not for spending. I'm so glad I know now that money is for managing first, and then for spending.

## Chapter Five

Caught in the Debt Trap

KNOW THE DANGER SIGNS

---

*Debt keeps you stuck in the trap of using
your future to pay for your past.*

Mary Hunt

There are lots of opossums where I live in California because it is unlawful to exterminate them. The ones that hang around our yard have developed quite an attitude about their private little reserve. They are fearless and consider our property as much theirs as ours.

The only lawful way to deal with these less-than-attractive marsupials is to trap and then relocate them to uninhabited areas. It is not difficult to trap an opossum if you have attractive bait because they are so gullible.

All you do is stick some opossum delicacy, like fruit (even cat food will do), inside the trap and set it out after dark. The trap's clever one-way entrance makes crawling into it nearly effortless for the opossum. Once he's in—*slam!* He's caught, with no way out.

Debt is a lot like an opossum trap. It is very attractive, easily accessible, and the bait can be irresistible.

If you've ever been—or are now—in the debt trap, you know what a horribly confining and stressful place it can be. That's why you need to know how to gnaw your way out. You also need to learn to recognize the traps so you never get caught in it again.

DEBT TRAPS

If you are going to avoid debt traps, you have to learn to recognize them. Some debt traps are not as obvious as others. Here are the most common debt traps:

- Credit card accounts
- Monthly installment plans
- Overdraft protection plans
- Past taxes
- Student loans
- Medical bills
- Dental bills
- Personal loans

Credit cards are by far the most common of all the debt traps. Currently there are *billions* of active accounts in this country, some 70 percent of which carry a revolving balance month after month, year after year. What's more, there are hundreds of companies doing their level best to see the numbers increase.

One way these companies lure unsuspecting consumers into debt is through those rascally preapproved applications. Billions are sent through the mail every year. These solicitations are often quite beautiful, with lavish use of color, photography, and foil stamping on high-quality paper stock. I get so many preapproved credit card applications that I've actually considered wallpapering my guest powder room with them to make my own whimsical statement.

To further my research on the matter of consumer credit— but more importantly to give myself an occasional humor break—I read these credit card applications thoroughly and with a magnifying glass. It's not that I have poor vision; nowadays it seems the really important information is graphically designed to fit on the head of a pin.

These appeals always begin with a cordial, often gushy, letter telling me how wonderful I am and why I deserve only the very best that life has to offer. There is always some kind of acceptance form with urgency written all over it, pressing me to act now! Then comes the preaddressed, postage-paid return envelope.

I have gone over every square millimeter of hundreds of these solicitations and have yet to find a single word that honestly describes what these companies are selling—debt. It is simply not there. So what's the deal? Why are they so afraid to call it like it is, to come clean and say that carrying a balance from month to month can be hazardous to your wealth? Beware, the debt trap!

For fun I looked up the word *debt* in my trusty *Roget's Thesaurus* (you might wonder about the mental stability of a person who thinks it is fun to read a thesaurus, but go with me on this). Mine is not your ordinary classroom variety but the five-inch-thick, 1,500-page, 49-pound, thumb-indexed version. Here's what it says:

> *Debt.* obligation, encumbrance, in the red, pound of flesh, arrears, inability to pay, bilked, bound, beholden, up to one's ears, over one's head, mortgaged to the hilt, in the poverty trap, unable to keep the wolf from the door, hard up, beaten down,

financially embarrassed, strapped, stripped, fleeced, busted.

Instead of any reference to *debt,* what I read in these solicitations are flattering and manipulative words such as *congratulations, easy, instant, preferred, deserve, prequalified status, spending limit, cash advance, buying power, do with as you please, accepted in a zillion places, convenience, reward, make life easier,* and my favorite—*you stand out in a crowd!*

Clearly we live in a culture where consumer credit has become an ordinary part of life. We don't think much about debt until caught in its trap. As I mentioned before, even widely accepted classroom curriculum used in many public school districts (prepared and distributed free of charge, by none other than our friends at VISA and MasterCard International) teaches kids it's OK to spend "up to 20 percent of your net income on consumer debt."[1]

Each one of these unsolicited credit card applications closes with some version of "Please respond today!" So I have made it a practice always to comply with that request (a practice I will need to reconsider if I do decide to take up wallpapering that powder room). First, I remove the preaddressed, postage-paid envelope that always comes with these unsolicitations. Then I take every other piece of paper including the envelope it came in, tear all of it into small pieces, and load them back into the prepaid envelope. I seal it and drop it right back into the mail as my way of responding to their invitation. My answer is "No, thank you!" (It occurred to me recently that my mailman must be a bit confused as to why I, the self-proclaimed, reformed credit card junkie, am accepting every credit card offer known to mankind.)

Debt Trap Warning Signs

While I suppose it is possible, it is not common for a person to wind up in the debt trap overnight. It is a process, a series of events and choices that brings one to that dismal place.

How can you know if you are headed in that direction? There are definite warning signs—red flags I wish I'd heeded back when I was moving at breakneck speed into debt's pit of despair.

Here are the danger signs that indicate you may be entering the debt trap:

1. *You are living on credit.* How can you tell if you are living on credit? I just happen to have a little test you can take:

- If you regularly pay for things with credit because you don't have enough money, you are living on credit.
- If the balance you carry from month to month is going up, you are living on credit.
- If you are applying for new credit cards, you are living on credit.
- If you ever pay one credit card bill with another credit card, you are living on credit.
- If, when you think of not having credit cards, you break into a cold sweat and fear you would never survive, you are living on credit.

2. *You pay your bills late.* What's paying your bills late? you might ask. Well, if you have to ask that question, I would suspect you are indeed a late-payer. But just to be on the safe side, here is a checklist:

- You write out your bills but don't mail them because you don't have enough in the bank to cover them.
- You count on next month's paycheck to pay for this month's bills.

- You pay half of your bills this month and half next.
- You pay late fees willingly because you think of them as the price you must pay for your pitiful financial situation.
- Your standards have slipped just a tiny bit to where you think anything within thirty days late is on time.
- You would never consider paying a bill before the final due date even if you have the money because you might need it for something else.

3. You are not a giver. One might think that this matter of giving is fairly straightforward: either you are a giver or you are not. But, here again, many of us like to think in gray rather than black-and-white terms. Here are the ways to tell you are not a giver:

- You like the idea of giving money to God, and will do that as soon as you have more than enough to cover your necessary expenses.
- You reason that you cannot possibly give what you don't have.
- You argue that because you give so much of your time— and since time is money—you are, therefore, a giver.
- You call yourself a giver-in-kind because you regularly dump loads of stuff at the thrift store drop-off station.
- You consider that payment of your kids' tuition to private school counts as giving.

4. You are not a saver.

- You like the idea of saving money and will do that as soon as you have more than enough to cover your necessary expenses.
- You reason that you cannot possibly save what you don't have, and once you cover your necessary expenses you will save a lot.

- Your home is gaining value every year, so that counts as saving as far as you are concerned.
- You think of your available credit as your savings because it will be there in case you run into an emergency.

5. You dream of getting rich quickly and living an extravagant lifestyle. When your mind is focused on winning the lottery or falling into a get-rich-quick opportunity, you become a magnet for discontentment. Your attitude becomes fertile ground for debt because easy credit tempts you to have the extravagant lifestyle now before your ship comes in or before that great get-rich-quick opportunity taps you on the shoulder.

6. You worry about money. When your mind is filled with worry about money, you become an easy target for debt because it masquerades as a reasonable solution. The following warning signs signal that your worrying is drawing you into the debt trap:

- You find yourself thinking about money.
- You are unable to sleep.
- You become obsessive.
- You are fearful when the phone rings.
- You think up ways to hide purchases or bills from your spouse.

7. You overspend your checking account. If you are living so close to the edge that you spend more money than you have in your checking account, you are flirting with the debt trap. If you fall back on the overdraft protection plan that is connected to your checking account, you may not feel you are actually bouncing checks—but that is exactly what you are doing. You are taking a loan to cover what you do not have. Your financial institution is charging you some whopping big fees and interest, and you are repaying it a little bit at a time. If you have done this more than twice in the past twelve months (I'll cut you a little slack for simply being human) that is a serious indication that you are about to be snapped into the jaws of the debt trap.

Do you recognize any of these warning signs in your life? If so, don't panic. Just know that you need to turn around. It's time to recognize the red flags, sirens, and flashing lights. You are headed for trouble.

If you've gone past all the warning signs and the trap door has slammed behind you, now is the time to start gnawing your way out. Don't think of your situation as impossible. It is not! I got out, and I've helped thousands of others get out as well. You can get out too.

Escaping the Debt Trap

If you are in debt, your assignment is fairly simple: *Get out!* Every day that you delay, you are transferring more and more of your future wealth to your creditors.

1. Get serious. Decide right now that you are going to do whatever it takes to get out of debt and stay out of debt forever. Make a commitment. Write it down and date it so you can refer to it often. Don't worry if you are afraid or don't think you know what to do. Remember, it is easier to act your way into a feeling than to feel your way into an action. God will give you just the amount of light you need for the step you are on. I too will help you get going and be right here with you all the way.

2. Start giving to God. If you are in the fast lane to the debt trap or have already arrived, you should see that as a pretty good indication that your method of money management could use an overhaul. If what you're doing isn't working, you might as well consider an alternative approach. The way I see it, trying God's way could only improve things. All he asks is that we obey him by giving back the first part of everything he's given to us.

That means that when you get paid, the first thing you do is give. Just do it. And there's a promise for those who choose to obey. God says he will bless them so much it will be as if the windows of heaven opened up and rained blessings on them.[2] Wow!

I don't understand how it is that in giving we receive—but I believe it. And I have proven it over and over again. God keeps his word, and if you plan to get out of debt and stay out, I suggest you start right now to trust him in this. It will make your goal attainable and the journey joyful.

3. Start saving. You cannot allow yourself to spend it all. You must start saving something for yourself. Even if you are deeply in debt, you need to give and save. These two activities are going to enable you to get out of the debt trap. When you give and when you save, you find contentment. That impulsive thing going on inside of you that seems never to find satisfaction is quieted. When you are satisfied, you won't be as driven to spend wildly. Your mind will clear so you can think before you buy.

4. Start tracking. One of the reasons you've landed in the debt trap is that you've allowed money to leak from your life. I know, because I've been there myself. I get nauseous when I recall how much money flowed through my hands year after year after year. Remember, it's not that you don't have enough money. The problem is you don't know how to manage what you do have. That's what sends you in constant search of new sources of credit. Let me tell you again: More will never be enough until you learn to manage what you already have.

Tracking simply means counting. It means keeping track of where your money goes. There's not a successful business in the world that doesn't keep track of the outgo and the income. They know where every penny goes—and so should you.

5. *Know what you owe.* If you are in the debt trap, you probably don't know exactly what you owe—exactly the extent of your debt. Therefore, if you want out, you have to make a list of your debts. All of them. I call it facing the music. While it may be very difficult to do this, you must take this big step in order to get a handle on where you are.

6. *Design a plan.* In the same way you would never dream of building a house without a detailed set of plans, you should not even dream of getting out of your debt mess without a plan—a written plan that is suitable for refrigerator posting. You need to know exactly how long your payoff plan will take, right down to the year and the month. You need a plan for how you will manage your money while you're getting out of debt. You need a plan for where you will go once you are debt free, how you will begin to invest. Just a simple plan that shows where you are, where you're going, and how you're going to get there! A plan brings a dream alive. Good planning and hard work lead to prosperity.[3] (You can find more information on creating a Spending Record and a Spending Plan in my book *The Complete Cheapskate,* chapters 4 and 9.)

7. *Know what you own.* As you work your way out of the debt trap, it is very important to know what you own—not only the contents of your closets, drawers, and home, but also your financial assets. Do you have insurance? Where are the policies? How about the savings bonds you received as a kid, or your family heritage documents, such as birth certificates and military records? Straightening out your records will give you a sense of where you are. This new awareness will bring order to your life and aid you tremendously.

8. Have a sale. Once you know what you own, you'll be in a good position to decide what you really need. Excluding family heirlooms and sentimental possessions, consider liquidating what you haven't used in the past year. If you do not find it useful or it does not bring beauty to your life, get rid of it. Organize a huge garage sale. Run ads in the local classifieds for items with a price tag of thirty dollars or more. Dejunk; unclutter; simplify. It will breathe a breath of freshness into your life to dig out, and a stash of cash will jumpstart your out-of-debt plan.

9. Incur no more new debt. Make a commitment that from this day forward you will incur no more new debt. Let me warn you: at first it will feel as if you are swimming upstream against Class VI rapids because credit is so available, so seductive. Depending on your situation, you and your credit cards may already be enmeshed. You may have established quite a dependence on them, and that is something I fully understand. Still, having said all that, let me say again: You need to decide today—no more new debt.

10. Look for the solution. God has created you uniquely. He has given you tremendous abilities and talents, some you might not be aware of. As you demonstrate your commitment to getting out of debt and living beneath your means, opportunities are going to come your way. Perhaps the solution to your debt problem is right in front of your eyes.

While working our way out of a huge debt mess, I got the idea of publishing a subscription newsletter as a means of raising the rest of the money we needed to complete our plan. Clearly, that wasn't an idea I could have come up with on my own. I'd lived for forty-five years and had never once dreamed of or aspired to becoming a writer. I believe now that God placed in me that desire and the ability to do things I'd never considered or even dreamed of. I didn't know I had any talent in that area. But as I searched for the solution, I made an amazing discovery.

I began publishing that newsletter in 1992. I have just completed eight years of continuous publishing of *Cheapskate Monthly*. That newsletter has been one of the means through which God opened the windows of heaven on our lives. But it did not happen until we stepped out on faith. I made a commitment to repay all the debt and to begin living beneath our means many years before I found the ultimate solution.

11. Persevere. Think of getting out of the debt trap as a journey. Some days the path will be rocky and steep. Other times it will seem much easier. Know that this is going to take perseverance. You cannot give up! Find someone who will be your encourager. Grab onto your plan and God's promises, and don't ever let go!

⌒

---

1. "Visa's Choice & Decisions: Kids, Cash, Plastic and You," produced by MasterCard International in cooperation with the U.S. Office of Consumer Affairs and the Consumer Information Center.
2. See Malachi 3:10.
3. See Proverbs 21:5.

## Chapter Six

Step Away from the Edge

CREATING A CONTINGENCY FUND

There is no new suit of clothes, no vacation, no new car that can offset the pain of being truly worried about running out of money. I have had that fear. It comes at about five in the morning, and it keeps you awake and makes your mouth dry and makes you hate the sound of birds singing. I don't want anyone I love to come even close to it.

Ben Stein

T he edge is a miserable place to live. People who exist from paycheck to paycheck live there. They spend all they have. And when something unexpected happens, they must either take a flying leap into the darkness below or run to the credit cards, the finance company, or worse, the bankruptcy court.

The antidote to living on the edge is simple: Move away! It starts with a single step away from the edge. Follow that with another and another until you have created enough space between where you live and the edge so that you can relax—and sleep at night.

CONTINGENCY FUND

That space is called a Contingency Fund. It is a tangible hedge of protection. It is a pool of money that you can get your hands on in a short period of time, and it is stored in a safe place that pays at least enough interest to stay ahead of inflation.

An important part of your plan to debt-proof your life is to create and then maintain a Contingency Fund.

A Contingency Fund has nothing to do with your savings or investments. It is not the money that you build up over the months to pay your unexpected, irregular, and intermittent expenses—ones that don't occur on a monthly basis, thereby catching us off guard (we'll talk about how to handle these expenses in chap. 8). A Contingency Fund is not for discretionary spending. It is a pool of money set aside for major catastrophes, when your only other recourse is to run for credit. It will be there if you lose your job or if your safety or health is at risk.

Financial experts typically suggest a family needs the equivalent of three to six months' living expenses in reserve. I find that recommendation too nebulous and prefer to take the advice of my colleague, Austin Pryor, author of *Sound Mind Investing,* who suggests a fund of $10,000. That seems about right for the average family. If your monthly expenses are high, however, you should adjust the amount to cover what you would need to live for a full three months without any income.

Think of your Contingency Fund as your personal debt insurance. Its short-term purpose is to give you an alternative to using credit to cover emergencies like auto repairs and medical bills for which you are not otherwise prepared. Eventually your Contingency Fund will become your second line of defense against debt (see chap. 8 for tips on creating the Freedom Account—your first line of defense). Once your Freedom Account is in place, the Contingency Fund has one primary purpose: to be the bridge you will need in the event you and your income temporarily part company. It is difficult enough to get out of debt, but if you are continually adding new debt, it becomes nearly impossible.

While you are in Savings Level 1, the 10 percent you pay to yourself from your income should be parked in your Contingency Fund. If you currently have a savings account, you can designate that as your Contingency Fund and then start adding to it on a regular basis.

The goal is to accumulate and then maintain a $10,000 Contingency Fund as your normal way of life. If you find it necessary to withdraw money from your fund, it should be replaced as quickly as possible—becoming your top savings priority until it is restored to a full $10,000.

MAINTAINING YOUR FUND

THREE BASIC CONSIDERATIONS

You will be tempted to start seeing your Contingency Fund as a long-term investment. Avoid doing that, because this isn't an investment. It is money to be available to you in an emergency. It is insurance that will keep you afloat. In looking for a place to park your Contingency Fund, you need to be concerned about safety, availability, and growth—in that order.

- Safety. It must be in an account where the principal is not at risk. This is why your Contingency Fund should not be invested in the stock market.
- Availability. Because of the nature of emergencies, this fund needs to be liquid, meaning you could get your hands on at least part of it within twenty-four to forty-eight hours.
- Growth. You will be maintaining your Contingency Fund for many years. As a good steward, you want to expose

it to the best compounding interest available while still
meeting the safety and availability requirements.

WHERE TO PARK IT

Whether you have no savings now or a have a great start
on accumulating at least $10,000, you'll want to start thinking
about where to put it.

If you have no savings now, you should open an account at
your credit union or bank with your next deposit. The type of
account will depend on the amount of money you have available to get started.

Credit Unions and Bank Accounts

Banks are for-profit corporations while credit unions are
nonprofit organizations that exist for the benefit of their members. When a credit union generates a surplus, it is paid out to
account holders in the form of either a small dividend or a
rebate of loan interest at the end of the fiscal year. Typically
credit union fees are lower while their interest rates are a bit
higher. Provided you are eligible to join a credit union, consider this an excellent place to park your Contingency Fund as
you are growing it. One caution: while deposits in banks are
federally insured up to $100,000, not all credit unions are.
Make sure you choose a credit union that is also federally
insured.

When you walk into a bank or credit union to open an
account for your Contingency Fund, you'll be given a choice
that may include the following:

Passbook savings account. This is at the bottom of the savings ladder but is a good place for first-time or new savers. You
can expect low interest and low minimum requirements.

NOW account. Even though this is an interest-bearing
checking account, you might consider it in the beginning. Just

make sure any checks they issue are put away in a very inconvenient, yet safe, place. You don't want to slip and think this is a checking account from which you can start making withdrawals. You will find the interest rate to be a bit higher than the passbook savings account, but expect a minimum requirement of $1,500.

SuperNOW account. Similar to the NOW account, the SuperNOW has better interest but a greater minimum deposit, usually $2,000 to $2,500. Ditto with that checkbook.

Bank money market accounts. Don't confuse these with money market funds that are offered by mutual fund companies. Bank money market accounts carry the same federal insurance provision as other bank deposits, but they typically pay lower interest than a money market fund.

Certificates of deposit. These are similar to a passbook savings account in that you deposit the money and are paid a set rate of interest. The difference is that in exchange for your promise to leave the money for a set period of time (90 days, 180 days, 1 year, etc.) you are guaranteed a higher rate of interest. If you must withdraw early, there is a penalty that will apply to the interest portion only. The penalty will never touch your principal. If you take a short-term CD, you will receive slightly less interest.

Alternatives to Banking

Another option is to lend your money to the U.S. government in the form of Treasury bills (short-term government bonds).

If this sounds like a place you'd like to park your Contingency Fund, you need to do a little homework. First you need to get a copy of *Buying Treasury Securities*. Call the Federal Reserve branch closest to you to request a copy plus a complete packet of forms and information available for first-time investors. If you cannot find a branch, call the Federal branch in Los Angeles: (213) 624-7398. You can open an account and make your purchases by phone by calling 800-943-6864 or online at http://www.publicdebt.treas.gov/sec/sectrdir.htm.

The minimum investment required is $1,000. Government securities are sold at auction, and there is a process you will need to learn to become an active participant.

Money Market Fund Accounts

A money market fund (not to be confused with a money market account at a bank) is a large pool of money managed by professionals and invested in safe and stable securities, including commercial paper (short-term IOUs of large U.S. corporations), Treasury bills, and large bank CDs. Money market funds are a very attractive place to grow a Contingency Fund because of:

- Safety. Even though not guaranteed by the federal government, this type of account is regulated by the Securities Exchange Commission.
- Liquidity. Deposits are not tied to any time frames, which means your funds are available at any time and in any amount. You can take out only the amount you need.
- Higher rates of interest. The return on money market fund accounts are typically 1 to 1.5 percentage points higher than bank or credit-union accounts.
- Check-writing privileges. This is a feature that allows access to the funds without going through phone calls and wire transfers. You cannot think of this as a checking account and that's good. Money market fund

accounts have restrictions against writing checks for small amounts, say less than $200. Typically there are no fees imposed or restrictions on the number of checks that can be written in a month.

If your funds are parked in a money market fund, you don't have to worry about maturity dates, the possibility of early withdrawal penalties, or getting in before the auction closes. The interest effective yield (interest rate) moves with the general state of the economy.

While most money market fund accounts require a minimum deposit of at least $2,500, some waive that requirement if you authorize automatic deposits of at least $50 a month.

There are literally hundreds of money market funds from which to choose if you decide this is a good place for your Contingency Fund. Before opening any account, you need to call for and read a prospectus so you fully understand the rules and risks involved. With the prospectus you will receive an application that looks daunting but is actually quite simple to complete. If you have any questions, you should call the toll-free customer service number.

I recommend that you consider a money market fund account for your Contingency Fund and that you also sign up for automatic deposit authorization. That way you have the best of all worlds with the least amount of babysitting your fund.

REPUTABLE MONEY MARKET FUNDS		
Fund Name	Minimum to Open	Telephone
Benham Prime Money Market	$2,500	800-472-3389
Vanguard Prime Portfolio	$3,000	800-662-7447
USAA Money Market	$3,000*	800-531-8181
Strong Money Market Fund	$2,500	800-368-3863

*Exception: The minimum deposit is waived if you authorize automatic monthly deposits of at least $50

AUTOMATIC DEPOSIT AUTHORIZATION

I cannot tell you what a huge proponent I am of automatic deposits, especially when it comes to building a savings or investment account.

With my busy lifestyle and my tendency to put things off, I know I would forget or find some reason to skip my savings deposits from time to time. Authorizing my bank or investment account manager to reach into my checking account on a specified day every month to take out the amount I authorize is one way I simplify my life. In a way it's like delegating work to someone else so I can be free to do what I do best. I think of it as hiring a staff person to handle the savings and depositing that I've committed to do.

If you have any tendencies toward procrastination and feel better when things are taken care of for you, I suggest you think seriously about arranging for automatic deposits into your Contingency Fund. Even more important than knowing you won't have to remember to make the deposit, if the money is gone before you see it, you won't miss it. I've proven this for myself and have had it confirmed over and over again by people who have tried it.

Months Required to Accumulate $10,000				
4 PERCENT ANNUAL INTEREST				
If you start with	Assuming you add this much each month				
	$100	$150	$200	$250	$300
$0	87	61	47	38	32
$500	82	57	44	36	30
$1000	77	54	42	34	29
$2000	67	48	37	30	25
$3000	58	41	32	26	22
$5000	41	29	23	19	16

Months Required to Accumulate $10,000				
6 PERCENT ANNUAL INTEREST				
If you start with	Assuming you add this much each month				
	$100	$150	$200	$250	$300
$0	81	58	45	37	31
$500	77	55	43	35	30
$1000	72	51	40	33	28
$2000	62	45	35	29	25
$3000	54	39	31	25	22
$5000	37	27	22	18	15

In the beginning you might feel the pinch of having your savings automatically deducted from your regular checking account and deposited into your savings vehicle. But before you know it this will become ordinary. You won't miss it, and you won't have to worry about remembering to make that transfer of funds. Some larger employers offer such a service as a payroll deduction plan. You simply fill out an authorization form with the specific account numbers and so on. Your pay stub will indicate that the money has been deposited automatically. Of course, you can change your automatic deposit authorization anytime. You can increase the amount, change the date, or even change your mind. You're the boss, and isn't that a wonderful feeling!

## Chapter Seven

Break Out of the Debt Trap

THE POWER OF THE RAPID DEBT-REPAYMENT PLAN

No investment is as secure as a repaid debt.

Austin Pryor

I f your kitchen is on fire, fireproofing your home is the last thing on your mind. All you can think about is getting that fire out. But while your efforts are directed specifically at the problem at hand, you are not purposely starting fires in other rooms of the house just to see how large a blaze you can get going.

The same goes for debt-proofing your life. Any stupid debt you have is tantamount to that kitchen fire. You need to devote your efforts to putting it out! At the same time you must do everything in your power to make sure you don't set other areas of your life on fire while battling the major blaze. When you get that fire out, I assure you you'll be a lot more interested in "fireproofing" the kitchen. In the same way, once you are out of debt, you will be seriously concerned about debt-proofing your life.

You Need a Good Debt-Repayment Plan

There are lots of plans available that will help you get out of debt. Some concentrate on debt with the highest interest rate; others start with the smallest debt. Some plans have provisions that require you to increase all of your payments from the get-go, while others work with the minimum monthly payments you have presently.

If you're in debt, you have to get out by whatever means works for you. So put your mind into high gear and put together a plan—then stick with it. Commit to do whatever is necessary to complete the plan. (If you want to do yourself the biggest favor of all, commit to completing it in half the time.)

Above all, remember: a plan is only as good as your ability to stick with it. Just like diets, all of them work in theory, even the hot dog/popcorn diet (so I've been told). The true test, however, is which diet will you stick with? No matter how effective the plan is on a daily basis, if the regimen is outlandish and impractical, you will not stick with it no matter how good it looks on paper.

When evaluating a get-out-of-debt plan, you should look for the following characteristics:

1. It is specific.
2. It is easy to prepare.
3. It is simple to understand.
4. It is visually pleasing and suitable for refrigerator posting.
5. Its results can be measured.
6. It has a specific finish date.

When it comes to this kind of effort, the simpler the better. But don't sacrifice quality on the altar of simplicity.

THE RAPID DEBT-REPAYMENT PLAN

Surprise! I have developed a plan that fits the above criteria. It's a simple plan and effective because it works. I call it the Rapid Debt-Repayment Plan.

This plan works with all debts, not simply those that are unsecured. You could, for instance, include your home mortgage, automobile loan, and any other secured debts in your plan. However, for our purposes and in keeping with the goal of ridding you of your debts, we'll use only unsecured debts in the examples that follow.

Let me show you how this plan works using Bob and Sally Green as our fictitious subjects. Below is a list of their unsecured debts: the current balance, the interest rate (APR), and the current minimum monthly payment.

Debt Name	Current Balance	Annual Percentage Rate (APR)	Current Minimum Monthly Payment
MasterCard	$3,897	16.9%	$115
Visa	$1,775	18%	$50
First Bank	$1,500	9%	$60
MNBA	$16,750	8.9%	$300
Optima	$900	18%	$50
Discover Card	$1,350	19.99%	$65
Totals	$26,172		$640

THE FOUR RDRP RULES

This plan is simple because there are only four rules. If you adhere closely to all four rules, you will get out of debt in record time. Just imagine how your life will change when you are completely stupid-debt free. It can happen—more quickly than you might have dared to dream. More than that, stick with it and it *will* happen!

Rule #1: No more new debt. Unless you are willing to stop adding to your unsecured debts, you're really out of luck when it comes to debt-proofing your life. Furthermore, if you don't stop adding to the problem, you'll be like the homeowner with the kitchen fire—except instead of putting out the blaze that's ready to destroy the entire structure, you'll be pouring gasoline on it. It might be manageable for awhile, but you'll be on your way to a full-on raging inferno. The rule is simple: add no new revolving unsecured debt.

Rule #2: Pay the same amount every month disregarding the declining minimum amount due as stated on the monthly statement until that debt is paid. If you are following Rule #1 religiously, you will soon notice something peculiar about your minimum monthly payment: it will start to shrink. Credit card companies in particular are not that interested in your paying off your debt. They'd like to keep you in the position of paying them a tidy sum of interest every month for the rest of your life. That is why your minimum monthly payment may be a percentage of the remaining balance, generally 2 to 3 percent. RDRP Rule #2 requires that you pay no less than the amount of your minimum monthly payment required for the first month of your repayment plan. In the Greens' case, their current MasterCard payment is $115, which is about 3 percent of the current principal balance of $3,897. Next month the required payment might drop to $113 or $110. Nonetheless, they will ignore the change and commit to paying no less than $115 every month to MasterCard until that debt is paid in full.

Rule #3: Line up your debts according to size, putting the one with the shortest pay-off time at the top and the one with the longest term at the bottom.

Rule #4: As one debt is paid, take that payment and redirect it to the regular payment of the next debt in line. This rule requires that until completely debt free, you pay the same total amount toward your debt (in this case $640) until all debts are paid. For example, when Optima is paid in full, the Greens do not absorb the $50 they have been sending monthly to Optima into their regular household funds. They redirect it to the next debt in line.

Are these rules important? Absolutely! The following charts show three different scenarios for the Green family. Look at how their financial picture changes if they pick and choose which rules to follow.

SCENARIO A

The Greens obey Rule #1, but not Rule #2. Instead they make their payments each month according to the creditor's desires, where the payment is always in the same ratio to the principal as it is in the first month. This is also referred to as "falling payments."

Debt Name	Principal	APR	Payment Amount	Total Interest	Total Number of Payments
MasterCard	$3,897	16.9%	$115	$3,373.26	205
Visa	$1,775	18%	$50	$1,773.13	174
First Bank	$1,500	9%	$60	$316.34	84
MBNA	$16,750	8.9%	$300	$11,608.89	396
Optima	$900	18%	$50	$297.67	62
Discover Card	$1,350	19.99%	$65	$653.60	86
Totals	$26,172		$640	$18,022.89	396

The total of the Greens' current payments is $640 in the first month. If they add no new debt and make their payments according to the falling payment method, whereby their monthly payment always bears the same relationship to the principal as it does in the first month, it will take 396 months (33 years) to pay off all of their debts. In addition to the $26,172 they will pay back, they will also pay $18,022.89 in interest, for a total payback of $44,194.89.

SCENARIO B

The Greens obey Rule #1 and Rule #2, but as one debt is paid off, the money they've been paying to that debt each month is absorbed into some other area of their lives.

Debt Name	Principal	APR	Payment Amount	Total Interest	Total Number of Payments
MasterCard	$3,897	16.9%	$115	$1,436.94	47
Visa	$1,775	18%	$50	$778.50	52
First Bank	$1,500	9%	$60	$167.37	28
MBNA	$16,750	8.9%	$300	$4,954.66	73
Optima	$900	18%	$50	$156.92	22
Discover Card	$1,350	19.99%	$65	$320.71	26
Totals	$26,172		$640	$7,815.10	73

The total of the Greens' current monthly payments is $640. Because they will now obey Rule #1 (no new debting) and Rule #2 (they commit to pay no less than $640 each month until debt free), they will be debt free in 73 months (6 years and one month) instead of the 396 months it would have taken in scenario A. They will also avoid paying $10,207.79 in interest by adding Rule #2 to their plan.

SCENARIO C

The Greens obey all four nonnegotiables: they stop incurring new revolving debt; they pay the same amount every month toward each unsecured debt (said amount determined by what the minimum required is on the first month of their plan); they put their smallest debt at the top of the list; and as one debt is paid, they take that payment amount and redirect it to the next debt in line, thereby accelerating the payoff plan.

Debt Name	Principal	APR	Payment Amount	Total Interest	Total Number of Payments
Optima	$900	18%	$50	$156.92	22
Discover Card	$1,350	19.99%	$65	$315.88	24
First Bank	$1,500	9%	$60	$164.80	26
MasterCard	$3,897	16.9%	$115	$1,221.88	33
Visa	$1,775	18%	$50	$678.90	36
MBNA	$16,750	8.9%	$300	$4,148.32	52
Totals	$26,172		$640	$6,686.70	52

SCENARIO COMPARISON SUMMARY			
Payment Plan	Number of Months	Total Interest	Interest Savings
A. Rule #1	396	$18,022.90	$0
B. Rules #1 & #2	73	$7,815.10	$10,207.79
C. Rules #1, #2, #3, & #4	52	$6,686.70	$11,336.19

As we compare the different scenarios, we see that there are definite advantages to following all four RDRP rules. If the Greens faithfully commit to the debt-repayment plan laid out in scenario C, their payment schedule will look like the chart on page 94.

RAPID DEBT-REPAYMENT SCHEDULE
(SUITABLE FOR REFRIGERATOR POSTING!)

#	Month/Yr	MBNA	Visa	M/C	First Bank	Discover Card	Optima
1	Jan 2000	300	50	115	60	65	50
2	Feb 2000	300	50	115	60	65	50
3	Mar 2000	300	50	115	60	65	50
4	Apr 2000	300	50	115	60	65	50
5	May 2000	300	50	115	60	65	50
6	Jun 2000	300	50	115	60	65	50
7	Jul 2000	300	50	115	60	65	50
8	Aug 2000	300	50	115	60	65	50
9	Sep 2000	300	50	115	60	65	50
10	Oct 2000	300	50	115	60	65	50
11	Nov 2000	300	50	115	60	65	50
12	Dec 2000	300	50	115	60	65	50
13	Jan 2001	300	50	115	60	65	50
14	Feb 2001	300	50	115	60	65	50
15	Mar 2001	300	50	115	60	65	50
16	Apr 2001	300	50	115	60	65	50
17	May 2001	300	50	115	60	65	50
18	Jun 2001	300	50	115	60	65	50
19	Jul 2001	300	50	115	60	65	50
20	Aug 2001	300	50	115	60	65	50
21	Sep 2001	300	50	115	60	65	50
22	Oct 2001	300	50	115	60	108	6
23	Nov 2001	300	50	115	60	115	
24	Dec 2001	300	50	115	97	77	
25	Jan 2002	300	50	115	175		
26	Feb 2002	300	50	277	12		
27	Mar 2002	300	50	290			
28	Apr 2002	300	50	290			
29	May 2002	300	50	290			
30	Jun 2002	300	50	290			
31	Jul 2002	300	50	290			
32	Aug 2002	300	50	290			
33	Sep 2002	300	113	226			
34	Oct 2002	300	340				
35	Nov 2002	300	340				
36	Dec 2002	579	60				
37	Jan 2003	640					
38	Feb 2003	640					
39	Mar 2003	640					
40	Apr 2003	640					
41	May 2003	640					
42	Jun 2003	640					
43	Jul 2003	640					
44	Aug 2003	640					
45	Sep 2003	640					
46	Oct 2003	640					
47	Nov 2003	640					
48	Dec 2003	640					
49	Jan 2004	640					
50	Feb 2004	640					
51	Mar 2004	640					
52	Apr 2004	218					

Notice that the debts are now sorted so that the loan with the fewest number of payments is in the first position. The Greens' monthly payment is still $640, which they commit to pay each month. They also agree to no new debt. However, as Optima is paid in full, the $50 that was going there is added to the regular payment going to Discover Card. When Discover is paid, both Optima's $50 and the Discover Card's $65 are added to the First Bank payment and so on and so on until all are paid in full. By adhering to all four RDRP rules, the Greens will avoid paying $11,336.19 in interest charges and will be debt free in 52 months, or 4 years and 4 months.

Oh, the power of a plan! Bob and Sally can see exactly when they will be finished paying their debts. And should they decide to accelerate their plan even more, they can simply add to the amount they pay to the debt at the top of the chart (or in the case of our chart on page 94, the debt on the right).

Once the Greens are debt free in April 2004 as their plan prescribes, they should immediately redirect the entire $640 to some other specific purpose, such as rapidly repaying their mortgage, or redirecting it into an investment program—or some combination of the two.

Let's see what will happen if the Greens (both will be 39 years old when they finish paying their debt in April 2004) redirect $640 a month ($7,680 annually) into an investment vehicle that earns 10 percent interest compounded annually until they retire at age 63.

HOW $640 MONTHLY INVESTMENT WILL GROW

#	Year	Age	Annual Investment	Interest Earned	Investment Value	Accumulated Investment	Accumulated Earnings
1	2005	39	$7,680	768.00	8,448.90	7,680.00	768.00
2	2006	40	$7,680	844.80	16,972.80	15,360.00	1,612.80
3	2007	41	$7,680	1,697.28	26,350.08	23,040.00	3,310.08
4	2008	42	$7,680	2,635.00	36,665.08	30,720.00	5,945.08
5	2009	43	$7,680	3,666.50	48,011.59	38,400.00	9,611.59
6	2010	44	$7,680	4,801.15	60,492.75	46,080.00	14,412.75
7	2011	45	$7,680	6,049.27	74,222.03	53,760.00	20,462.03
8	2012	46	$7,680	7,422.20	89,324.23	61,440.00	27,884.23
9	2013	47	$7,680	8,932.42	105,936.65	69,120.00	36,816.65
10	2014	48	$7,680	10,593.66	124,210.32	76,800.00	47,410.32
11	2015	49	$7,680	12,421.03	144,311.35	84,480.00	59,831.35
12	2016	50	$7,680	14,431.13	166,422.49	92,160.00	74,262.49
13	2017	51	$7,680	16,642.24	190,744.74	99,840.00	90,904.74
14	2018	52	$7,680	19,074.47	217,499.21	107,520.00	109,979.21
15	2019	53	$7,680	21,749.92	246,929.13	115,200.00	131,729.13
16	2020	54	$7,680	24,692.91	279,302.05	122,880.00	156,422.05
17	2021	55	$7,680	27,930.20	314,912.25	130,560.00	184,352.25
18	2022	56	$7,680	31,491.22	354,083.48	138,240.00	215,843.48
19	2023	57	$7,680	35,408.34	397,171.83	145,920.00	251,251.83
20	2024	58	$7,680	39,717.18	444,569.01	153,600.00	290,969.01
21	2025	59	$7,680	44,456.90	496,705.91	161,280.00	335,425.91
22	2026	60	$7,680	49,670.59	554,056.50	168,960.00	385,096.50
23	2027	61	$7,680	55,408.65	617,142.15	176,640.00	440,502.15
24	2028	62	$7,680	61,714.21	686,536.37	184,320.00	502,216.37
25	2029	63	$7,680	68,653.63	762,870.01	192,000.00	570,870.01

If after paying all their unsecured debts, the Greens invested the $7,680 they had been sending to the creditors each year at 10 percent interest compounded annually, in 25 years their investment would grow to **$762,870.01.**

CALCULATING YOUR RAPID DEBT-REPAYMENT PLAN

UTILIZING CYBERSPACE

When I first developed the RDRP it was great, but not nearly as specific as I would have preferred. Thankfully, since then we've entered cyberspace and now enjoy the power of super technology. Available in the members' area at our website—www.debtproofliving.com—is what I call the amazing Rapid Debt-Repayment Plan (RDRP) "calculator." This is not the kind of calculator you can hold in your hand, but rather software that resides on my Internet website. This particular online calculator (one of several dozen that reside there) has revolutionized our ability to offer a plan that meets and exceeds all of the characteristics listed above. The RDRP theory has not changed over the years; only our ability to offer it in a more refined and usable format has changed. (See page 386 for specific information on how to get online membership access to the RDRP calculator and many others.)

MANUAL METHODS OF CALCULATION

If you do not have access to the amazing RDRP calculator at www.debtproofliving.com, do not consider that an excuse for not getting busy with your RDRP. There are other ways, albeit a bit more difficult, to work your plan equally efficiently.

Financial calculator. There are financial calculators out there (these are the kind you hold in your hand and can buy at an electronics store) that will help you come up with the numbers you need for your plan. Using Sally and Bob's smallest debt, Optima, as an example, the following is the type of question you need to ask of that calculator (or of the really smart person who owns it and is willing to help you): I have a debt of $900. The annual interest rate is 18 percent fixed, and I will pay $50 once each month. How many months will it take to pay the debt in full? Repeat for each of your debts.

Use that information to make a chart just like the one you see on page 94. I suggest you have handy a fist full of pencils and a really big eraser. I've done this manually more times than I like to recall, and I assure you it can be done. It just takes a long time and is very tedious. Your debt-free future is worth it, so persevere!

No calculator method. If you can do the foregoing calculations in your head, bless you. And call me—I want to tell you just how amazing you are. If you, however, cannot do this in your head, do not have a financial calculator, do not know anyone who has one, do not have access to the Internet, and you basically live on a deserted island in the middle of the Pacific, still you can do this! You will likely sacrifice the benefit of being able to project with specificity which month and year you will be debt free, but then again, if you're on the deserted island, you probably don't know what month and year it is right now anyway.

Here's what you should do: Get a really long piece of paper and make up a blank form similar to the one below. Make enough columns to accommodate the number of your unsecured debts plus two extras to the left for the Payment Number and the Month/Year. You are going to fill in your payments as you make them.

Below are examples that illustrate the progression of your Rapid Debt-Repayment Plan.

This is how your chart will look the first month.

#	Month/Year	MBNA	Visa	Master-Card	First Bank	Discover Card	Optima
1	Jan 2000	300	50	115	60	65	50

You will add the payment information in the second month, making sure you pay exactly the same amount (or more but never less) each month.

#	Month/Year	MBNA	Visa	Master-Card	First Bank	Discover Card	Optima
1	Jan 2000	300	50	115	60	65	50
2	Feb 2000	300	50	115	60	65	50

Third month, same thing.

#	Month/Year	MBNA	Visa	Master-Card	First Bank	Discover Card	Optima
1	Jan 2000	300	50	115	60	65	50
2	Feb 2000	300	50	115	60	65	50
3	March 2000	300	50	115	60	65	50

. . . and the fourth.

#	Month/Year	MBNA	Visa	Master-Card	First Bank	Discover Card	Optima
1	Jan 2000	300	50	115	60	65	50
2	Feb 2000	300	50	115	60	65	50
3	March 2000	300	50	115	60	65	50
4	April 2000	300	50	115	60	65	50

Fast forward to month 22. You get your statement from Optima and see you owe only $6 and then you will be paid in full. Do a cartwheel, throw a little confetti, and be sure to write and let me know (I will celebrate too!). What fun you will have filling in the chart in month 22 because finally something is going to change. You write 6 in the Optima column and $108 in the next debt to the left because you are going to send Discover Card far more than they really want. You will send the $65 to which you have committed plus the $44 you didn't send to Optima. (Note: All of the figures in the RDRP charts are rounded off. I am following the computer-generated chart in this manual illustration. Don't write and tell me that $44 and $65 don't equal $108. I know. It all works out in the end, trust me.)

#	Month/Year	MBNA	Visa	Master-Card	First Bank	Discover Card	Optima
20	Aug 2001	300	50	115	60	65	50
21	Sept 2001	300	50	115	60	65	50
22	Oct 2001	300	50	115	60	108	6

In month 23 the entire $50 Optima used to get goes to rapidly repay Discover Card to the tune of $115.

#	Month/Year	MBNA	Visa	Master-Card	First Bank	Discover Card	Optima
20	Aug 2001	300	50	115	60	65	50
21	Sept 2001	300	50	115	60	65	50
22	Oct 2001	300	50	115	60	108	6
23	Nov 2001	300	50	115	60	115	

In month 24 you look at your Discover Card statement to realize your total balance remaining is now only $77, so you pay it off and move the difference over to the First Bank payment.

#	Month/Year	MBNA	Visa	Master-Card	First Bank	Discover Card	Optima
20	Aug 2001	300	50	115	60	65	50
21	Sept 2001	300	50	115	60	65	50
22	Oct 2001	300	50	115	60	108	6
23	Nov 2001	300	50	115	60	115	
24	Dec 2001	300	50	115	97	77	

About this time I predict you are going to get anxious to see how the plan is going to work in the future, so you will either get yourself to a library that has Internet access so you can become a member of my website—www.debtproofliving.com— and use the RDRP calculator, or you will find a friend with a financial calculator. Keeping track is remarkable, but seeing into the future is exhilarating! As you approach month 25 in your plan, you will not know exactly how many months you have to go. It will feel like an eternity. However, if you have the computerized printout, you will see that you are nearly halfway there—and in April 2004 you will be debt free.

THE QUESTION

If you haven't already asked the following question, you probably will at some point: Wouldn't it be better to line up my debts according to interest rate, with the highest interest rate debt in the first position rather than the debt with the smallest balance?

Theoretically, perhaps that would be the way to go. And you are going to hear many financial experts who advise that method. Keep in mind that I have designed this plan according to what works for me. I acknowledge that I am an emotional being. When tackling a job this challenging, I need gratification as quickly as possible—and right now would not be too soon. If I approach my debt-repayment plan with the largest interest rate as the first priority, I might be working on my largest debt. It could be many years before I reach my first zero balance. That would be like going on a diet and not losing any weight for three years . . . maybe four. Who would stick with such a plan?

I have worked these plans every which way possible, and still believe that the potential difference in interest is miniscule compared to the benefit of using a plan that has a high probability of taking me across the finish line—or to the starting line, if you know what I mean.

The RDRP is a plan that works because it is something you can live with. It is both economically and emotionally sound.

OPTIONAL RULE #5: REPORT

Many, many people have reported using the RDRP successfully. I know because they write to me and tell me of their progress and when they pay that final debt. If you are carrying unsecured debt, I hope to hear from you too. Please let me know when you cross the finish line. I do care, and I do celebrate your victory.

Just last week we received a call at the office. I was out at the time, but my assistant Cathy spoke with this caller who was experiencing a particularly emotional moment. She explained to Cathy that she couldn't give her name or number, but she needed to speak with someone . . . anyone!

Seems she began working on her RDRP several years previously when she had more than $24,000 in unsecured debt. She explained that just prior to calling, she'd mailed the last check. Her RDRP was complete. She made it. She needed to tell someone who would care. I'll never know who this dear lady was, but I am still doing my mental cartwheels—and throwing confetti too.

So no matter when it happens, you must let me know. Write, E-mail, send a carrier pigeon. I don't care what method you use (provided you don't go into debt to pay for it). Just do it.

TURBOCHARGE YOUR RDRP

One reason the RDRP is such a great tool is that it does not require you to increase any of the payments beyond the current minimums you are making right now. If you are making your current payments, you *can* get out of debt. I hope that is encouraging if you, like most people, assume that you need some major financial intervention—like an unexpected inheritance, or Ed McMahon and Dick Clark knocking at your door—even to consider getting debt free. Now, having said that, let me suggest that there are ways you can speed up the process.

INCREASE THE MONTHLY PAYMENT

If you are able (it would be advisable to stretch yourself if at all possible), increase the amount you commit to the RDRP total monthly payment. Using the Greens' example, let's say they could realistically increase that $640 monthly commitment to $700. That would change the Optima payment from

$50 to $110 (applying the full $60 additional commitment to the first debt). Here is how that technique would affect their plan: instead of being debt free in 52 months, the time would be reduced to 46 months, and their interest savings would increase to $12,031.19.

INCREASE PAYMENTS OCCASIONALLY

The beauty of this plan is that even the smallest windfall can be applied to a specific and noble cause—getting out of debt! Let's say you work overtime one month and see an additional $50 in your paycheck. You can direct that amount to the regular monthly payment of whichever debt is farthest to the right (or on top) as a one-time boost. Then you simply recalculate your plan (if you have RDRP calculator access) to get a current printout for the refrigerator, or recalculate by whichever method you used in the beginning. Because at this point you are always paying more than the minimum required by the creditor, to go back next month to the amount required by the RDRP will not get you into any kind of trouble with the creditor. To be perfectly honest, I have a feeling they are confused beyond belief by your odd payments anyway, and that should keep you chuckling all the way to the end. I have one reader, in fact, who, with a sense of joy, writes "Ha-ha!" in the memo area of her monthly check that is going to the creditor farthest to the right (or the top, whichever way you position your RDRP). She loves the idea of them having to accept more money than they actually require.

CONVERT TO A BIWEEKLY RDRP

Unlike many mortgage holders, credit card and other unsecured debt holders will accept partial payments at any time during the billing cycle. The theory is to pay one-half of your payments every two weeks. This has two benefits:

1. By using a biweekly schedule, you will make 26 half-payments in a year, or the equivalent of 13 monthly payments. By prepaying an additional month's payment each year, you will significantly cut the time and interest required to get debt free.

2. By paying early in the month, you stop the effect of compounding interest. The credit card companies must, by law, process payments of any size as received.

At this writing, a Biweekly RDRP Calculator is under construction at our website. We will keep you posted.

GO AFTER LOWER INTEREST RATES

I've saved this tactic for last because it is the least likely to happen. However, if you have a debt with an outrageously high interest rate, it cannot hurt to ask for a reduction.

For high interest rate credit card balances, start with customer service. Just call the toll-free number and tell them you are distressed by the high rate you are being charged. Point out to them that you are being offered considerably lower rates all the time and you are thinking about switching. If you have been a good customer (and you are if you've been paying lots of interest over the years), chances are great that they might accommodate your request.

TRANSFER CREDIT CARD BALANCES TO A LOWER RATE CARD

OK, I've made the suggestion, but let me quickly follow with all the reasons this is not only risky but potentially hazardous to your wealth. What could go wrong? Plenty. And most all of it can be found in the fine print on the typical credit card application. If you choose to consider this tactic you'd best get a magnifying glass.

1. The low interest rate could be only introductory. Read carefully to see how quickly that 3.9 percent rate morphs into something closer to 9.9 percent or 12.9 percent.

2. The low interest rate that captured your attention could be very restrictive. Does it really apply to balance transfers or only new purchases or both?

3. Does that new card have an annual fee? If so . . . there goes the benefit of switching.

4. What about late fees and over-limit fees? Here is where the companies are making up for what they're "losing" on that low interest rate on the front end. Read all of these provisions very carefully, because in many instances not only will you be hit with a huge late penalty, you can kiss that low interest rate good-bye. And if you are late twice, watch out. The interest could zoom to 22.99 percent or more.

5. Watch out for balance-transfer fees. Some issuers charge transaction fees as high as 4 percent of the transferred amount. That is significant.

6. Too many credit inquiries can spell trouble for your credit report. Card-hopping shows up as a suspicious activity. Say you apply for a real estate loan in the future. The lender may see any open credit lines and multiple applications as potential outstanding debt. Even though you may not be heavily in debt at the time, you have the potential to run it up overnight, and that would be considered a negative.

It is really tough these days to qualify for low-rate card offers, and holding onto those low rates is even more difficult. Some companies now have fine print that gives them permission to look into your credit history file whenever they like. And if they find that you have been late with other debts you carry or have significantly increased your total debt, your rates may increase.

While transferring balances to lower rate cards may be a beneficial tactic in a rare case, it is important to remember that these companies are in this for the money—not to make your life easier or to decrease the amount of interest you will end up paying. On the contrary, they are looking for excuses to charge you more and recover the interest rate they may be losing. If you do not have perfect credit and do not maintain an impeccable payment schedule, they are going to take advantage of you.

Getting out of debt is unlike any other kind of recovery program I know of or have participated in. In other kinds of endeavors, such as weight loss, which I'm very familiar with, the joy is not in the recovery itself but in reaching the goal. Rapidly repaying debt, however, seems to be a different kind of recovery. The joy is in the recovery. The joy comes from sending those checks every month, in seeing the balances decline, in knowing that you're traveling in a different direction than the one that got you into the trap.

For myself, I can report that repaying debts in a conscious and reasoned manner brought me the same kind of exhilaration that spending did. I cannot explain that in rational terms; I can only testify to you that it is true. I have had many readers confirm this in their lives as well. Getting out of debt is an important part of the journey.

For those of you who are not now in debt, nor have ever had a problem with debt, this is still an important part of the debt-proof living process that you need to know about. You never know when it might be a child, spouse, or relative who needs your wisdom and encouragement to get out of debt. Perhaps you will someday find yourself in the position of counseling others in this regard. Your encouragement and effectiveness will come from your understanding. And you cannot understand what you do not acknowledge and then know to be true.

RDRP TESTIMONIALS

"We are just beginning our RDRP and are so excited about it. My husband has always been one just not to get involved when it comes to the bills (except to accumulate them), but now since I have shown him your plan, he is ready to start!"—Lisa

"My husband and I have finally started our RDRP. I have been literally at the point of waking up nights in a sweat because of financial worry. It has taken us a long time to take the first step of putting the plan into action, but what a freeing feeling! According to the calculations, we will be debt free in 26 months. It will be a long road for us, but a journey which will—and already has—taught us many lessons. Thank you for sharing your life with us and for those awesome calculators at your website!"—Karen

"Just wanted to drop you a note and say thank you for having an influence on my life. I just wrote my last credit payment and am now debt free except my home. That's my next major hurdle to be completely debt free. I have followed your advice for two years. You have been a major impact in my life and I will ever be so grateful. Thank you for caring enough to share your heartaches and experiences."—Brenda

"I am a sixty-three-year-old woman on a retired fixed income. All my adult life I have had credit cards and revolving balances. Last August I decided to develop my Rapid Debt-Repayment Plan. I made a commitment not to charge anything else and began paying down my debts—more than $5,000. In

less than one year I have completed my plan; I am debt free for the first time and much happier for it. Indeed this year was my turning point."—Tracy

"I must tell you that I have figured my Rapid Debt-Repayment Plan using the online calculator. You showed me how to save $7,113 in interest and cut my payoff time from 118 months to 21 months using the same amount of money I always use to pay my bills. I can't begin to express how happy that has made me and how much it has inspired my husband to help me with becoming debt free!"—Dana

"Today is independence day for our family. We are out of debt except for our home and one final round of truck payments. We have followed the RDRP to the letter for the past two years. I am so proud to be able to stand here and say it's possible and what freedom you acquire when you're finished. It's amazing how much money is suddenly coming our way to invest and save now that the bills are paid."—Linda

## Chapter Eight

Expect the Unexpected

FREEDOM ACCOUNT

That which we call our necessary expenses
will always grow to equal our income
unless we protest to the contrary.

George Clason

Have you ever noticed that no matter what size your apartment, condominium, house, garage, drawers, closets, hard drive, handbag, or briefcase is—it is mysteriously filled to capacity?

Our first apartment was three hundred square feet. We were newlyweds, didn't have much, and were still in the cozy stage, so it wasn't a problem. Three years later we were packed to the gills and longed for a little breathing space, so we moved into a twelve-hundred-square-foot house. Wow, so much extra room. In what seemed like the time it took to unpack, the place was mysteriously filled to capacity.

A year later we moved into an eighteen-hundred-square-foot house that had a big family room addition and two-car garage. Again, whatever-that-is kicked in, and soon we were full to the rafters.

Twelve years later we moved into our present house which is twice the size, and—you guessed it—we're full. Paring down, cleaning out, and simplifying has become an unrelenting challenge. We must be in a constant mode of "protesting to the contrary" to maintain control of our possessions and our lives.

This great mystery of life operates in the area of finances as well. It goes like this: No matter what your income, your necessary expenses will be equal to it.

Think back to your last pay increase. I have a feeling that before you could even enjoy the extra money it was mysteriously absorbed into this nebulous thing we call necessary expenses.

Just like the problem with stuff that fills closets, drawers, homes, and hard drives, unless you protest to the contrary, the forces that are at work constantly to ratchet up your "necessary expenses" will send you down in defeat.

Most people, without actually thinking about it, assume their necessary expenses are those that repeat every month. But they are wrong. Not all necessary expenses are as systematically recurring as the rent, grocery bill, telephone bill, and car payment. When we assume, however, that those are the only necessary expenses and allow them to grow to equal our income, everything falls apart when the nonrecurring expenses appear out of the blue with all the urgency of a baby ready to be born.

This is the way most of us think: *The expenses I have right now—this month—are my necessary expenses. Everything else is optional. If an expense is not in my face at this moment, I have a choice whether to pay it or not.*

Before we can hope to find the solution, we have to understand fully the problem and why it is so unique to these times in which we live.

Before the advent of easy credit, people had no choice but to anticipate. They had to save up for everything because there was no alternative. Anticipating expenses and being prepared for those rainy days was the only way to deal with the reality of running out of money. Whether you had a lot or only a little, you never spent all of it. Anticipation meant survival.

The advent of easy consumer credit perpetuated a dangerous, albeit most welcomed, message that we didn't have to worry anymore. Running out of money was no longer a possibility. Running out of cash? Sure, but that didn't mean running out of money. We were assured that if we could spend money, it was the same as having money.

The message was that as long as we had the umbrella of credit, we would stay dry no matter how rainy the days became. Our incomes were now freed from all thoughts of tomorrow and were available to make the present just as wonderful as possible.

It was the new wave of the future and seemed far superior to the past. The convenience and security of plastic made everything else seem old-fashioned. We rolled our eyes as our grandparents lectured about how things were "in the old days," the importance of frugality, and not buying on credit. We thought we were up-to-date and modern in our thinking. Our grandparents worried that we were headed for trouble.

We learned that while *emergency* was once defined as a situation in which one's health or safety was in imminent danger, the new meaning included much more—the twice-yearly sale, a brake job on the family automobile, Junior's preschool tuition, the Christmas holidays, and anything else, provided it was on sale. We turned into a nation of spoiled consumers who overconsume and overspend because we believe that what we have is ours to spend now, and the purpose of credit is to be there whenever life takes us by surprise.

During my wild spending years, anticipation was something I counted on, but only if it was personally beneficial. I anticipated that my husband should receive regular pay increases and bonuses. I expected and acted on it. I anticipated that the home we purchased in 1975 for $38,000 would be worth—and this was only a rough estimate—between 5 and 10 million dollars someday. I anticipated king-sized tax refunds and a future free of financial worries.

On the other hand, it didn't cross my mind that I could possibly anticipate an urgent trip to the dentist or the cost of a new set of tires. I loved my new Cadillac sitting in the driveway, but in my wildest dreams I could not anticipate the $600 price tag tied to that first required maintenance appointment or that my land yacht was no more mine then than it would be in three years when the lease was up.

Not once did I anticipate the expenses of clothing a family of four, but somehow I consistently managed to avoid anything close to a fashion risk. Anticipate a burned-out water heater? Get real. A trip to the emergency room to repair the damage sustained during a boy's maiden voyage on his new bike? No way.

Thanks to available credit, I began labeling all kinds of things as emergencies and felt completely justified in doing so. The provision was there, so why not take full advantage of it?

All you have to do is look at the horrible amount of debt I amassed to understand how often we ran into problems we'd not anticipated. And I must admit that the credit card companies came through quite nicely.

Most people just don't think of allowing each month for all the things that will happen on an occasional or unpredictable basis. The failure to anticipate has become a pervasive financial problem in this country, evidenced by the fact that in 1998 outstanding consumer debt hit an all-time high of $1.4 trillion. That is not what the government owes; that's what individuals owe as a result of impatience and failure to anticipate.

If you are like most, your financial situation looks pretty good on paper. When you add up your necessary expenses and deduct them from your income, it looks as if there is at least enough there. Ends should meet. On paper it might even appear that you have a surplus. Rarely does that scenario play out in real life. Without fail, it seems something always happens. There's never enough money to get through the month, or if there is, it is a very rare thing indeed. If it's not a brake job, it's a busted water heater or soccer sign-ups or a million other little things that catch you by surprise. So much for any surplus you've managed to accumulate.

The diagnosis is clear: You have a case of selective amnesia. Selective amnesia is a condition that attacks your memory in the irregular, intermittent, and unexpected expenses region. You've lost your ability to anticipate those things that you should anticipate as a normal part of life, and in so doing, you've conveniently lost your memory.

Your predictable monthly bills are not the problem. Somehow the rent or mortgage and utilities get paid, and the family is fed. Some months it's tight, but you manage to get by. Once in a while there's even a bit of money left after the current bills are paid. You breathe a sigh of relief, and you automatically assume every month from now on is going to be as easy. *Wow! It feels great to have the bills paid. And money left over. Finally we're getting ahead of the game. Let's get a big-screen television!*

Next month, to your utter amazement and complete bewilderment, everything falls apart. The car breaks down, your young soccer player breaks his arm, the quarterly insurance premium is due, three family members have birthdays, the dog gets sick, and the washing machine dies. Expenses you've not planned for are screaming for money you don't have.

Selective amnesia allows us to forget that every day we are incurring expenses we choose to forget. We are using up and wearing out our cars, our clothes, our homes. We are clicking away at our prepaid insurance and inching ever closer to vacations, Christmas, and college educations.

When these kinds of expenses appear to come at us seemingly from out of nowhere, we collapse into a pitiful heap and bemoan the fact that once again we've been broadsided by an emergency. Another financial crisis.

And where do these financial crises send us? To the credit cards, of course. After all, we've been educated to believe that this is the purpose of a credit card. We've been suckered into believing that plastic was invented to rescue us from life's financial emergencies.

Imagine this: It's the middle of March. Spring is poking its way through the ground; thoughts are turning to summer fun. You sit down with a pile of bills and your checkbook. You line them up in order of priority (past dues first, then whatever else you can work in—you know the routine). How much are you thinking about the expenses of next Christmas? Not much. It's understandable since some of those past due bills are from *last* Christmas.

Let's try another scenario: It's September 16. Yesterday was the final day to mail your semiannual property tax installment. How much are you thinking today about the next installment that will be due March 15? As little as possible, I have a feeling. You are so relieved that yesterday is over and you scraped together enough credit to cover the big check you had to write.

One more: It's any day of the year. You're driving home from work, the car is running perfectly, the weather forecast is nearly too good to be true, and you're looking forward to a restful weekend. How much are you thinking about your brakes that are going to brake their very last time in just seven weeks from now?

At this point you might be thinking, *Sure, I can understand planning for Christmas and for the property taxes, but you can't expect me to plan for totally unpredictable expenses like brake jobs.* Yes I can, and so should you.

You have to agree that every time you step your foot on that brake pedal you are using up part of your brakes' useful life. You are in fact "spending" your brakes one day at a time. Contrary to the way you choose to think on a daily basis (or not think as the case may be), they will not last forever. And the chances that you'll be any more prepared financially to replace them seven weeks from now as you are today are not very good—perhaps worse since you don't know what else might happen between now and then.

My point is, and let me repeat this, we regard anything that is not in our face right now as an optional expense. Only when an unexpected, irregular, or intermittent expense brings our lives to a screeching halt does it get our full attention.

So how do you handle it when a big unexpected car repair bill or semiannual insurance payment comes along and at the eleventh hour you finally concede that it is not optional, that this is serious? More than likely you find justification in using the credit cards. For some people, I would enlarge that to say they feel "righteous justification" because they look at their available credit line as a providential provision to take care of the problem. I have actually had people tell me that all of their debts are not their fault because they were necessary to pay for car repairs and "other big things like that."

As a person who ran up debt rivaling the net worth of a small nation, I know about this kind of thinking because I've been there. Believe me, not all of the debt I amassed went to pay for luxury cruises and shopping sprees on Rodeo Drive. In fact, none of it went for that. We used credit to pay for property taxes and car repairs and Christmas and clothes—all perfectly essential expenses. The reason we went into debt for those things was because we didn't view them as essential every month, but only as they occurred. And because our regularly occurring expenses grew to equal our income, there was nothing available for the other kinds of expenses. So we relied on credit to bridge the gap.

This problem does not affect everyone in the same way. Some people do not run for credit when the unexpected, irregular, and intermittent expenses happen. Instead, they pull the funds from their meager savings or fledgling Contingency Fund. While certainly not as damaging as going into debt, this same problem keeps them forever stuck in a financial rut. They just cannot seem to get ahead. While they might handle the problem a bit differently—and might I say, much more intelligently—the underlying problem is the same as those who go into debt to survive.

If you see yourself in any of these scenarios, you are not alone. I have a strong suspicion that most people face this challenge because they do not accurately identify their necessary expenses. They allow their regular monthly expenses to grow to equal their income and then there is nothing available for expenses that are unexpected, irregular, or intermittent.

The antidote for selective amnesia is to find a reasonable and practical way to make every expense a recurring monthly expense—even those expenses you do not yet know about.

THE FREEDOM ACCOUNT

To treat my own case of selective amnesia, I developed something I call a Freedom Account. It is a simple, personal money management tool that makes unexpected, irregular, and intermittent expenses as ordinary, predictable, and necessary as your rent and grocery bill. A Freedom Account eliminates financial surprises.

I have written about the Freedom Account in previous books and repeatedly in *Cheapskate Monthly* because the Freedom Account is the heart and soul of debt recovery and debt-proof living. It is a reasonable and practical way to eliminate what many people feel is their only defense against financial emergencies: credit cards.

A LOT LIKE A CHRISTMAS CLUB ACCOUNT

Perhaps you once had a Christmas Club account or knew someone who did. Lots of banks, even schools, offered Christmas Club accounts as a way to encourage people to save for their Christmas shopping. The plan was relatively painless because you saved just a little bit throughout the year. You decided how much you would save and then authorized the club automatically to take that amount out of your paycheck or bank account before you ever saw it. You forced yourself to save for Christmas.

The fun was in forgetting about it. You knew this sneaky thing was going on behind the scenes, but you took pleasure in pretending you didn't notice. You didn't miss the money because of the same mysterious law that lets you disregard expenses that are unexpected, irregular, or intermittent: *Out of sight, out of mind.*

The reward for faithful membership in the Christmas Club was that big check that came in the mail every year right around Thanksgiving. Even though you knew you were contributing a little bit at a time, it was great fun to experience the joyful surprise. It was always bigger than you thought it would be, and it felt somehow noble or righteous because this check was tangible proof that you'd done the right thing—you anticipated the expense of your Christmas shopping.

The Freedom Account takes the simple principles and joyful rewards of a Christmas Club and applies them to all of your expenses that will come—you can count on it—but do not recur every month. It also makes a provision for those expenses that have a high likelihood of occurring.

I promise that if you will start a Freedom Account, build it gradually, and then manage it diligently, you will experience a freedom in your financial life that you have not known before.

It will be a gradual process, but eventually your Freedom Account and Contingency Fund are going to switch places. The Freedom Account will become the first line of defense against emergencies and unexpected expenses, while the Contingency Fund guards you from financial ruin in the event of the mother of all emergencies: the temporary loss of your income.

STEP-BY-STEP INSTRUCTIONS

Before heading into these specific instructions, we need to be very clear on the definition of unexpected, unpredictable, and intermittent expenses. These are expenses that do not recur every month. Your mortgage payment, car payment, and telephone and grocery bills do not fall into this category because they are regular expenses that you deal with every month.

Setting up and then maintaining a Freedom Account is simple. But let me caution you to do it exactly as outlined below. I've tried variations or shortcuts, and I can assure you, they will not work as effectively or as consistently as these simple steps.

Step 1: Determine your irregular, unexpected and intermittent expenses. This will be the most challenging step in the process. Let me encourage you to start with the obvious and work your way to the more remote. For example, if you have an automobile, maintenance and repair is a glaring irregular expense that you ignore until something goes wrong.

Using your check registers for the past twelve months, your credit card statements, your tax return, or—if all else fails—your memory, make a list of your expenses that you do not pay on a monthly basis. These might come quarterly, every six months, or annually. They may occur so sporadically that you have no idea when they'll pop up again, if ever. The past year or two will be the best indicator of the future. Remember, you are searching for expenses that do not recur on a monthly basis. If you already pay a portion of your property taxes every month, that does not qualify for the Freedom Account. If you pay your life insurance premiums every six months, that does qualify.

Once you have a reasonable list (it will probably not be complete, but that's OK—you can add and adjust later), do the math so you end up with a number for each category that represents 1/12 of the total projected annual expense. You will first have to multiply as appropriate to reach an annual figure and then divide by twelve.

Here is an example of five typical Freedom Account categories that I will use for illustration purposes.

Auto Maintenance/Repair: $765/year ÷ 12 = $64/month

Life Insurance: $520/year ÷ 12 = $44/month

Clothing: $480/year ÷ 12 = $40/month

Property taxes: $600/year ÷ 12 = $50/month

Vacation: $800/year ÷ 12 = $66/month

Total: $264/month

Step 2: Open a second checking account. I'm assuming you have a checking account already, so open another one at the same bank or credit union for now. Order checks for your new account (you can save a bundle if you order from a printer, not the bank. Try Current, 800-533-3973 or Checks-in-the-Mail, 800-733-4443). Have your checks personalized as usual, adding a special line above your name that says "Freedom Account."

Consider carefully the different types of accounts available. If the bank or credit union offers an account with check-writing privileges that also pays interest once you reach a minimum balance, consider it seriously. If a $500 or $1,000 minimum balance is required, check to see if you can convert to the interest-bearing account once your account reaches that level. An account that limits the number of checks that can be written in a month, say 10, will work just fine.

For this to work, you must have two active checking accounts. Your regular checking account will continue to accommodate your monthly expenses and typical day-to-day needs for which you presently use a checking account. You will continue to deposit your paychecks and other income into your regular account.

Under no circumstances should you accept overdraft protection, ATM privileges, or a debit card for your Freedom Account.

Step 3: Authorize an automatic deposit. At the time you open the account, request an Automatic Deposit Authorization form (some banks call this an Automatic Money Transfer) instructing the bank to transfer the monthly total of your irregular expenses (in our example it is $264) from your regular checking account into your Freedom Account on a specific day of the month. Think carefully about this. The selection of your transfer date is very important because once established, you can be sure the bank will never forget to make the transfer, nor will they be late.

Step 4: Get a notebook. Any three-ring binder will do. Fill it with notebook paper. Now, as far as the bank is concerned, you have a second checking account. But you are going to treat your new Freedom Account as a collection of *subaccounts*.

Prepare one page per subaccount you've chosen, similar to the illustration below, including five columns labeled *Date, Description, In, Out,* and *Balance.* Fill in the title of the account, and enter the amount to be deposited into that subaccount in the upper right-hand corner.

$ per month: __$66__

Vacation

$ per month: __$50__

Property Taxes

$ per month: __$40__

Clothing

$ per month: __$44__

Life Insurance

$ per month: __$64__

Auto Maintenance & Repair

Date	Description	In	Out	Balance

Step 5: Make a deposit every month without fail. Once a month, deduct the amount of your Freedom Account deposit ($264 in this case) from your regular checking account register just as if you'd written a check for that amount. Because the bank will transfer that amount, you must treat this as a regular monthly expense the same way you treat your rent and car payment. Don't even think about forgetting, because the bank never will. You will have a royal mess on your hands if you bounce your own automatic deposit.

This is going to feel weird in the beginning. You won't like making this big debit entry in your regular checkbook because it feels like you're throwing money away. You're spending but not getting anything in return. But no, you are managing your money, controlling money instead of letting it control you.

Next, go to your Freedom Account notebook and enter the individual subaccount deposits. Using our illustration figures, it would go like this: On the first page, which is Auto Maintenance & Repair, enter a deposit of $64; enter $44 on the next page, which is Life Insurance; $40 into Clothing; $50 into Property Taxes; and $66 into Vacation.

$ per month: __$66__

Vacation

$ per month: __$50__

Property Taxes

$ per month: __$40__

Clothing

$ per month: __$44__

Life Insurance

$ per month: __$64__

Auto Maintenance & Repair

Date	Description	In	Out	Balance
05-5	Opening Deposit	64		64.00
06-5	Deposit	64		128.00
07-5	Deposit	64		192.00
08-5	Deposit	64		256.00
09-1	Chk #101 - Jiffy Lube		19.95	236.05
09-5	Deposit	64		300.05
10-5	Deposit	64		364.05
10-15	Chk #102 Sam's Club		132.25	231.80
10-16	Chk #103 A-1 Battery		45.87	185.93
10-16	Chk #104 Joe's Big Tow		45.00	140.90
10-17	Chk #105 Al's Electric		98.44	42.49
11-5	Deposit	64		106.49
12-5	Deposit	64		170.49
01-5	Depsit	64		234.49
02-5	Deposit	64		298.49
02-10	Chk. #110 Trak Auto		22.50	275.99
03-5	Deposit	64		339.99
04-5	Deposit	64		403.99
05-5	Deposit	54		467.99
06-5	Deposit	64		531.99
06-28	Chk #115 - 50,000 Servc		300.00	231.99
07-5	Deposit	64		295.99
08-5	Deposit	64		359.99
09-5	Deposit	64		423.99

Referring to the illustration on the previous page, let's go through the Auto Maintenance & Repair subaccount.

May 5 was the launch date for this Freedom Account. The first deposit was made that date, and $64 was added to this particular subaccount. Same thing on June 5, which brought the balance to $128. Two more months went by with the same $64 deposits bringing the balance in this subaccount to $256 on August 5.

On September 1, it was time to get the oil changed, so our account owner took the Freedom Account checkbook to the place she always has her oil changed, wrote out check #101 to Jiffy Lube for $19.95, wrote the entry into the subaccount book when she got home, and did the subtraction to come up with a new balance of $236.05. Regular monthly deposits occurred again on September 5 and October 5, bringing the new balance to $364.05.

Have you ever noticed how car trouble seems to come in waves? Some insist it comes in "threes," but I'm not so sure about that. Nevertheless, it always hits when you least expect it.

Notice on October 15 our account owner had to buy two new tires. But because she had the cash available and didn't have to rely on whatever shop she could find that would take the only credit card she had available, she could shop around. Apparently the best deal was found at Sam's Club, so she wrote check #102 accordingly, entering $132.25 in the "out" column, and calculated the new balance of $231.80.

The very next day, the battery died, requiring a replacement to the tune of $45.87. As you may have already predicted by looking ahead on the form, it wasn't the battery that was the problem after all, evidenced by the fact that the next day, October 17, the car died and had to be towed by Joe's Big Tow for the amount of $45. But does our account owner panic? Not at all. The Auto Maintenance & Repair subaccount is properly funded and is handling expenses just the way it should. She uses the Freedom Account checkbook to disperse the funds.

Later that day, October 17, the real problem causing the car to malfunction is discovered, requiring yet another payment of $98.44 to the electrical shop for a new generator. Now, after three days of car trouble, is our account owner stressed? No. Car repairs and maintenance are a part of life. The money is already in place for such an occurrence.

The next four months are trouble free, so the balance builds back. In February the account owner decides to save a few bucks by changing her own oil, writes out the check for $22.50 for enough oil for four changes, and calculates the new balance of $275.99.

Things continue to go well; the balance grows so that on June 28, more than enough is in the account to cover the 50,000-mile service on the car. She makes a few phone calls and finds that the prices of this kind of service required to protect the warranty can vary greatly. She selects the best deal, has the work done, and pays for it with $300 from her Freedom Account. How freeing to know that the money is in place, ready to go. To me it is still amazing the kind of freedom and peace of mind that a simple $64 monthly deposit set aside for a specific purpose can bring to your life.

OTHER IRREGULAR EXPENSES

Any potential expense, including those that are not as predictable as auto maintenance & repair and property taxes but ones that have a way of hitting you over the head when you can least afford it, would qualify for the Freedom Account.

Insurance Deductibles

An excellent way to keep insurance premiums low is to carry higher deductibles. But what happens if you are in an auto accident that requires you to fork over your $1,000 deductible? Ouch! I would advise adding a new subaccount: Insurance Deductibles. This Freedom Account subaccount should grow until its balance is equal to the annual deductible of your health, homeowners, and auto deductibles. If you are nervous raising your deductibles in the beginning without the funds in place to cover them should the need arise, go ahead and start funding that subaccount. When its balance reaches the amount equal to whatever your deductibles are currently, then you'll be in a good position to instruct your insurance agent to increase deductibles in exchange for lower premiums.

Imagine the peace of mind you will have knowing that the deductibles are there ready to be used if necessary, and if they're not used, thank God and know the account is drawing interest. That is freedom. Once your subaccount reaches the amount you determine is adequate to cover your deductibles, you are now free to divert future deposits into some other subaccount.

Clothing Account

You cannot imagine how many families do not list clothing when asked to list their expenses. Ironically, I have noticed that those in the worst financial shape are often the best dressed. Where does that money come from? I can only assume that many people load huge clothing expenses on credit cards or write checks using funds that were supposed to pay for groceries or utilities.

With a Freedom Account, clothing becomes a dignified and legitimate monthly expense. You may want to set up a general clothing account for the entire family, or three separate accounts: His Clothes, Her Clothes, Kids' Clothes, or some combination thereof.

Christmas/Holiday Account

Probably nothing in the world throws more of us into a debting depression faster than approaching the month of December. Broke! And every January you say that next year you are going to save a little bit every month for Christmas. And do you? Well, lest I sound like a broken record, your Freedom Account is the perfect way to join your own Christmas Club.

Dream Accounts

What is it that you hope to have enough money to do or be someday? Perhaps you'd like to take a class, redecorate the master bedroom, go on a special trip, start a stamp collection, or take up skiing. If you are like most of us, these things remain a dream to be fulfilled "when we get some extra money"—which is usually never. Well, not anymore.

The Freedom Account is the way you turn those dreams into achievable goals. Let your mind run wild. Insert new pages in your Freedom Account notebook and title them accordingly: Redecorate Master Bedroom, Room Addition, John's Woodworking Tools, Caribbean Cruise, [your name]'s Dream Account, [spouse's name]'s Dream Account. Maybe you won't be able to start funding these accounts right now, but little by little you will find it possible to fund more and more pages in your Freedom Account.

One added benefit of a Freedom Account is that it is a fabulous marriage tool. By having individual accounts, both partners can manage their own money without feeling a need to sneak around or wallow in self-pity.

UNSCHEDULED INCOME

You receive unexpected and unpredictable money all the time, such as rebate checks, tax refunds, freelance payments, and gifts. It may be only a dollar here or ten dollars there, but what happens to it? You put it in your pocket and it is absorbed into your daily spending so fast you hardly remember getting it. Larger amounts, such as tax refunds and consulting payments, usually go into the checking account with the intention they will be used in some special way. Before you know it, however, they are gone too, but who knows where?

The Freedom Account is a wonderful solution to the case of the vanishing funds. Make it a habit of depositing unscheduled income—big or small—into the Freedom Account. Selecting the subaccount to which they will be credited suddenly gives new meaning to surprise money.

Let's say, for instance, that you misjudged your Federal Tax withholding, and you end up with a refund of $1,000. If you put it into your regular account, it will disappear as it slips through your fingers via the ATM machine or some other phantom maneuver. But if you immediately put it into your Freedom Account, you will be able to decide which goals to nourish.

A word of caution: you may be tempted to think of your Freedom Account as a savings or investment account. You may find yourself skipping your true savings in favor of funding your Freedom Account. But it is not a savings account. This money has been committed for a specific purpose and is meant to be spent. Prepare yourself, because this new account will give new meaning to the term *ebb and flow*. That's the way it's supposed to work. It is strictly a financial management tool. This is what money management is all about. By following these basic instructions and then customizing your Freedom Account to reflect you, your family, and your lifestyle, you will become a very skilled personal finance manager.

I heard from a man who diligently set up and funded his Freedom Account. However, his hesitation to use it became his downfall. In the beginning, when he had a minor auto repair, rather than using the Freedom Account as he should have, he thought he was being especially good to fund the expense from his pocket money. I can understand his way of thinking—that paying for the expense from his general fund forced him to leave money in the Freedom Account. But he kept doing it, and each time, the righteous feeling he got from not using the Freedom Account prompted him to keep doing it. Well, eventually the expenses he was funding outside the account, for which he'd already set aside the money, became more than he could pay from his regular account. Believe it or not, he had come to see his Freedom Account as some kind of sacred investment—he couldn't bring himself to use it. Instead, he put irregular expenses on a credit card, thinking he could somehow pay it off in the grace period and still be the "good boy" who was not touching the Freedom Account. By the time I heard from him, he was all messed up and was on the verge of dumping the whole idea as totally unmanageable.

Clearly the problem is that he refused to use his Freedom Account for the purpose he created it. Do not let this happen with you. Understand exactly what this account is for—to be spent for the purposes for which it was created. Of course this does not imply that you spend wildly—that if you have accumulated $1200 in your Christmas subaccount, you must spend every last penny. That's not at all what I mean. The point is that when Christmas comes around, you must use the Freedom Account funds to cover your Christmas expenses as opposed to sneaking money out of the grocery funds. You might get away with that for awhile, but I can assure you this kind of sloppy management will land you back from whence you've come—all mixed up and letting your emotions guide you rather than your newfound financial management sense.

COMMON QUESTIONS ABOUT A FREEDOM ACCOUNT

Q: Have you lost your mind? I don't have extra money every month to fund anything new, let alone a Freedom Account.

A: Listen to yourself. You are acting as if maintaining your auto is optional or you can skip paying your insurance if you're a little short. Do you really have a choice whether to pay your property taxes or buy clothes? But you are driving a car, your taxes were paid, and you dress fairly well. Exactly how did you do that? You came up with the money somehow, and you probably have a few battle scars or credit card payments that help you remember the trouble you went through to do it.

This step is too important to pass off as something you cannot afford. I suggest you start out with the bare minimum number of accounts, limiting them to your most essential irregular expenses. You may have to reduce your spending in other areas in order to get started with a Freedom Account, but whatever the sacrifice, no matter how painful, this is one of the nicest things you will ever do for yourself.

Q: Won't I incur new expenses caused by this new Freedom Account, expenses like fees for checks and service charges?

A: Yes. However, as your total balance (the balance the bank sees is the total of all of your subaccounts) grows beyond the minimum amount required, all service fees may be waived, provided you have selected an account with that kind of benefit. You will be writing very few checks from this account, so check costs will be minimal. I suggest that you choose your favorite subaccount (in my case it would be Decorating or Vacation or Mary's Stash) and designate it as the account from which you will deduct any administrative charges. And, very importantly, this favorite subaccount will also be credited all of the *interest* your Freedom Account will earn.

If you are diligent in locating a bank that pays interest on checking accounts (NOW Accounts being a good example), you are going to make some money, and that's going to be a great bonus for your favorite subaccount. Granted, the Freedom Account balance will fluctuate over the course of a year, but since you are adding to it every month, this has a positive effect on your average daily balance. In time you will earn a nice sum of reportable interest that should give your favorite account a mighty boost and more than offset any costs incurred.

Q: How do I balance the Freedom Account each month?

A: Add up the current balances of the subaccounts. They should match the bank statement's closing balance once you have made allowances for checks that haven't cleared and deposits not yet posted. Balance it just like any other checking account. If you've never done this, step-by-step instructions can be found on the back of your monthly checking account statement.

Q: Couldn't I create my own Freedom Account at home without opening up another checking account?

A: Sure, you could get a series of envelopes and put cash into each one every month. But problems with this are obvious. Because keeping large sums of cash is not smart from a security standpoint, you'd need a home safe or vault. Remember, if you are contributing, say, $264 a month, you could quickly accumulate up to several thousand before it begins to fluctuate. Also, having the cash readily available and held in such a casual way would tempt you to engage in impulsive borrowing. When things got a little rocky, you might be tempted to skip contributing some months. The Freedom Account should be a serious business activity, not a simple no-one-knows-if-I-do-and-no-one-knows-if-I-don't kind of thing.

If you're at all like me, you need the discipline and pressure of an automatic withdrawal. It puts everything on a much higher, businesslike, professional level. Besides, you probably won't pay yourself interest like the bank or credit union will. (I really like that interest.) Record keeping is easier, too, when you have canceled checks at tax time.

Q: What happens if my Freedom Account gets too large? Shouldn't I be investing the money?

A: Your goal is to have a full year's requirement in each of your subaccounts. That's not going to happen overnight. Also, remember that this is not an investment vehicle; this is simply a money management tool. Most of your subaccounts will be self-reducing. Subaccounts such as insurance deductibles or other items that may not be self-eliminating should have a cap. For instance, your insurance deductibles may total $1,000. Once you have reached the designated amount in that subaccount, discontinue deposits until you must make a withdrawal. You might have a High School Reunion account. Once you've funded it and have attended the gala event, you can rip that page out and adjust your monthly contribution accordingly.

If you set up the Freedom Account properly, it is not going to present a problem of surpluses. Besides, I would hardly call that a problem. You will be amazed at how financially functional you'll become once you have the opportunity to manage your money.

Q: In the beginning as the subaccounts have low balances, what will I do if I have an expense that is greater than the current balance in that subaccount?

A: Ideally, you should find a way to open each subaccount with a larger initial deposit to cover this situation. Example: you open your Freedom Account on October 1. Your semiannual property tax bill is due on December 10. If your monthly property tax deposit into the Freedom account is $75, you will hardly have the $450 necessary to make the payment. You will have contributed only $225 total ($75 X 3) into that particular subaccount. You should make an initial deposit into the subaccount to jump-start the process. By contributing an additional $225 into the account on October 1 to anticipate the shortfall, the problem would be solved. As you set up the Freedom Account, you might see where a few hours of overtime or a moonlighting position for a few weeks would raise the funds necessary to launch your Freedom Account in such a way that you'll be fully prepared for the first expense. However, even if you can't manage the additional funding in the first month, don't let this become an excuse not to get started.

Let's look at another scenario. Say you have a $64 balance in your Auto Maintenance & Repair account and you incur a $100 repair item during the first month. What do you do? Write a check out of your Freedom Account for the $64 and supplement the balance from your regular account. Do *not* borrow from other freedom subaccounts. While it pains me to suggest it, if you have absolutely no other way to come up with $36 (try hard—I mean *really* hard), I feel it would be better this one last time to put the balance on a credit card and then pay the credit card payment from the Auto Maintenance & Repair subaccount. I would recommend this only if the borrowed funds can be repaid within the following thirty days. Example: your Auto Maintenance & Repair account has a balance of $64. Your repair bill is $100. You write a check for the $64 from the Freedom Account and pay for the balance on your credit card. By the time the billing comes, you will have made another $64 deposit into the Auto Maintenance & Repair subaccount, allowing you to write a check from the Freedom Account to pay off the credit card in full without incurring an interest charge. Going through these steps of depositing into the Freedom Account and writing a check out of it to cover the $36 credit card bill is necessary in order to keep everything straight and your subaccount page correct.

Accept the fact that it will take a little time to get the Freedom Account working smoothly. But don't let a little rough water in the beginning convince you to abandon such a wonderful, life-changing tool!

Q: Would it make sense for my Freedom Account to be held in a money market fund account rather than at a bank or credit union?

A: Yes, that is an excellent idea because of the greater rate of interest you can expect in a money market fund. But remember, these accounts typically have high minimum requirements. Select one that has a low requirement if you sign up for automatic deposits, such as the USAA Money Market, 800-531-8181 (no minimum requirement as long as you have an automatic deposit of at least $50 a month). But keep in mind that money market fund accounts have minimum withdrawal guidelines. You will not be able to write checks for less than, say, $250 (fund guidelines vary).

FREEDOM ACCOUNT TESTIMONIALS

"We have no consumer debt now and a $10,000 Contingency Fund in a money market account. We will be able to pay off the mortgage in just 5 more years and we are so excited! We have had our Freedom Account since 1995 and it has changed our financial life! Thank you."—Bill and Tracy

"I love the Freedom Account! I set mine up this past January, and I actually have the money set aside for our property taxes. In the past I would try to save the money and would

always come up short. Then I would be forced to write a cash advance check from my credit card. How pathetic. The first two months of having $300 a pay period transferred into the Freedom Account was really hard, but now I'm used to it. Once my car is paid off in a few months, I will set up a couple more subaccounts for household repairs and one for furniture we need. The Freedom Account is incredibly liberating! If you haven't set one up yet, do it, even if it's for $20 a month. Having the money socked away has really helped me, and my husband is very impressed by my change in behavior."—Lucy

"Just this past month I was able to pay the six-month auto insurance premium instead of the usual three-month. I think I will have enough to do that on the other car by the time it is due. I love the freedom the Freedom Account has given us. We used to have to scrape by, and my husband would have to work overtime when the 3-month premiums were due. Also, we had a $100 co-pay at the hospital when my daughter was born that I paid for with cash. Things certainly are looking up." —Jennifer

"Back in February we had to replace our garage door. Actually, it needed to be replaced as early as the previous May, but we put it off because of the expense. It was our first major dent in the Freedom Account—$790—but boy, did it feel good not to incur a charge of that amount. And we just paid a full six-month auto insurance premium out of the Freedom Account as well. The Freedom Account is such a great idea." —Elizabeth

"I am proud of myself today. Our water heater went out yesterday. We shopped around and came up with the best

water heater for us and the future. It, however, was not cheap! But when it came time to pay, we paid for it with the Freedom Account. It all but wiped out my Freedom Account, but now we know it is paid for and we are done with it. It really felt great. Now back to the grindstone to rebuild that subaccount."
—Marie

"It's been more than two years since I first read about your Freedom Account. I wanted to start one but my husband was very skeptical. One year later we officially opened our Freedom Account. It is now more than a year later, and boy, where would we be without our Freedom Account. Even my husband loves it! At first, I thought it would take forever to start adding up, but before I knew it, we had enough money to cover every 'surprise' bill that appeared. It makes so much sense to have a Freedom Account because you have to pay for those bills that come every six months or once a year anyway, so why not save for them instead of wiping out your checking account? We have lots of subaccounts, including ones for taxes, insurance, auto maintenance, Christmas, and even a toy fund for my husband. It has been so nice getting the car serviced and not worrying about how we are going to pay for it. Believe me, the Freedom Account has reduced stress in this family. Thank you for such a great idea."—Virginia

## Chapter Nine

Debt-Proof Your Attitude

IT'S 10 PERCENT ABOUT MONEY, 90 PERCENT ABOUT ATTITUDE

You cannot tailor-make your situation in life, but you can tailor-make your attitudes to fit those situations.

Zig Ziglar

Attitude, the way you respond to life and all of its circumstances, is more important than anything. It is more important than the past, than struggle or success, than education or experience. It is more important than how much money you have, how much you owe, what you would like to do, or where you would like to go.

While I have never actually experienced them in person, I've seen pictures of the cables leading to the top of Half Dome in Yosemite National Park. Those I know who have completed the climb tell me the final ascent up the sheer granite surface of that majestic landmass is by far the most challenging. The cables are there to make sure climbers reach the top safely and with a modicum of ease. (However, I understand the term *ease* is terribly relative.)

Once you begin the last leg of the journey and finally see the cables, you stand there, tilt your head to the sky, view the final hundred yards or so that lead to the top, and experience terror like you've never known. You realize you have no choice but to finish the trip.

At that moment you are more thankful than you could ever imagine for the cables that will become the guardrails you need to pull yourself to the top—not only to a spectacular view, but also to the feeling of accomplishment the likes of which you cannot begin to fathom from your current vantage point.

We need to erect cables in our lives so that when we face the difficult climbs on the journey—and they will come, you can count on it—the guardrails we need to make it to the top will be there waiting to protect us from our own fears and self-defeating attitudes.

ERECT SAFEGUARDS AGAINST QUITTING POINTS

All of us have quitting points in our lives—those times or situations that become so overwhelming or challenging that we simply quit. No matter what you call them—brick walls, insurmountable obstacles, predictable or complete surprises, financial crises—without erecting cables ahead of time, you most likely will continue to give in to defeat.

BE PREPARED

You can erect cables for your financial circumstances by memorizing a list of all the reasons you will not give in to debt. Drilling them into your mind so deeply that you could repeat them in your sleep will give you those cables to hang on to when you feel weak and vulnerable. Some examples:

- I don't choose debt because it presumes unfairly on my future.

- It is wrong for me to spend money I do not have.
- There is always a way out; I will not stop until I find it.
- When I step out on faith, I unleash God's power in my life.
- I trust even when I do not understand.
- I do the right thing even when I don't feel like it.
- This credit card company doesn't really care about me the way this letter indicates; they are looking for a new sucker.

CRASHING THROUGH

Another way you can erect cables is by identifying your unique quitting points and then figuring out how to crash through them. What past circumstances and situations have caused you to throw in the towel and turn to credit as the easy way out? Perhaps it was Christmas or vacation or your fickle feelings of dissatisfaction when you saw what others had that you want.

Once you discover your quitting points, you have to prepare to deal with them. You have to do this ahead of time, not at the moment you come face-to-face with the overwhelming desire to quit. People who set out to climb Half Dome are notified before they ever leave camp whether or not the cables are up for the summer season. Experienced hikers would never set out on that seventeen-mile trek without the assurance that the cables are in place and ready to go. Moreover, I can tell you that long before they need them, those hikers are already counting on the cables to be there when the going gets tough.

It takes practice to crash through your quitting points. Let's say you identify the holidays as a time you are likely to give up and give in to credit.

Year after year, even though you say it will never happen again, you end up shopping with your credit cards, promising that "this will be the last time ever." It's July, August—or later—and you've still not paid the bills from last year even though the gifts are long forgotten and the season is but a foggy memory. The load of debt has become a pile of resentment and something you'd rather not think about. Now is the time to practice crashing through that quitting point, because next Christmas will be here before you know it.

Using the Christmas example, you can decide to start earlier. Make a commitment way ahead of time as to how much cash you have to spend and promise that you will not go over that amount. During the spring or summer—when the holidays are not breathing down your neck and robbing you of your good sense—is the time to practice crashing through that quitting point. Anticipate; prepare; shop early. There are dozens of things you can do to get in shape for that particular quitting point.

Perhaps your quitting points (or those of someone you love) come in monthly cycles—if you know what I mean. You have three weeks of every month to practice crashing through the difficult time you know is on its way. Anticipate those feelings of defeat and sadness. Practice rejecting attitudes of defeat and purposely replacing them with appropriate thoughts and behaviors. Know exactly what you will do even when you don't feel like it, when every emotion in you begs to stay in bed and pull the covers over your head or suggests that a trip to the mall—credit card in tow—will make you feel better. Gather all the determination you have to crash through those quitting points. Each time you do, it will be easier to do it the next time. Soon it will become a habit on which you rely, and then you will begin to experience tremendous progress.

One of the human freedoms we enjoy is to choose our attitude in any given set of circumstances. We can alter our lives by altering our attitudes. That is an amazing concept and one that should fill you with confidence and joy.

When it comes to debt-proofing your life, I believe 10 percent is about the money you have and 90 percent is about your attitude toward it. How else could I possibly explain the amazing financial feats of people like Vikki and her husband, who not only survived but thrived during a very difficult financial season of their lives. Here's their story:

> After twenty-four years of service, my husband learned his job was in jeopardy. So we sat down and worked out a six-month plan. We lived by it religiously.
>
> First we took all the money from our regular savings account, which was enough to pay off two credit cards. We took those payments and added them to the next highest balance credit card bill and paid it in full in two months.
>
> We tackled the next largest credit card bill. We increased its monthly payment by the amount we'd been paying toward the other bills each month plus $50 more, which we really didn't have to spare.
>
> We did not go out to eat, to the movies, or rent videos. We altered our seams and hems to be able to extend the useful life of our clothes. The adults went on a diet (we needed to shed some pounds along with the debt).
>
> We went through our house and assessed every single belonging. If it hadn't been used in a year it became part of our huge garage sale. We made $2,500, which we immediately paid toward the next credit card account.
>
> We called the credit card company and asked them to lower the interest rate. They said no; we

said adios. Then they agreed and lowered it to 7.9 percent for six months. Our big payment (plus $50 every month) began to make a huge impact.

On January 29—no more job. We also learned the same day there would be no unemployment benefits or child support from our granddaughter's parents. Wow. A triple-whammy.

We sat down again and went over what was left to pay. At this time, excluding the mortgage, we still owed about $30,000. We were scared, but decided we could do it.

We went through the house, garage, and attic again and purged. We had another garage sale. We made another $1,400, which was enough to pay off the last credit card.

The next debts in line were the doctor, dentist, and optician bills. We made arrangements to pay as much as we could on a weekly basis.

To our complete amazement, my husband got an unexpected severance package, so we paid off all outstanding unsecured debts. We split the remaining amount into three: one-third into the checking account for monthly expenses, one-third into a contingency account, and one-third into savings.

On May 1st we were completely debt free except for the house. We even paid past-due property taxes. We rolled the 401(k) account into an IRA. We closed all of the credit card accounts (and will never, never have another one by the way), and have three months' living expenses in the bank.

I reopened my home business, which generated food money. I used every trick in the book to get our grocery bill at rock bottom.

We made it. We stuck to our plan. We are debt free, fat free, and much, much wiser. We are patiently waiting and excited to know what our next employment opportunity will be.

We can learn so many lessons from Vikki's story, but I believe the most important is about attitude. She and her husband, upon learning that his employment situation was on shaky ground, had a choice: they could fall into a deep funk, or they could see this wake-up call as the opportunity to rise above their circumstances. They could plan a pity party complete with whining, blaming, complaining, and a long list of all the reasons they were doomed, or they could pick themselves up and make a plan for survival.

Out of all the possible reactions available, this family chose happiness. Instead of a situation they could have labeled *disaster,* they turned their situation into a launching pad and their positive attitudes became the fuel to initiate a season of financial accomplishment.

DON'T PLAN TO QUIT; DO IT

When you keep credit cards with a just-in-case attitude, you are planning to quit. I have seen this happen many times: someone will consolidate all of their credit card balances into a new home equity loan (HEL) or on a new low-interest credit card, leaving the previous cards with a $0 balance. The problem? They don't cancel those old accounts. They keep them "just in case" or justify the credit as a cushion if things get tight. As reasonable as that might sound, it is nothing but a sugarcoated plan to quit (see chap. 13).

As long as you leave yourself these kinds of escapes, you will find it difficult to summon the strength, stamina, and courage to crash through your quitting points.

Endurance is counter to our have-it-all-now culture, but it establishes our hope and builds the courage we need for those times when the situation appears impossible.

STOP WHINING

When we find ourselves in challenging financial situations, our backs against the wall for any number of reasons, it is easy to default to victim status—which is often the first sign of quitting. Oh, how easy it is to start whining, blaming, and complaining. Although that does nothing but make the matter worse, for some reason resorting to self-pity is, in some sick way, comforting. Unfortunately, that attitude is also self-defeating and destructive.

As long as you see yourself as a victim, things will not change. Your attitudes will continue to bring you to the quitting point. You will never fix your problems while you blame others for your circumstances. Whatever your situation, regardless of the details, you are accountable. You are responsible.

You can either give in to your circumstances or rise above them. You can remain in your misery or climb out of that rut and look around.

You can reward your whining, blaming, and self-pity with your full attention, or you can completely ignore yourself when you slip into that debilitating mode.

You can choose thoughts that support your misery or those that will lead you to action and a solution. You can keep living in denial, or you can find the courage to face the truth.

You can dig your pit of despair a little deeper, or you can make the commitment to do whatever it takes to turn your financial life around. The choice is yours.

ATTITUDE OF THE DAY

The single most significant decision you make on a daily basis is your choice of attitude. It's the difference between letting life happen to you or taking control and making it happen. Debt-proofing your attitude is the difference between your financial situation controlling your life or you taking control of your finances.

Every morning when you wake up, you put on your attitude of the day, whether you do it consciously or simply default to whatever your emotions hand you.

Allowing our emotions to dictate our attitudes can be very dangerous because emotions are so fickle. They cannot be trusted. They will lie to us. That is why you consciously need to choose happiness, contentment, joy, optimism, trust, love, peace, and confidence while rejecting fear, denial, anxiety, pessimism, anger, and resentment.

Happiness is an ability. It has nothing to do with what you have—whether that's a little or a lot. If you have not chosen happiness, more money is just going to magnify who you are already. If you are bitter, more money will only intensify your bitterness. If you are greedy, money will make you even more self-centered and selfish.

If you choose to embrace your situation as an opportunity to experience God's power in your life, you will have chosen happiness.

You have to want what you already have or more will never be enough. Purposely choosing to be content is an important ingredient in debt-proofing your life.

TAKE CONTROL OF YOUR MIND

In the same way you can take control of your actions, you can control your thoughts, because thoughts are behaviors too.

You cannot allow your feelings to guide your actions—particularly your financial decisions—or you will spend your life on an emotional roller coaster. If you make your financial decisions based on what feels good, watch out.

The way to take control of your mind is to choose good thoughts and positive attitudes and banish every thought and behavior that is contrary to them.

Chalkboard and Eraser

When I have difficulty falling asleep, it's because I have overwhelming thoughts racing through my mind. I've discovered a way to get rid of them. (Actually this works well any time of day, not only as a way to get to sleep.) I visualize my thoughts written on a chalkboard. Just as quickly as those thoughts appear on the board, I start erasing. Typically I make one or two end-to-end passes on the chalkboard in my mind, and I'm either sound asleep or ready to replace those thoughts with what I know to be right and positive.

File this silly technique away in your anti-debt toolchest and reach for it whenever negative and destructive thinking begins to crowd in or when you are threatened by waves of desire. It really does work well.

Counterdestructive Attitudes

Let's say your neighbor just came home with a brand-new sports utility vehicle. You are overwhelmed by feelings of desire and envy. There was a time when you would begin immediately to find a way to get a new car too. But things are different now. You have a new set of values. You no longer make financial decisions impulsively. The car you have already is paid for and meets your family's current needs. But still those feelings bubble up. Just as soon as you recognize them, start erasing. Replace those destructive attitudes with thoughts of your Freedom Account and the way you are committed to the cash purchase of your next vehicle. Think about *not* making huge monthly payments, *not* paying triple insurance premiums, *not* paying $400 for the annual registration fee, and *not* forking over $600 for that 50,000 mile tune-up.

A good way to counter negative attitudes is to replace them quickly with positive ones. Here are some examples:

- I never have enough money. *I am so thankful for a regular paycheck.*
- It's not my fault. *Even though I wasn't 100 percent to blame, I take full responsibility—I will find a way through!*
- This is too difficult. *This is challenging!*
- I work hard, so I'm entitled to have what I want. *I work too hard to let money leak out of my life.*
- I want it now! *Waiting builds my character.*
- Maybe I'll win the lottery. *I'd rather save $5 a week than throw it away on the lottery.*
- It won't matter just this once. *Even the little things add up.*
- If only I had more money, then everything would be OK. *More money is not the answer—managing well what I have is!*
- If I didn't have to worry about money I'd be happy. *I choose to be happy regardless of my present circumstances.*
- What's the use, I'll never get out of this mess anyway. *I can do all things because God strengthens me.*
- They wouldn't give me the credit if they didn't know I can handle it. *I have the confidence to make my own financial decisions.*

THE BEST DEFENSE

I'm not much of a sports enthusiast, but I do know that the best defense is a good offense. I can't think of a better way to think about dealing with this matter of debt-proof living. You dare not wait for a surprise attack by some overwhelming desire to go back to your old way of living. You need to build your offense ahead of time so you have it handy as a defense and a prevention.

Identify Your Slippery Places

Slippery places are situations, events, or locations where you could easily trip and fall, financially speaking. For example, one might be at the mall, where you could easily slip into an old habit of shopping mindlessly and running up a lot of debt before you take time to analyze what's going on.

Seeing your checking account statement in the mail might represent a slippery place because without thinking you could easily return to your old habit of making it disappear into a drawer or cupboard.

As you debt-proof your attitude, you need to identify your slippery places and then devise a counterattack—a specific behavior to counteract the potential negative effect on your commitment to debt-proof your life.

I have identified lots of slippery places in my life. I realized early on that there were some behaviors I could eliminate from my life. For others, like the grocery store and department stores, I've come up with alternatives to my thinking as well as purposeful behaviors that help keep me from falling.

Mail order catalogs are one of my most slippery places. I can need absolutely nothing, pick up a catalog, and in the time it takes to flip a few pages, have about 157 urgent and critical needs. My original antidote for this slippery place was quite gentle. I made a deal that as long as I followed a few new rules, I could "shop" to my heart's content.

As I went through a catalog, I allowed myself to order anything and everything I wanted. I would fill out the order forms for all the items I just could not live without, including all the order numbers, color codes, sizes, prices, shipping and handling, and tax. Once I came up with the total, I would write that amount on the outside of the envelope, indicating the amount of the check I needed to enclose. I would also write the mailing date—one week in the future. The deal: I could order whatever I wanted as long as I waited a full seven days and I could pass a simple test—I had to remember what I ordered without opening and reading the order form.

It makes me laugh to admit that in all the times I did this, never once did I carry through. I would either forget about the order altogether and find it months later, or fail my test of remembering what in the world I ordered. Clearly, my joy was in the "shopping," not in actually acquiring all that stuff.

Curiously, the exercise was so tedious, the rules so confining, that my catalog problem has all but disappeared. Now I go through my mail next to a trash can and toss the catalogs without even a glance.

Jump-Start Your Attitude

Getting off to a good start in the morning sets the tone for the whole day. There are lots of ways to select your attitude before one selects you. Read a verse from Psalms or the Book of Proverbs first thing in the morning. Ask God to renew your mind. If you have access to the Internet, log on to my website at www.debtproofliving.com. I log on every day to share what's going on in my mind. We can help each other with our attitudes.

Come up with your own unique attitude starters. Make a list so you can refer to them often. Here are some ideas:

- Today I am grateful for . . .
- The small sacrifices I will make today pale in comparison to the more worthy goal ahead.
- Today is the tomorrow I worried about yesterday . . . and all is well!
- Nothing can happen today that God and I can't handle together.

Develop an Arsenal of Alternative Good Feelings

I'm the first to admit that spending money is a lot of fun. It feels great to buy all kinds of stuff and pretend that money is no object. It's particularly enjoyable to spend someone else's money—the way it feels when you use a credit card instead of cash. I purposely came up with alternative activities that didn't have such negative consequences, activities I could do instead of shopping and spending whenever that urge came over me. My alternative activity of choice has become—you're going to laugh—ironing. I am not kidding, and I cannot believe I am actually admitting this.

I have an unusual respect for fine textiles, and I thoroughly enjoy ironing them. For me there is something soothing about the sound of a good steam iron gliding over high-quality cotton or linen. I find the activity to be calming and pure joy. When my old defeating attitudes and destructive thoughts start to crowd my mind and insist that I throw caution to the wind in favor of an all-out shopping binge, I often iron instead. It works for me.

You would do well to come up with your own arsenal of alternative activities so when you get the urge to go back to your old ways you'll be able to deal with it quickly, logically, and responsibly.

CHOOSE TO SEE THINGS IN A DIFFERENT WAY

Of all the techniques to debt-proof your attitude, this might be the most difficult, but also the most rewarding: Choose to see things in a different way. It is difficult because you may have to confront attitudes and beliefs you've had all your life.

Some years ago my husband Harold and I desperately wanted off the car-leasing treadmill. We'd repaid our unsecured debts, and we wanted to free ourselves from car payments.

We'd been leasing cars, two at a time, for far too many years. But how to stop? Each time a lease ended, we had no money for a down payment on another car. We always owed more than the car was worth (overmileage penalties and the like), so we did what any typical car salesman recommends today: We "rolled over" any remaining balance into new leases on bigger and better cars—models that elevated our minimum standard ever higher. But finally, we said, "Enough! No more leases!"

Our plan to get out was drastic. We would take our lumps on the last lease ever. With the cash we had—$4,000—we would buy the best car we could find for that amount and we would continue saving to buy a second car—all cash. In the meantime we would become a one-car couple. This was possible since we share an office and followed each other to work anyway.

Understand that for more than twenty years we'd always supported two cars—late-model, high-end, leased vehicles. Every marketing campaign's dream consumer, I bought into the myth that I was what I drove. Having my own car provided my freedom and spontaneity. But for now, we would share.

The best we could find for the money we had was a 1986 Chevrolet El Camino. At the time it was nine years old—a major step down as far as I was concerned. I consoled myself, however, in the temporary nature of the situation and thought it was worth the trade-off: *no more car payments!*

I tried to hide just how miserable I was. After all, for twenty-two years I had my own car. I didn't have to check with anyone or ask permission. Now I had to ask my husband to drop me off or ask to use what felt like *his* car. I hated the feelings of dependence and my loss of freedom. I wanted to control the radio and decide when to get in the fast lane. I wanted to select the parking space. All my little quirks and control issues were without outlet. Now I had to compromise, but mostly it felt like I had to give in.

After about three months of this miserable arrangement it came down to this: I could either change my attitude or go stark raving mad. Choosing the former (mental institutions are expensive), I sat down for a heart-to-heart with myself. I said: *Oprah has a driver. She never concerns herself with mundane things like parking spaces, pumping gas, car washes, and oil changes. Her driver takes care of everything. You too have a driver. You no longer have to concern yourself with mundane things like parking spaces, pumping gas, car washes, and oil changes. Your driver takes care of everything. You can talk or sleep; you can listen to music or read. Your driver is always available and makes your transportation needs his top priority. What's not to love about this?*

I then moved to the financial ramifications of not having a car of my own: no car payment, no additional insurance, no annual registration and licensing fee, no biannual smog inspection (California thing), no maintenance and repair on a second car, no worrying about parking tickets for forgetting to move it on street-sweeping day, four less tires to replace, fifty-two less car washes each year. The list got longer and longer, and my conclusion was clear: *You are a blessed woman.*

My attitude changed in a heartbeat, and it remains that way to this day, by choice. We are still a single-car couple, and I do not want now, nor can I ever imagine wanting, the responsibility or expense of owning a second car.

One of the most powerful debt-proof tools you have at your disposal is your attitude. It can become your best ally or your worst enemy. You hold all the cards. It's up to you.

## Part Two

Debt-Proof Living in Action

In the first part of this book, we've been dealing with philosophy and theory—the foundation and basic structure for debt-proof living. Now comes the matter of practical living, the furnishing and decorating—the living part. Part 2 is about applying the philosophy and theory of part 1 to everyday financial decisions and activities.

Due to the limitations of space and my desire that this book will actually have an ending, I will address those specific topics that I am asked about most often. In the thousands of letters I've received since 1992, certain subjects and specific questions have come up over and over. Not surprisingly, those have become the matters on which I've done the most research and personal investigation. Accordingly, the chapters that follow represent the subjects I expect you will have questions about as well. Hopefully, by making this preemptive attempt, I can save you some time and postage.

Some of the chapters will be much more comprehensive than others, and that should be seen as a direct reflection of the importance of that particular issue in the beginning phases of debt-proofing your life. Credit reports, for instance, seem to hold a great deal of mystery for many people—and with good cause. It is difficult to find clear and concise information on these rascals that have such a hold over us. One might conclude that the credit industry prefers for us to be in the dark and therefore ignorant as to what really is going on in this area of credit reporting. I want to shine as much light and give you as many tools as you need to approach your credit report with confidence and understanding.

One of the first things you will do after finishing this book will have to do with groceries or some other source of food. Next to your mortgage payment or rent, you spend the most money each month on eating in or eating out. Money is being sucked out of your life by grocery stores, fast-food joints, restaurants, coffee bars, diners, and street vendors. Taking control of that spending category will greatly impact your ability to rein in your expenses to fit within 80 percent of your income. That is why you're going to find a chapter devoted to the matter of food.

If a subject isn't covered and you have a specific question, just follow the conventional wisdom that is readily available in lots of other good books on the market—including a couple of my own—or send me a note. You will find my address in the back of this book.

Every day I answer readers' questions in my monthly newsletter, *Cheapskate Monthly,* on my daily radio show, and in monthly magazine columns. And there's always a chance that you'll get a personal response. Perhaps your question will be the catalyst for another book someday.

The way I see it, if you take the time to write to me with a specific question, there are thousands of others who are asking the same thing. I place great importance on my mail and love to hear from people just like you. You are the reason I do what

I do, and hearing from you is like plugging myself into a quick-charge battery recharger.

By all means, start reading. If you don't have a subscription to *Consumer Reports,* make sure you get one or get into the habit of reading it at the library. Not only will you learn specific and fascinating information, it will teach you how to be a responsible and savvy consumer. And while you're at the library, peruse the personal finance and consumer reference sections. Pay attention to the business and personal finance sections of your newspaper. Browse the *Wall Street Journal* and make yourself read even those parts you don't fully understand. The light will click on one day. You'll be amazed at how quickly you can get up to speed when you expose yourself to excellent, relevant information.

## Chapter Ten

Taming Your Household's Runaway Expenses

ESPECIALLY THE FOOD BILL

The typical American family spends $10,000 to $15,000 per year on food—more money than it cost to buy a car or even a new house just a generation ago!

Mark Miller

If you've been keeping a spending record for any period of time, you know about the I-can't-believe-it mode. Keeping track of where the money goes on an hour-by-hour basis can be quite revealing. Perhaps that's what Benjamin Franklin was doing the day he uttered his now famous words: *Beware of little expenses. A small leak will sink a great ship.*

As you move out to debt-proof your life, it is, of course, important to take control of large expenses. But I can assure that if you pay attention only to the large expenses, your ship may still sink from all the small leaks.

For years now I've been learning and writing about all the little things you can do to reduce expenses. I like that idea—plugging the leaks, and in so doing, reducing everything a little rather than eliminating some category altogether. As most families commence to get their outgo in line with their income, they eliminate entertainment because it appears too frivolous and therefore expendable. Don't do that. Life is to be enjoyed and lived abundantly. Cut back, but don't entirely eliminate the joyful parts of your life, or you'll never stick with it.

HOUSEHOLD FINANCES

MAJOR HOUSEHOLD EXPENSES

Typically the largest monthly expense for a family is housing—the rent or mortgage payment. Second largest, believe it or not, is food. Expendable, consumable, here-today-and-gone-to-the-ocean-tomorrow food.

Another large expenditure for most families is the category we call utilities—electricity, gas, telephone, and water. Of course these days many families have added cable or direct television and Internet access to that list.

An interesting thing is going to happen to you as you begin to live by a spending plan and shop with cash: You're going to start paying attention to what things cost. You won't be able to help yourself. I don't know what it is that allows us to throw caution to the wind when paying with a check or plastic, but it works the other way too by drawing our attention into amazing focus when we know we'll be handing over cold, hard cash.

MAKING CHANGES

Basically there are only two ways to change your financial situation: earn more or spend less. You can increase your income or reduce your expenses. Sure, you could sell something to pay down debt and that could be considered a third way, but I want to stick to what you can do now.

Increasing your income is not simple. Of course you could work overtime or pick up some weekend/evening work. You could start a home-based business or hit the job market, resume in hand, to see what kind of better-paying job you could land. All of these things would accomplish the goal of increasing income, but there is also a downside that should be considered in this method of changing your financial picture. If you add hours or pick up additional work, you will also increase your job-related expenses. Also, this additional income could push you into a higher tax bracket. By the time you earn the money and actually receive it, weeks could go by; and due to that irritating thing called withholding, you could actually net a bit less than you earned. Still, all things considered, increasing your income remains a viable way to turn things around.

Reducing expenses, on the other hand, is easy. Let's say that you typically spend about $125 a week on groceries. What if I could help you find reasonable ways to cut that to $100 this week? You would walk out of the store with $25 in your hand. Right now. No waiting. The money has already been taxed so there's no further reduction. You have this money immediately to direct into some other area. Think of your long-distance telephone bill. If you could cut that in half, you'd have the difference between what you usually pay and your new and improved reduced amount in your hand.

For my money, reducing expenses is definitely the way to go.

REDUCING FOOD EXPENDITURES

In the remainder of this chapter, I am going to offer practical ways to begin slashing that second largest household expenditure: food. I will give you a jump-start.

Many people assume their food expense is represented by the groceries they buy at the supermarket. That's part of it, for sure. But the average American family spends far more than the grocery bill on food. There are fast-food places, delis, restaurants, diners, coffee bars, donut stands, sidewalk vendors, cafeterias, and vending machines.

Surveys indicate that the typical family spends only half of their total food expenditure at the grocery store. The other half goes for food eaten outside the home. So, if you've been assuming all along that the $125 a week at the grocery store is what you are spending to feed your family, double that and you may be much closer to the actual cost.

If you find your food spending to be out of line, there are lots of things you can do to reduce it. But first you need to understand what's going on to influence you in this area of spending.

CHOOSING WHERE TO SHOP

Grocery stores these days are in fierce competition for your business. Millions and millions of dollars are spent each year by the supermarket industry on marketing alone. They conduct tests to psychoanalyze customers. They videotape the habits of customers and then study them at length to figure out why people do what they do. They arrange stores according to what they learn from surveys and statistics. They know the percentage of customers who turn to the right more often than to the left and where they look as they make a right-hand turn at an aisle endcap before they proceed down the next aisle. They have scrutinized the eye level of the typical customer, which type of music promotes greater sales, and how much a wider aisle affects the bottom line at the checkout. They arrange the produce according to marketing data and customer data. From the color of the walls to the irresistible cooking odors of the bakery and hot food deli (interestingly, most businesses pump odors to the outside through the ventilation system, but many supermarkets trap them and return them to the store), to the music playing, to the position of the checkout stations, to the exact location of the high-impulse items— everything has been carefully orchestrated. You may believe that is because they care about you and want your shopping experience to be pleasant. The truth is that all of these things are part of a single purpose: to separate you from more money than you intended to spend.

Your choice of food stores is very important. Get your decorating ideas and good feelings somewhere else—don't look to the grocery store to make deposits into your feel-good bank. Instead, select the store(s) where you will spend your food dollars on the basis of value and economy.

Most communities have a very expensive supermarket, a no-frills cheap market, and then a few in between. I suggest that you do some research (see the price book section later in this chapter) to find out which store in your area has the lowest prices on a consistent basis. In making your determination, don't let sale prices and specials taint your thinking. You want to determine this information based on regular, everyday prices. You will probably find this store does not double coupons or participate in sweepstakes and frequent-buyer programs. All of those features are expensive to administer, and the costs are passed to the customers. You may find that the cheapest store overall in your area is indeed a supermarket. That is fine. The point is, you need to *choose* the stores in which you shop, not approach the matter mindlessly.

In addition to the store with the lowest prices overall, add to your arsenal of locations a produce market and a bakery outlet, if you are fortunate enough to have óne of these where you live. (A bakery outlet is where the delivery trucks take the products they didn't sell to the regular markets that day. The truck is unloaded and the bounty offered at rock-bottom prices. These are not inferior or old products—just manufacturing goofs on products with a short shelf life.)

Try to do your major shopping at the one store with the lowest prices. Then supplement by making occasional visits to the produce market and bakery outlet to supplement your regular shopping. You may even want to pop into the super-duper market from time to time to pick up loss-leaders (an item priced below the store's cost that is advertised as a way of baiting customers to come into the store and hopefully dump a load of money on other stuff they cannot resist). I don't suggest, however, that you travel from store to store buying only the sale items. You will do better in the long run if you stick to one store, taking full advantage of their sales and weekly specials.

IMPORTANT SHOPPING TIPS

Shop with cash. At the risk of sounding like a broken record, let me say again how important it is to show up at the store with cash. Take only the amount you intend to spend on groceries at that visit. Leave the checkbook and plastic at home. If you come across a fabulous bargain and don't have enough cash, you can always return to the store to stock up. Bring a calculator if you're concerned about being embarrassed at the checkout. As an aside, I think the ideal is to use your checkbook only when sending a payment through the mail, opting to use cash on all other occasions. Realistically, I know that probably won't happen because most people are hooked on the convenience and safety of writing checks. But do everything to wean yourself from anything but cash at the grocery store. You go there often and spend a large percentage of your income on food. Anything you can do to eliminate impulsive purchasing is going to impact your bottom line tremendously.

Take a list. Arrive at the store with a specific plan in mind. As much as humanly possible, do not buy anything that is not on the list, but be willing to substitute. Make your list using the week's newspaper sale ads as your guide. If chicken is this week's loss-leader, don't plan meals around beef and turkey.

Eat first. Just a simple reminder of something you already know. If you are starving, you can be sure everything you put into your basket will be what you want right this minute. Believe it or not, those grocery store marketing types actually survey this particular quirk, and their studies find you will spend at least 17 percent more if you arrive hungry than if you eat first.

Price book. One of the most useful tools you will ever use in reducing grocery spending is something you must make for yourself. A price book is a way to track the prices in two or three different stores of the products you buy most often.

Once you know for certain the regular price of something, when you see it advertised as a "Special," you'll know immediately whether it is a bargain or not. Remember, "Special" may have nothing to do with a sale or a price reduction. Store owners know that if they pile anything at the end of the aisle and top it with a "Special" sign, customers will assume it's on sale and buy it. When you find a fabulous loss-leader, stock up so you have enough on hand until the next time it goes on sale.

Warehouse clubs. They are great and I do a lot of my grocery shopping there. But the discount warehouse club can present quite a financial snare if you are not sure of what you're doing. I call it the $200 Store, because if you're not careful, it's hard to get out of there without spending $200. Unless you are quite certain you can recoup the membership

fee (about $35 a year) in normal savings (as opposed to con-
trived savings you might claim on impulsively buying, say, a
big-screen television because you are "saving" so much
money), why bother with the club? Chances are high that if you
don't exercise extreme discipline, these kinds of megashopping
opportunities will actually cost you money in unplanned purchases and impulsive buying.

Bulk buying. Buying in bulk has become the new buzz, and
while in theory it is advisable, in practice it's costing people a
lot more than they would spend otherwise. The thing you must
know is: Just because some item comes in a box the size of
Nebraska does not guarantee it is a good deal for you. First, is
the unit price really better than the grocery store price (your
price book will quickly reveal this information)? Also, the pres-
ence of so much of a particular item may create a sense of
abundance that negates a need to make it last. Face it, if you
have 24 rolls of paper towels within arm's reach, you are not
going to think frugally as you use the roll on the counter. Your
kids will think there is no need to stop drinking soda if they see
five cases of the stuff in the pantry. (By the way, soda pop is not
a very good deal at the warehouse clubs.) Will you be able to
consume those 497 chicken breasts before their recommended
use-by date? If you find yourself searching for ways to use
them before then, you are not working the bulk-buying thing
to your advantage. Keep in mind the following tips to make
bulk buying work for you:

1. Buy in bulk only when you will realize significant sav-
    ings. Generally speaking (I'm sure your price book will
    turn up exceptions from time to time), food items that
    will be cheaper when purchased in larger quantities at
    a warehouse club include milk, butter, cheese, bread,
    ice cream (the containers are mammoth), condiments,

tuna, meat, poultry, pet food, trash bags, and laundry detergent.

2. Do not outshop your storage space. You should be able to find creative places to "hide" the bounty. "Out of sight, out of mind" works even if you're the one who puts it out of sight. You want to create a sense of scarcity. You can hide cases of canned goods under a bed. Nonperishables can be stashed in the garage. If you have inadequate storage, you'll find yourself pressed to use it up just to gain some room.

3. Do not outshop your reasonable ability to consume. No matter how good the deal, if you cannot consume the items within a reasonable period of time, forget it. There's nothing like throwing away spoiled or stale food items to wipe out any savings you might have realized.

4. Do not create need. There is something seductive about 55-gallon drums of industrial-strength, high-quality shampoo concentrate for the great price of only $89. But come on! How will you ever use that prudently and judiciously? I've been guilty of coming home from the club with a few things I never dreamed I needed. That is not good and will quickly erode the purpose for which I joined in the first place.

Trip timing. Avoid shopping the first of the month and right before holidays. Some stores regularly adjust prices upward on the days they anticipate heavy traffic. Stick to the two or three cheapest stores in your area and then rotate your shopping trips. Force more time between your shopping trips. One of the best things I did in the beginning to get a handle on our food costs was to stop those daily trips to the store. Before, I would go to the store when I needed something, and often that was daily. I would go in for something small and come out with bags of things I obviously "forgot" I needed—and still I'd have nothing to fix for dinner.

Start with no more than once a week in the grocery store. Then get tough with yourself and move that to ten days, then two weeks or longer. If you practice this discipline, you will be a more effective shopper and you will spend less. A lot less. You'll be more careful about what you buy and more diligent to use it.

Use it. Check the contents of your pantry, cupboards, and freezer. Most of us have a lot of money tied up in pantry staples, canned goods, and freezer fodder—stuff we've been hanging on to for years (and with some items that could be many years). While I've heard that a can of Spam is still edible after twenty-five years, not many other things are. (I can't say I'd be too crazy about verifying this with Spam.) Discipline yourself to use what you have before you buy more food.

Couponing. It takes a lot of time, organization, and discipline for your couponing efforts to be cost effective. Some important rules to follow are:

- Only use a coupon if you would have purchased the product anyway.
- Save a coupon until the item goes on sale.
- Buy the smallest size or quantity that the coupon allows for the greatest percentage of savings.

Anticipate that even after all of your efforts, a sale item may still be cheaper than the other brand with a coupon.

Expiration dates. Most items are now printed with a "best if used by" or expiration date. Look for the date farthest into the future if you have a choice. The items with the closest expiration date will be toward the front of the shelf, so look at the items in the back to find the date farthest out.

Consider store brands. Many times the store brand and the brand name item come off the same factory line. The only difference is the label and the price. The store brand reflects no advertising costs.

Shop solo. Being distracted can be costly. Leave the kids, friends, neighbors, and spouse at home, and you'll be much more effective.

Find the marked-down bins. Produce, bakery, and meat are regularly marked down when the expiration date is near. They can be a good deal, but only if you can reasonably use them before they turn into penicillin. Meat items close to expiring should be frozen within twenty-four hours. Dented cans should show no sign of puncture, and packaged goods must be fully sealed.

Look high and low. Expensive brand names are purposely positioned at eye level. Manufacturers pay a premium for the prime shelf space, and that creates a lot of competition. While that is good for the store owner perhaps, it is not so good for you, particularly if you are on the short side. You can be sure that what you see first is the most expensive and that you will have to look high and low for the real bargains.

Avoid individual servings. As a general rule, anything with intense packaging is going to be more costly. Rather than individual-size packages, buy the big bag or size and divide into smaller portions at home. Buy cereal in a bag instead of a box and cut your cereal costs by half.

Learn sale cycles. Study sale flyers until you recognize predictable cycles, and keep track of them in your price book. Buy enough when it's on sale to last until the next sale.

Less meat. Plan meatless menus a couple of times a week. That's good for both your diet and your wallet.

Make it yourself. It's more cost effective to make your own salad dressing, chicken-coating mix, cakes, brownies, and other mixes you may be used to buying. Make your own. It will taste better, be better for you, and be much less expensive.

Brown bag it. If you eat lunch out every day, take your lunch to work two or three days a week. You'll save a huge sum of money over a year's time and probably a pile of calories too.

Make it a special occasion. If the family eats out often, put the brakes on that activity. Saving your restaurant experiences for a once-a-month treat or something you do on birthdays or other special occasions will make a huge difference in your overall spending and in your kids' attitudes. Too much of a good thing may not be good for you or your bottom line.

Chapter Eleven

Solving the Deep, Dark Mystery
CREDIT REPORTS

A good credit rating takes time and effort to obtain, but it is easy to lose. Unless you were born with a silver spoon in your mouth and a bag of gold ingots in both hands, you will need to borrow in order to meet your personal financial objectives.

Jonathan Pond

F ew things in life are more mysterious or dreadful than one's credit report. I know people who would gladly endure a root canal without benefit of anesthesia if they could get out of a one-on-one encounter with their credit report.

Why are we so intimidated by what lurks in that dark hole known as our credit files? For me it was a combination of ignorance, fear, and denial. I acquiesced to a system I didn't understand and ended up feeling like a helpless victim.

Over the years, I've come to the conclusion there are three main reasons for credit report phobia.

1.   Fear. Some people are so fearful of the unknown that they choose denial over reality. It's easier not to face it because there's always a chance it's not that bad.

2. Ignorance. A lot of people simply do not understand what a credit report is, if they really have one, where it is, who can look at it, or why it even matters.

3. Blind faith. Believe it or not, many people naively trust some supreme credit-bureau-in-the-sky to have their best interests at heart. These folks believe they have done nothing "wrong." They pay their bills faithfully and have never had a problem.

Here's a letter from a *Cheapskate Monthly* subscriber whose blind faith in the system and in her and her husband's exemplary money management turned out to be misappropriated:

> We carry no debts and have always prided our-selves on having a spotless credit report. Recently I applied for a credit card so I could get the freebie they were offering—a round-trip plane ticket. Imagine how shocked I was to be rejected because of poor credit.
>
> We immediately ordered a copy of our credit report only to find that someone had stolen my hus-band's identity, received three credit cards in his name, and run up $15,000 in bad debts.
>
> What a nightmare. We're having to file forgery affidavits and who knows how long it will take to restore our good credit standing. The problem is this happened two years ago. It looks a little odd that after all this time we're telling the companies, "Hey this isn't us—we are not responsible!"
>
> I am thankful I applied for that free airline ticket or we might not have found out what was going on for a very long time. We are regretful, however, that we didn't take your advice to keep an eye on our credit reports all along.

THE IMPORTANCE OF GOOD CREDIT

A credit report, also known as a credit file or credit history, is unfortunately not one of life's options. You have to have one. Like it or not, somewhere along the line some individual or business is going to receive information on you that will trigger the creation of a file with your name and Social Security number on it. They will not seek your permission or your blessing. Your role in all of this—and one that few people are willing to accept—is to monitor your credit report and make sure the information in it is a fair and honest representation of you. Adopting a proactive attitude is the way to win the credit-reporting game.

If you want to buy a house, a car, or even apply for that one, good, all-purpose credit card (which you will pay off each month), you need a good credit report. Even an insurance company will want to check your credit file when you apply for additional coverage.

More and more, prospective employers are checking the credit ratings of job applicants because it says a lot about a person's character. You never know when your credit report will be the deciding factor on the job of your dreams.

CREDIT BUREAUS

Credit bureaus, or credit reporting agencies as they are also called, are not governmental or law enforcement agencies. They are businesses in the private sector that collect consumer data for their customers—credit grantors like banks, finance companies, merchants, credit card companies, and others with a need for this type of information. There is no law that requires a history of your credit transactions be collected and maintained.

HOW IT ALL STARTED

Here's my version, loosely told, of how all this got started.

Back in the olden days (think *Little House on the Prairie*), when a person wanted to buy on credit, he walked into the local mercantile, and if the owner recognized him, they shook hands and the deal was done. As things progressed and business became more sophisticated, credit transactions were done in writing. The store owner wrote down a description of the credit sale and the customer signed his name. Simple as that.

As time progressed and more and more people needed credit, someone came up with a nifty form called a credit application. It contained a few extra blanks to complete that revealed the person's financial situation, employment, maybe a reference or two.

Somewhere along the line—and I can only imagine it was because so many people were filling out these applications—companies saw the need to verify the information on those applications. They called employers and references to find out all they could about an applicant's character. Credit would be granted if they determined there was a high likelihood he would repay the debt.

In time, lots of stores jumped on the credit bandwagon. And why not? If they allowed customers to buy now and pay later, their sales doubled, even tripled, almost overnight. Many businesses, however, overextended themselves by granting too much credit, causing them not to have the resources to pay their own bills. And of course some debtors failed to keep their promises, so debt collection became a new headache.

Before long, every store in town was on the credit-granting bandwagon. Reviewing applications and checking out the applicants became full-time jobs for lots of people.

One day a clever business-minded fellow saw this situation as a great business opportunity. Instead of every store checking the history and background of each of their customers, why couldn't he offer a service where he collected information on individuals and then stored that information for future use? By setting up permanent files for each person who was applying for credit, he could build a credit history, something that would become quite useful if that person ever applied for credit again at some other store.

He started his clearinghouse business, and it was wildly successful. Every merchant in town signed up for his services, agreeing to pay fees that turned out to be far less than if the company had hired individuals to do the work from scratch.

Soon banks, finance companies, merchants, credit card companies, and other creditors became paying customers, or "subscribers," of the credit bureau. The credit collection business exploded because the consumer credit industry was growing by leaps and bounds. Many credit bureaus opened their doors, and the competition heated up.

Employers jumped on the bandwagon because, they reasoned, looking into a person's credit file would give them a candid picture of this job applicant's character.

Landlords began relying on credit information as a way of predicting what kind of tenant a person applying to rent might be.

Insurance companies soon learned they could predict potential liability exposure by looking at a person's credit report.

Credit bureaus, looking for more ways to load up information in individual credit files, thereby making them more useful to their subscribers, began including items of a legal nature that were gleaned from public records, such as tax liens, judgments, and bankruptcy filings.

In time, credit bureaus realized they were sitting on very valuable marketing data. Credit scoring and the sale of marketing data became new profit-making centers, turning these companies into more than just credit-collecting agencies. They have now become information businesses that deal in all kinds of data.

Today there are thousands of credit bureaus collecting credit information about consumers. They are connected to centralized computer files that contain data on millions and millions of individuals. More than *two billion* pieces of information are put into these files every month, and much of it is done manually. While credit bureaus boast a 1 percent error rate, actual independent studies reveal a true error rate of closer to 40 percent. This should give you some indication of why it is important that you keep your eye on your credit report.

THE FAIR CREDIT REPORTING ACT

When the credit reporting industry was about thirty years old, things began to spin out of control. Credit bureaus would often report incorrect information. Private citizens began complaining that their rights were being violated. They accused the credit bureaus of ruining their lives by being so reckless with sensitive information. People who had no business looking into files could get information quite easily and then use it in inappropriate ways. Finally the government entered the picture.

In 1971, Congress passed into law the Fair Credit Reporting Act, which was subsequently amended in 1996. The FCRA granted consumers access to the contents of their credit reports, knowledge of who receives copies, and the right to dispute inaccurate, nonverifiable, and obsolete information.

The FCRA also placed restraints on the credit bureaus, limiting the length of time they can report negative information and requiring them to correct misinformation. Among many other requirements, it set up a process by which all credit bureaus must share corrected information with every other bureau.

YOUR CREDIT REPORT

HOW TO GET IT

You need to know what is being said about you, and the only way you can find out is to read your credit report. It is your right to review your report as often as you desire. Not knowing exactly how to do that is the biggest reason many of us are content to remain ignorant. (I believe that's called denial.) While there are thousands of credit reporting agencies, you need to be concerned with only the "big three" (see p. 181). More than likely, each of them has a file on you. They may not have the same information, however, which means you will want to get a copy of your report from all of them.

Even though credit bureaus are required by law to share corrections made to an individual consumer's record with other credit bureaus, don't assume that if one of your reports is correct all three will be. You should check your credit history in all three systems.

For now, I suggest you start with Experian because their report is more user-friendly than the others. It's a good one to learn on. Then start rotating.

If you are married, your spouse should also order his or her report. It might be identical to yours, or it might not be.

There are three ways you can get your report: by mail, by phone, or by Internet. You will be charged up to $8 for your report unless you've been denied credit within the past sixty days or you live in Colorado, Georgia, Maryland,

Massachusetts, New Jersey, or Vermont, in which case there will be no charge. (Note: Experian, formerly TRW, at one time offered consumers one free copy each year without restriction. That policy ended in 1996.)

Once requested, it will take ten days to two weeks for your report to arrive in your mailbox. When you get it, make one or two photocopies for note taking. You will not want to write anything on the reports themselves.

REVIEW YOUR CREDIT REPORT

Before the advent of computers, consumer data was actually handwritten on three-by-five-inch cards and stored in file cabinets. Now everything is stored digitally in what I can only imagine are the biggest computers known to mankind. Your credit report, therefore, will show up as a computer printout. Each bureau has its own style and format, but basically the information is the same.

At the very minimum your report will contain your name, current address, birth date, and Social Security number. Beyond that there may be enough data to choke a horse or just some basics like

- Your current employer
- Your current position
- Your current income
- Your former address
- Your former employer
- Your data as listed above
- If you own your home, rent, or board

GET YOUR CREDIT REPORT. GET IT NOW.

You've put it off long enough. It's time to make friends with your credit reports. Contact the bureaus listed below to order a copy. You can call, write, or go online. If you've never done this before, start with Experian because their report is the most user-friendly.

When ordering by mail, be sure to enclose a copy of your driver's license, credit card bill or utility bill along with your full name, address, and Social Security number.

If you live in Colorado, Georgia, Maryland, Massachusetts, New Jersey, or Vermont, or if you have been denied credit or services within sixty days because of the information found in your report, you can receive a free copy of your report(s). Otherwise, each report will cost $8.

Experian (formerly TRW)
P.O. Box 2104
Allen, TX 75013-2104
800-682-7654
www.experian.com

Equifax
P.O. Box 105873
Atlanta, GA 30348-5873
800-685-1111
www.equifax.com

Trans Union Corporation
750 West Sproul Road
P.O. Box 390
Springfield, PA 19064-0390
800-888-4213
www.transunion.com

I know what you're thinking: *Where do they get all of this private information?* Somewhere along the line you gave it to them. Perhaps you applied for a real estate loan or automobile loan. Think of the information you revealed when you took that student loan or when you applied for a job. Perhaps the information was gleaned from an insurance application. Chances are there was fine print that disclosed to you that by signing the form you gave your permission to have it shared with the world.

A lot of information about you that shows up in a credit file is public record, such as marriage licenses, court records of bankruptcy filings, real estate transactions, judgments, and decrees of divorce.

Like it or not, your privacy is a thing of the past, and the blame can be placed on the credit bureaus. There's not much you can do but accept it and then do what you must to make sure your credit report is a true reflection of reality.

Your credit report will contain detailed credit information. If you have open lines of credit, all of them will be listed stating the high limit allowed, current status, and payment history. Previous late payments, even if you are now current, will stick out like black eyes. You may see you have open credit lines at stores you don't even remember or credit cards you forgot you had.

The report will show different versions of your name, if any, under which information has been reported. Note: From now on, whenever you sign anything of a legal and binding nature like an application for a loan, employment, housing, insurance coverage, and so on, use the same version of your name—the way it appears on your Social Security number and federal tax return. This will eliminate confusion down the road such as when you apply for Social Security benefits or you discover there are 4,896 other people in the world who share your name or some version thereof.

Check all of the historical data on your report. You may see previous addresses as well as current and former employers. Is all of the information correct?

SCRUTINIZE ALL INQUIRIES

Inquiries, listed at end of the report, are companies or individuals who have received a copy of your report in the past years. Do you recognize these entries? Did you authorize those inquiries?

Every time you apply for credit, and the credit grantor checks your credit report, a credit inquiry is placed on your file. Even if you receive a credit offer in the mail and you respond, your credit will almost certainly be checked and a credit inquiry will be added to your credit report.

Too many credit inquiries indicate a person is credit hungry and perhaps in financial trouble. Worse, it could be assumed that you received many of the credit lines that show as inquiries and that they have not yet appeared on your credit report, but will in time. At the very least, most people who review credit reports find inquiries to be red flags.

HIGHLIGHT ALL ENTRIES

Using three different colored highlighters, go through your report marking the positive entries in one color, the neutrals in another, and the negatives in still another, using the information on page 186 as your guide.

Positive entries. Make sure you mark these in your most favorite color. While you're at it, go ahead and put a gold star by them too. This is what positive entries say about your character: I keep my promises; I am a person of integrity. Before you go nuts thinking that if two positives are good, then twenty-two

CREDIT REPORT ENTRIES

These are the only positive entries:
Paid as agreed or paid satisfactorily
Current account with no late payments
Account closed at consumer's request

These are considered neutral entries:

Paid, was 30 days late	Refinance
Current, was 30 days late	Settled
Inquiry	Paid
Credit card lost	

These are considered negative entries:
Bankruptcy—Chapter 7 or Chapter 13
Judgments
Liens
Account closed at grantor's request
Paid, was 60, 90, or 120 days late
SCNL (subscriber cannot locate)
Paid, charge-off
Bk liq reo (bankruptcy liquidation)
Charge-off
Collection account
Delinquent
Current, was 60, 90, or 120 days late
CHECKPOINT, TRANS ALERT, or CAUTION (potential fraud indicators)

Any item on an Equifax report proceeded by a ">>>" icon.

Any item rated higher than I1, M1, or R1 such as R2 or I9 (this applies to Trans Union and Equifax only).

Any item listed as repossession, foreclosure, profit and loss write-off, charge-off, paid profit and loss write-off, paid charge-off, settled, settled for less than full balance, or included in bankruptcy.

Any item on Trans Union or Equifax reports showing one or more 30-, 60-, 90-day late payments in the column to the far right.

Excessive inquiries (looks like everyone in town has turned you down).

would be that much better so let's get a new set of credit cards—understand that you do not need many positive entries to have an excellent credit rating. One or two are just dandy.

Neutral entries. Theoretically, these entries neither help nor harm your credit report. In reality, however, anything less than positive is considered by some as negative.

Negative entries. These are the most damaging to your credit standing. Check them very carefully. As regretful or embarrassing as they might be, there's only one question you can ask yourself about a negative entry: Is it accurate? If it is not, mark it as one you will be disputing or correcting. If the entry is, unfortunately, correct, make a note of the first reporting date and then calculate the date seven years hence (ten years for bankruptcy) on which it will disappear. As you monitor your credit report each year from now on, you will want to verify its disappearance.

REPAIRING BAD CREDIT INFORMATION

As bad as that negative entry may be, you cannot erase, repair, correct, amend, or fix it if the information is correct. The law defines incorrect information as that which you "reasonably believe" to be inaccurate or incomplete, information that cannot be verified, or information that is obsolete. Everything else is an allegation. Think of it this way: you've been accused. You have the right to defend yourself and plead "not guilty."

Look at your highlighted negative entries, including the inquiries you have highlighted as neutrals. Which, if any, fall in the category of information that is inaccurate, can no longer be verified, or is obsolete? These are the ones that should get your attention.

How to Dispute Inquiries

First, you need the name and address of the entity that made the inquiry. You should be able to find this on your Experian credit report, unlike Trans Union and Equifax. If you are looking at all three of your reports, you may see the inquiry has shown up across the board. Match them up against Experian to get the address. If you are still missing any, call toll-free directory assistance, 800-555-1212, and request the toll-free number for the inquiring creditor.

Write a letter to each inquirer asking them to remove the inquiry from your specific report. If it's on all three or just one or two, state that. The FCRA allows only authorized inquiries to appear on one's consumer credit report. In your letter you must challenge whether the inquiring creditor had proper authorization before pulling your credit file.

Following is a sample letter to challenge an inquiry. It should be sent to the inquiring company, not to the credit bureau that simply reports what the subscriber submits. Rather than copying this letter verbatim, use your own words to make your request. Keep your letter professional and courteous.

Re: Unauthorized Credit Inquiry
Dear Sirs,

I have recently reviewed my [Experian, Trans Union, Equifax] credit report and it shows a credit inquiry by your company. I do not recall authorizing such an inquiry into my credit file. It is my understanding that without my authorization you are not allowed to put an inquiry into my credit history file.

Please instruct that this inquiry be removed from my credit file.

I'm sending this letter by certified mail so you can understand the urgency of this matter. Kindly forward to me documentation that will verify the inquiry has been removed.

If I am incorrect and you did have my authorization to make such an inquiry, please send proof of that fact.

Thank you in advance for your earliest response.

Sincerely,

[Your name as it appears on the report]

You may receive the documentation that the inquiry has been removed, or the company might respond with proof that carries your signature (then you can kick yourself for having such a poor memory). If thirty days pass from the date they received your letter (you will have the certified mail receipt) and you have not had a response, you have ample grounds to demand the inquiry be removed.

Here's the bonus benefit you will receive from this time-consuming activity of disputing inquiries: In the future you will think long and hard before allowing anyone access to your credit history.

OPT OUT OF DIRECT MARKETING LISTS

Credit bureaus increase their profit margins tremendously by selling marketing and direct-mail lists based on the information stored in their data bases. All kinds of companies that deal in direct-mail marketing, including credit card companies, pay a lot of money to get specifically targeted lists. Credit bureaus have at their fingertips very important—and what many feel to be private—information about the majority of people in this country.

If you've ever wondered why you get so many pre-approved credit card applications in the mail, it's because the credit bureaus have put your name on lists they sell to companies looking for likely candidates and potential customers. If that makes you crazy, you should be happy to know that the FCRA as amended in 1996 gives you the right to opt out, to tell the credit bureaus and other direct-mail marketing list brokers that you do not give permission for your name to be on their lists.

In accordance with the provisions of the FCRA, you can call a single phone number (800-353-0809) to exercise your opt-out option. This completely automated system will prompt you to answer questions that will identify you. It will take about three months for your opt-out instruction to reach the "big three" credit bureaus.

If you would like to opt out of other direct-mail marketing lists in an effort to stop the deluge of junk mail that flows into your home, write a letter giving your complete name, name variations, and mailing address to:

Mail Preference Service

Direct Marketing Association

P.O. Box 9008

Farmingdale, NY 11735

To remove your name from many telephone solicitation lists, send your complete name, address, and phone number with area code to:

Telephone Preference Service

Direct Marketing Association

P.O. Box 9014

Farmingdale, NY 11735

HOW TO DISPUTE INACCURATE INFORMATION

When you dispute or challenge negative entries on your credit report that you reasonably believe are inaccurate, you can either correspond with the credit bureau reporting the false information or the creditor from whom they received it. If you have several problem entries, you should probably start with the credit bureau.

Here's an example of an item that warrants a dispute: Let's say you have a debt that went to collection. You know and can verify that the amount was $564. Your credit report, however, shows the amount to be considerably more, at $750. This is inaccurate, and according to the FCRA, you have the right to dispute the entry in its entirety.

Fill out the dispute form that came with your credit report. If you do not have one, call the credit bureau to request one or write your dispute in the form of a letter. Be sure to include all the necessary information: the names of the creditors (they call them subscribers) and the account numbers. Using your own words, tell why you believe the information has been reported erroneously. Perhaps the amount reported is incorrect or the account has been paid in full. There's always the chance this isn't even your account at all. If the number of late payments is incorrect, state that. Whatever the situation, just state the facts. Don't get emotional, accusatory, or threatening. Don't get into details or state dollar amounts. Simply state that the information is inaccurate or erroneous.

Make sure your letter includes your name, identification number as stated on the credit report, address, daytime phone number, Social Security number, and date of birth.

You should receive something in the mail indicating the results of the credit bureau's reinvestigation within six weeks.

If you hear nothing, repeat the process. You may have to do this two or three more times.

Make sure you keep good records of all your correspondence and take notes on any phone calls, noting the date and time of the call and the name of the person with whom you spoke.

If on the off chance you do not receive responses within satisfactory periods of time (remember the FTC has interpreted "reasonable period of time" as thirty days), threaten to take legal action. Send a copy of your letter with copies of documentation to the Federal Trade Commission and to your state's local office of the attorney general.

You also have the option of dealing directly with the creditor, and that can be effective because the creditor has the authority to change or delete items from your credit report. Follow the same procedure recommended for dealing with the credit bureau. You can also deal with creditors on negative items that were reported correctly, but you now want to go back and make right.

Let's say they sent your account to collection and it is still outstanding in the amount of $500. You can completely ignore the collection agent and make the creditor an offer to satisfy the debt and at the same time negotiate to have the item removed from your credit report. There is no law that states a creditor must report negative information to a credit bureau, nor one that prevents them from removing information already reported.

How to Improve or Reestablish Credit

If your credit report does not represent your proudest accomplishment, take heart. You are on your way to turning your life around, and it's going to take a little time. The best thing you can do is change your ways now so that in the future it will be evident on your report that there was a significant change at a certain point in time.

Here are nine steps you can take to improve or reestablish your credit.

1. Pay off your debts. No matter how you got into credit trouble, paying off your unsecured debts will help restore your credit.

2. Learn to be a good money manager. Analyze your spending habits, create financial goals, and set spending priorities. Taking control of your finances will reduce the likelihood that you will get caught in the credit crunch again.

3. Pay with cash. Even if you have credit available, you are more likely to change your spending habits by not using it. When you pay with cash, you learn the joy of owning, not simply acquiring. Cash lets you stay in touch with your money, as opposed to plastic that is only a stand-in.

4. Obtain your credit report. Follow the instructions in this chapter to get control of your credit report aversion.

5. Dispute with confidence. Once you have your report, question the validity of every negative entry. You have the right to dispute any remark on your report that you "reasonably believe" to be inaccurate or incomplete.

6. Close accounts. If you have multiple credit card, department store, or other types of credit that you forgot about or are not using, close them. Then it will show up on your report as "closed by consumer," and that's a positive entry.

7. Apply for secured credit. If you are trying to reestablish credit or get it for the first time, one tactic is to obtain a secured credit card. This requires a security deposit to be placed in an interest-bearing savings account equal to the credit limit offered. The deposit is frozen by the bank and acts as collateral from which the bank can draw if you do not pay on time. Make sure you never carry a balance from month to month, and in a year or so, your credit report will reflect this account as "paid as agreed." Then you'll be ready to . . .

8. *Apply for unsecured credit.* Your goal is eventually to have one good, all-purpose unsecured credit card with these attributes: no annual fee, a twenty-five-day grace period, a credit limit no larger than you could pay in full in a single month, and one that is accepted at many places. Never allow a balance to revolve from month to month. Pay your balance, if any, during the grace period. Decline future credit limit increases.

9. *Educate yourself.* Read everything you can about personal finance and money management. As you continue to educate yourself, your confidence will increase and you will take control of your finances. As you look for ways to live beneath your means by spending less than you have, you will find financial freedom. And it will happen more quickly than you ever dreamed possible.

HOW TO ESTABLISH CREDIT

If you have no credit history at all, the most sure way to start a file is to apply for a secured credit card (see chap 12). You will be required to put about $300 into an interest-bearing account that will serve as collateral for a credit card you will be issued with a credit line of the same amount.

Once you have the card, use it once or twice, making sure you pay the entire balance during the grace period. In a few months your new credit report will list this one item with a positive rating of "paid as agreed." In about six months you should become eligible to convert to an unsecured credit card account. Make sure you follow the debt-proof living principles to stay out of debt. And prepare yourself. Now you'll begin to get preapproved credit card applications in the mail, trying to get you to fall into a life of debt.

Remember, you—not the credit bureaus—control your financial destiny.

HOW TO MAINTAIN A GOOD CREDIT REPORT

Once you are satisfied that your credit report fairly reflects you and your true credit history, it is important that you move into maintenance mode. The key to maintaining good credit is to follow a few simple rules:

1. Pay your bills on time. While some potential lenders may be lenient, tolerating a maximum of thirty days late, others— such as a potential employer or landlord—will not be so charitable. Late payments indicate a sloppy lifestyle and a lack of personal discipline. If you are currently behind on your accounts, catch up as quickly as possible. You want to fit the profile of the people who pay their bills on time.

2. Don't be too close to your credit limits. Lenders and others looking at your credit report will compare your credit card balances to your available credit. The closer you are to the total limit, the greater risk you appear to be.

3. Cancel any credit cards you do not absolutely have to use. It's best that you have only one good, all-purpose credit card. That's all you need. Many open lines of credit on your credit report—even if they are all currently at a zero balance— become a negative cloud over your credit report. Anyone looking at your credit report would quickly realize that you could be in major debt before tomorrow night if you went nuts with all of that available credit.

4. Once a year get copies of your credit reports and correct any errors. It is estimated that one in four credit reports contain mistakes. There are three major credit reporting agencies and chances are each of them has a file on you. In addition to your credit history, these credit reporting agencies have most of your financial information as well—your salary, bank accounts, credit cards, and loan information. And each report could be different; that is why you'd be smart to check all three on a rotating basis. Be sure to follow up to see that any corrections you've made are made promptly.

5. Be careful to limit the number of inquiries on your credit report. The more inquiries there are, the less likely you are to get the credit you're seeking, the job you want, or the insurance policy you need. For example, every time you apply for a credit card, an inquiry about your credit application is included in your credit report. If too many credit card companies inquire at once, or too many employers are taking a look, they may be suspicious about your intentions or wonder why you're still looking for a job.

THE FAIR CREDIT REPORTING ACT

The Fair Credit Reporting Act of 1971, amended in 1996, grants consumers certain rights with regard to individual credit reports. The following is an overview of the provisions. The full text of the FCRA can be found on the Internet at http://www.ftc.gov/os/statutes/fcra.htm.

1. You must be told if information in your file has been used against you in credit extension, employment, etc. Also, you must be told the name, address, and telephone number of the bureau furnishing the information.

2. You can find out what is in your file and a list of everyone who has requested it recently. You can request a free copy of your report within sixty days of being

adversely affected by information in your report. You are also entitled to a free report every twelve months if you certify that (1) you are unemployed and plan to seek employment within sixty days, (2) you are on welfare, or (3) your report is inaccurate due to fraud. Otherwise, you can be charged up to $8.00. In addition, some states have enacted legislation that requires the three major credit bureaus to provide consumers with one free credit report per year. These states are Massachusetts, Vermont, Maryland, New Jersey, Georgia, and Colorado.

3. You can dispute inaccurate information. If you dispute information in your report, the bureau must investigate the item(s) by presenting to its information source all of the relevant information you submit. The source must review your evidence and report its findings to the bureau, advising the bureau of any errors. If the investigation results in any change in your report, the bureau must notify you in writing and give you a copy of your new report. If the dispute is not resolved, the bureau must allow you to add a brief statement to your report. If your report is changed or a dispute statement is filed, you may ask that anyone who has recently received your report be notified.

4. Inaccurate information must be corrected or deleted. The bureau must remove or correct inaccurate or unverified information from its files—generally within thirty days after you dispute it. However, the bureau is not required to remove accurate data from your file unless it is outdated or cannot be verified. The bureau cannot reinsert into your file a disputed item unless the information source verifies its accuracy and

completeness. If the bureau reinserts the item, it must give you written notice that it has done so and must give you the name, address, and phone number of the information source.

5. Outdated information may not be reported. In most cases, the bureau may not report negative information that is more than seven years old; ten years for bankruptcies.

6. Access to your file is limited. A bureau may provide information about you only to those with a need to know and who are recognized by the FCRA.

7. Your consent is required for reports that are provided to employers or for release of reports that contain medical information.

8. You may choose to remove your name from bureau lists for unsolicited credit and insurance offers. Such offers must include a toll-free phone number for you to call to have your name removed from future lists for two years. If you request from the bureau the form provided for this purpose and return same, you must be removed from the list indefinitely.

9. You may seek damages from violators. If a bureau, a user, or (in some cases) a provider of data violates the FCRA, you may sue them in state or federal court. For more information, contact the Federal Trade Commission, Consumer Response Center—FCRA, Washington, DC 20580 (202-326-3761).

The following is an Internet site where you can learn more about your credit report, your rights, and how to monitor and manage credit in the best way possible: http://www.creditinfo-center.com.

## Chapter Twelve

Protect Yourself from Explosive Plastics

CREDIT CARDS, CHARGE CARDS, AND DEBIT CARDS

Plastic is not the real thing—it is only a stand-in for money. To think of plastic as having intrinsic value of its own is to believe a myth.

Mary Hunt

Many things we live with, rely upon, and enjoy—things like automobiles, prescription drugs, pesticides, and even fire—are intrinsically dangerous. They have the potential to harm. We would be horribly misguided if we did not take necessary precautions to prevent potential devastation. But that doesn't mean they should be banished from our lives.

We don't let kids play with matches. We keep highly flammable items stored safely and choose not to attach lighted candles to the Christmas tree. We wear seatbelts, enact traffic laws, stay on the right side of the highway, and teach our young people to drive defensively. We lock up prescription drugs and keep harmful pesticides and cleaning products out of harm's way.

Our lives are filled with things that are useful and at the same time inherently dangerous. But we do not banish them because of their potential danger. Instead, we handle them appropriately and with great respect. The same is true of "plastic"—credit, charge, debit, and ATM cards. They can be highly "explosive" if handled carelessly or very useful tools when we treat them appropriately and with great respect.

Here's the deal: Every adult, or family, needs one good, all-purpose, well-chosen, and equally well-managed piece of "plastic"—to be handled with all the care of a highly explosive yet powerful tool. With that privilege comes the responsibility to know and fully understand everything about the consumer credit industry and how to play its game. We need to know why the industry exists, how it functions, the designs it has on us and every member of our family, and the ways we can use that industry to our advantage.

I do not condone living completely plasticless. That is simply not realistic these days. In these high-tech times you will need your plastic tool to do things like buy airplane tickets, check into a hotel, or rent a car. It will provide consumer protection in case you have a problem when ordering things through the mail, by phone, or online. Used wisely, this tool will give you interest-free credit just long enough to transfer funds to pay a bill or get reimbursed for business expenses. But consumer credit is serious business, something that should not be considered lightly.

Whether a credit card becomes something useful or something terribly dangerous for you depends on how you use—or abuse—it. Like a rope, you can use it to help you, or you can turn it into a noose and hang yourself. I prefer to help you manage the former.

WHY THEY EXIST

All consumer credit companies—whether they offer credit, charge, or debit cards—exist for a simple purpose, and it's time we get it out in the open: They are in it for the money. There is nothing wrong with that, per se—I am quite fond of the capitalistic free-enterprise system myself. Still, I want to arm you with the knowledge you need to make the choice that is right for you so you can participate with this industry in a reasoned way. Then if the powerful industry snatches a lot of your hard-earned money, you will at least know that it happened by your choice, not theirs.

THREE TYPES OF PLASTIC

Basically, there are three types of "plastic" available. A *credit card* creates high-interest loans by allowing the cardholder to buy now and pay later, over time, with small monthly payments. Generally there is no annual fee for a credit card, and the interest is waived if the entire balance owing is paid each month during the grace period.

A *charge card* has no provision for incurring debt because it requires the cardholder to pay the balance in full each billing period. A charge card is a pay-as-you-go device for which you pay an annual fee.

A *debit card* looks much like a credit card but offers electronic access to your bank account and often doubles as an automatic teller machine (ATM) card. It is not a credit device. When a purchase is made using a debit card, the purchase amount is immediately deducted as if a check had been cleared against the account.

While any one of these three choices of plastic fulfills the basic need for electronic access to funds, there are pros and cons for all three types of plastic. The decision of which is best for you will depend greatly on your specific situation and lifestyle. Your needs may change with time as your financial picture changes. It is important that you know the difference between the three, the strengths of each as well as the pitfalls.

CREDIT CARDS

Of the three types of plastic, the credit card is by far the most widely used. That's because of the three choices it is the greatest income producer for the issuing company. More advertising and marketing schemes are devoted to credit cards, and that makes them by far the most complicated and difficult to manage.

More people are tripped up by credit cards than by any other type of plastic. Still the credit card offers the wise consumer the best deal possible—all the benefits of plastic without any of the costs. To achieve that end, however, you must become adept at nibbling the bait without getting hooked.

If you—now or in the past—have had a consumer debt problem, most likely the culprit was this slick invention known as the credit card. There is a high price attached to the so-called convenience of having things now and paying for them later. According to the American Bankruptcy Institute, there were 1.4 million personal bankruptcy filings in 1998, 90 percent of which were the result of excessive credit card debt. Still, the average American receives twenty credit card offers each year.

The Credit Game

When you signed that credit card application and accepted a credit card—or two or ten?—you agreed to participate in a kind of game. It is a one-on-one competition in which your opponent writes the rules. You even agreed that he could change those rules at will. Worse, your competitor isn't very interested in helping you learn how to play the game. He prefers that you remain ignorant—always paying, never questioning. Consumer ignorance drives the consumer credit industry.

The only way you can turn the tables and win the credit card game is to level the playing field. First you have to figure out what the rules are, find out what's in your opponent's game book, and then develop your own winning strategy.

A credit card company's goal is to develop each of its cardholders into a "revolver" (industry lingo for someone who carries a balance from month to month). The company's success is found when they can get consumers hooked on credit and over their heads in debt.

Credit card companies reluctantly tolerate those of us they call "deadbeats"—cardholders who always pay their balances in full and do not participate in the payment of interest and fees. The practice of letting deadbeats off scot-free, however, is showing the early signs of disappearing—several companies are testing an annual deadbeat fee of $25 to $35 for those cardholders who are not carrying their weight. There goes the no-fee feature if this practice is allowed to take hold.

Unfortunately, most credit card holders live in a fantasy world, choosing to believe the following credit card myths:

- Credit card companies want to make my life better.
- Consumer credit is a socially acceptable way to bridge the gap between my inadequate income and the amount of money I need to live on.
- The credit card company would not give me a credit limit I could not afford.
- My credit limit is my money. I'm entitled to spend it any way I choose.
- I trust the company to deal fairly with me, so I don't need to understand the terms and conditions of my credit card account.
- An increase in my credit limit is a reward for good behavior. It's a merit increase.

- It is not possible to live without consumer credit.

The Company's Ideal Customer

Credit card companies are always looking to develop and add excellent customers. Their ideal customer is one who

- has a perpetually revolving balance and considers that monthly payment as an ordinary and necessary expense;
- carries a balance that is higher than he could reasonably repay in a single month;
- makes only the minimum required payment each month;
- always pays on time;
- accepts and then spends up to credit limit increases.

No matter your debt-proof living (DPL) level, whether you are in the process of getting debt free or you are in full prevention mode, you must think of a credit card as a loaded gun—it is good to have when you need it but not something you should treat casually. You don't make false moves, act recklessly, or treat it lightly. It is something that commands your respect.

Debt-proof living strategies are rigid when it comes to the care and use of a credit card. There's little latitude, if any, if you intend to play the game and always win. Follow the rules without compromise and your credit card will enhance your life without out-of-pocket expense. Slip up and you'll find yourself in a lot of financial trouble.

The DPL Rules of the Game

If you choose to own a credit card, make it one good, all-purpose credit card and destroy the rest. The card you choose should meet the following criteria:

- No annual fee

- Twenty-five-day grace period
- Single-cycle billing method
- Wide acceptance
- Low interest

If you use a credit card ideally, you will never pay fees or interest. Therefore, the interest rate will be lower in priority when selecting a good, all-purpose credit card. Most likely the card you select will be either a Visa or MasterCard since these are accepted in the greatest number of places. When you destroy the other cards, do more than cut them up. Call the company and insist that your account be closed. Expect a hassle, but stick to your guns.

If you are now, or once were, a well-established revolver, you have been targeted by the industry as a very desirable customer. You will continue to receive unsolicited invitations, preapproved applications, and prequalified credit card offerings in the mail. There are probably three in your mailbox right now. Until you can get off the lists (see chap. 11) you will be hounded, so just expect it and determine to resist.

Understand the terms and conditions. Every credit card account operates according to specific terms and conditions. Some of these are disclosed at the time you complete the application; others are written on the monthly statement. Never forget that what the big print giveth the small print taketh away, and that is true both of the application and the monthly statement. Enlarge that small print on a photocopy machine. If you don't fully understand everything or information is missing, call customer service. Here's a rundown of what you need to know about your credit card account:

- Annual Percentage Rate (APR)
- Monthly interest rate (punishment for late payment)
- Punishment fee for going over limit

- Grace period guidelines
- Fees for cash advances
- Balance transfer guidelines
- Billing method basis
- Single- or two-cycle billing
- Statement closing date

Once you know the rules and the consequences of breaking them, you'll be less likely to slip up. You'll find a way never to incur late or over-limit fees and learn how to pay the least interest possible—hopefully none. Read your statement very carefully every month. Scrutinize every square millimeter, and question any charge or entry you do not understand.

Take control of the credit limit. Insist on a credit limit in an amount no more than you could reasonably repay in a single month. If you do not have an extra $10,000 lying around to blow on a credit card statement, don't accept a $10,000 credit limit. For most situations $500 to $1,500 is more than adequate to cover potential charges but low enough to discourage momentary lapses in purchasing judgment. Remember, you will have your Contingency Fund (see chap. 6) and your Freedom Account (see chap. 8) for emergencies.

It is important to note that large amounts of available credit (not debt, but open available credit) appearing on your credit report can be seen as a negative because potential lenders look at not only how much debt you have but how much you could incur in a short period of time. It's just one more reason to reject the large credit limits credit card companies are trying to push.

Leave home without it. This rule should apply particularly to those who are still paying off unsecured debt or are just newly debt free. To go back to living on credit can be so tempting at times that just carrying the card with you can present an overwhelming temptation to use it. Instead, keep it in a safe place—a bank deposit box or home safe. You can even freeze it in a block of ice and keep it in your freezer—any place that it is safe from you. As an alternative to actually carrying the card, record the number, expiration date, and toll-free number of the company (you will find this on the back of the card) in a secret place in your address book or wallet. Now if you have a true emergency or an unexpected need to buy a plane ticket, you have what you need to call the company directly to authorize the charge.

A word of warning: Credit card companies are not anxious to reduce credit limits. On the contrary, they want your credit limit at the highest possible level they can justify. They push for a higher credit limit, all the while making it appear to be a reward for good behavior.

Never use a credit card to buy something because you do not have the money to pay for it. This is the mentality the credit card industry desperately wants you to adopt. For them, this is the way to huge profit margins; for you, it is financially deadly. They want you to make the purchase today and then find you cannot, or do not choose to, pay for it within the grace period. They know (and can prove it statistically) that if you don't have the money today you are not likely to have it twenty-five days from now either. Even if you do, once you have put that must-have purchase on credit, statistics show that you are less likely to use your cash to pay for this purchase, choosing rather to roll it over.

Let's say you are absolutely sure beyond a reasonable doubt that you will have the money and that you will use it to pay for this purchase you're about to put on credit. Great. So what's the big rush? Force yourself to wait the few days until you do have the money. As a bonus, you'll give yourself the gift of time—time to think and time possibly to change your mind.

Don't be late. Just because you mailed your payment on time doesn't mean it won't be late. Take Capital One for example, where sorting the mail is no simple task. The Virginia-based credit card issuer sorts and processes anywhere from 100,000 to 600,000 customer payments each day. Three hundred employees and a number of machines make it happen. There are any number of things that can happen to delay your check on its journey to being processed the day it is received—if it is received. Remember, you are depending on something called the mail to get your payment to the processing center. Only after a payment is physically posted to an account is it no longer considered "in the mail." Being late will mean a double whammy: you will have to pay interest and the late fee. It will be a triple whammy if the interest plus the late fee plus the balance puts you over your credit limit. Then you'll get socked with an over-limit fee as well.

Pay early. If you carry a balance, making your monthly payment early in the billing cycle (even before the stated due date on the billing statement) will save you money. Why? Because most credit card issuers use the average-daily-balance method to figure monthly interest or finance charges. If you make your monthly payment early in the billing cycle, you reduce the daily balance for more days in that cycle. This also reduces the total balance used to figure the average daily balance for that month. On the next page are two examples. In the example on the left, the $400 payment is made at the end of the billing cycle, just before the due date. The second example shows the very same beginning balance, but the activity is reversed—payment is early in the billing cycle. That immediately reduces the average daily balance, so more of the payment goes toward the principal. Compare the charts carefully. This is how credit card companies figure how much interest a revolver pays. There are two reasons you should get into the habit of paying credit card bills as soon as they arrive. First, you will avoid incurring horrendous penalties for being late if there are mail delays, and second, you'll pay less interest.

Date	Activity	Balance
4-1		2500
4-2		2500
4-3		2500
4-4	$32 purchase	2532
4-5		2532
4-6		2532
4-7	$117 purchase	2649
4-8		2649
4-9		2649
4-10	$52 purchase	2701
4-11		2701
4-12		2701
4-13		2701
4-14		2701
4-15		2701
4-16		2701
4-17		2701
4-18		2701
4-19		2701
4-20		2701
4-21		2701
4-22		2701
4-23		2701
4-24		2701
4-25		2701
4-26		2701
4-27		2701
4-28		2701
4-29	$400 payment	2301
4-30		2301
Total Balance:		$78,964

$78,964 ÷ 30 days = $2632 avg. daily bal.
$2632 x .015 = $39.48 Interest
New Balance: $2340.48

Date	Activity	Balance
4-1		2500
4-2	$400 payment	2100
4-3		2100
4-4		2100
4-5		2100
4-6		2100
4-7		2100
4-8		2100
4-9		2100
4-10		2100
4-11		2100
4-12		2100
4-13		2100
4-14		2100
4-15		2100
4-16		2100
4-17		2100
4-18		2100
4-19		2100
4-20	$32 purchase	2132
4-21		2132
4-22		2132
4-23	$117 purchase	2249
4-24		2249
4-25		2249
4-26	$52 purchase	2301
4-27		2301
4-28		2301
4-29		2301
4-30		2301
Total Balance:		$64,948

$64,948 ÷ 30 days = $2165 avg. daily bal.
$2165 x .015 = $32.47 Interest
New Balance: $2333.47

Notes: Previous balance $2500, annual interest rate 18%, monthly interest rate 1.5%

Don't fall from grace. Many credit card issuers are nibbling away at interest-free grace periods. If you do not carry a balance from month to month but depend on those interest-free days, a change from a 25- to a 20-day grace period could be very expensive. Some companies are doing away with grace periods altogether. That means that even if you pay in full, the clock starts ticking the minute you make a purchase.

Death to cash advances. Interest rates on cash advances can be very steep (19 to 27 percent, sometimes more), plus there's an outrageous cash advance fee. There is no grace period on cash advances, so they begin charging interest from the day the money is taken out. Taking into account the high interest plus the horrible fees, some issuers are effectively charging more than 30 percent for cash advances. That is ludicrous. What's worse, most issuers now reserve the right to allocate a customer's payment toward any portion of the balance with lower APRs first. That means if you take a cash advance, it will continue accruing big interest until you get the lower APR balances paid in full. Don't even think about cash advances on a credit card.

Watch the mail. Credit card companies reserve the right not only to write the rules, but also to change them whenever they like. Always read your statement each month because this is where you will likely be notified of a change. Grace periods are disappearing, and this is where you will be notified if yours is headed south. If your grace period is shortened significantly or eliminated altogether, cancel that account immediately. Here's another reason to watch the mail: Your account could be sold to another company. You will be notified, but you might think it's junk mail. If you don't like being sold like a piece of meat, make a call to the new customer service department (the number is given in your notification). You won't be able to change card issuers, but you can put up a fuss and possibly negotiate new terms at least equal to those you had prior to being sold.

Know where you are. The worst thing you can do with a credit card is lose track of what you've spent and how much you owe. If you use a card (may I say that it would be better if you didn't), get into the habit of recording every transaction the same way you record checks that you write. You've spent the money, so write your credit purchases in your checkbook as if you wrote a check for that amount. Include the exact amount of the purchase and deduct it from your bank balance.

Refer to the illustration on page 210. This is a page from Frank's checkbook register. Notice that he treats credit card purchases the same as writing a check (his Visa activity items are printed in bold for clarity). Whenever he writes a check or makes a Visa purchase, he records the item and deducts the full amount from the current balance.

When Frank receives his monthly Visa credit card account statement, he reconciles the charges on the statement with his checkbook register. Frank uses the column headed by *T* (a column most people don't use but which is provided to mark items that may be tax-deductible) to check off credit card purchases that appear on his monthly Visa statement as they match his record. In this example Frank found everything to be correct. He checked off the eight purchase amounts and added them up to find the total of $346.48 to be the exact amount Visa said that he owed for the month.

Notice that on May 13, after he made sure all the transactions he was charged for on his Visa statement were correct, he wrote "Visa Total" and entered $346.48 as a credit in the "Additions" column. He had to do this reverse action so that when he paid the Visa bill in full by writing check #106, he wouldn't end up deducting all of his credit card purchases

Item No. or Trans Code	Date	Transaction Description	Subtractions Amount of Payment of Withdrawal (-)	✓ T	(-) Fee If Any	Additions Amt of Deposit or interest (+)	Balance
							1250 00
101	5-1	Electric Company	65 38				1184 62
VISA	5-1	Gasoline Company	13 60	✓			1171 02
VISA	5-2	Store No. 1	35 88	✓			1135 14
102	5-3	Telephone Company	19 00				1116 14
103	5-4	Cable Company	25 00				1091 14
VISA	5-4	Clothing Company	76 00	✓			1015 14
VISA	5-5	Store No. 2	15 75	✓			999 39
104	5-6	Water Company	35 00				964 39
VISA	5-7	Vitamin Store	61 20	✓			903 19
VISA	5-8	Computer Store	56 00	✓			847 19
VISA	5-10	Gasoline Company	12 95	✓			834 24
105	5-10	Church	100 00				734 24
VISA	5-13	Car Repair Company	75 10	✓			659 14
	5-13	VISA Total	346 48				
106	5-13	VISA - Full Balance/Statement	346 48			346 48	1005 62
107	5-15	Cash	100 00				659 14
VISA	5-17	Gasoline Company	13 75				559 14
	5-18	Paycheck				800 00	545 39
VISA	5-20	Airline	175 00				1345 39
							1170 39

twice (simply a debit/credit function required in order to make everything balance).

Of course when Frank receives his monthly checking account statement he will need to ignore all Visa entries—both debits and credits—he's made to manage his credit card use, but that should be simple to do. Then he can reconcile his bank statement without a problem.

There's something very important about writing down credit card transactions as they occur. It's called reality.

Become a deadbeat—and soon. If you are a revolver, develop a plan to repay the balance in full (see chap. 7) so you can lose that designation. If the card requires an annual fee, get rid of it. There are still lots of no-fee cards.

Specialty Credit Cards

Among the hundreds of different credit cards available, there are two specific types we need to discuss: affinity cards and rebate cards. Both types of cards usually require annual fees, and that pretty much puts them out of the running to qualify as the one good, all-purpose piece of plastic you need to own.

Affinity cards. Affinity cards are marketed to a group of customers with a common bond, such as a membership in an organization. You might have a credit card issued by your college alma mater for example. Typically a small portion—heavy on the word *small*—of the fees you pay to the credit card company for your affinity card goes back to the organization. You are not going to find a no-annual-fee affinity card. If you justify the fee by saying you are supporting the organization, you are really fooling yourself. Only a small bit of the fees you pay goes to the organization. You'd be better off to stick with a no-fee card and send the organization a donation occasionally.

Rebate cards. This is probably the most misunderstood of all credit card issues. Consumers are often willing to pay annual fees and make frequent use of the card because they believe they are getting paid to do so. The most popular of the rebate cards is Discover card, which has no annual fee and rebate one percent of annual purchases. Here's my objection to the Discover method. First, Discover is not a card I would classify as being accepted in most places, so it doesn't meet that criteria of an all-purpose piece of plastic. Secondly, if one percent of your annual purchases is significant at all, you need to rethink why you are putting so much stuff on a credit card throughout the year. Statistics prove that you will spend at least 23 percent more simply because you have the credit card mentality when it comes to paying for things. If you use it occasionally to purchase a plane ticket or rent a car—the purpose for which you have this one, good, all-purpose credit card— you will be lucky to get a one-dollar rebate a year for your efforts.

The second most popular rebate-type card is one that earns frequent flyer miles. Cards that earn miles almost always charge a significant annual fee of $50 to $85 or more. Here's the problem: You get one mile for each dollar you charge to your credit card. It takes a minimum of 25,000 miles to get one round-trip airplane ticket. Work it out: You have to put $25,000 of purchases on this single credit card to get enough miles to do anything with them. That means each dollar you charge on that card is worth one cent toward a plane ticket. By that calculation, one round-trip ticket is worth $250. That's a pile of required charging just to get a $250 benefit (remember, you had to pay at least $50 just to get the credit card), and that's assuming you will rack up $25,000 in credit card purchases in a twelve-month period. The companies involved know for certain you will acquire the tendency to justify charging in order to collect miles.

Another problem is that often the miles expire—you don't have an unlimited time frame in which to redeem them. This is a marketing ploy designed to create a sense of urgency. Of course each situation varies, but typically the miles expire after two or three years. The cardholder who is paying $50 to get something for nothing now must also charge at a high rate in order to collect enough points to turn this rebate fiasco into something useful.

I recommend that unless you earn miles by traveling a lot *in addition* to putting the cost of said travel on the rebate card (meaning you travel at least 50,000 miles a year on the same airline), you are far better off to go with a no-fee, nonrebate card and then shop for good airfare deals when you do want to travel.

The rebate card industry is growing and changing on a daily basis. I'm certain that if I listed every rebate program available at the moment, by the time you finish this sentence the list will have changed. Just remember that when all the smoke clears, the reason for the rebate plans is to increase the credit-granting company's bottom line—not yours. They are not in business to give you free gasoline or free plane fares or a rebate check at the end of the year. They are in business to turn a huge profit; and if returning a miniscule portion to the customer is the way to do it, that's exactly what they'll do. But it is not reasonable to think one of these companies would give away more than they receive. Rebate programs increase bottom lines or they would not exist. If in spite of everything you are able to make a rebate program work for you, and you are not incurring debt to get the rebates (it can be done—I've seen it from time to time), bless you. Just remember the company is banking heavily on the statistics that say one day you'll charge more than you can repay in a single month and then they'll cheer because they have you as an interest-paying customer.

CHARGE CARDS

A charge card differs from a credit card in the following ways:

- There is no stated spending limit.
- The balance, if any, must be paid in full within 30 or 60 days, depending on the charge card (which can be thought of as interest-free credit). There is no rollover privilege or opportunity for debt on a charge card.
- There is an annual fee of $55 to $300, depending on the card.

Because of the strict limitations, a charge card is simple. You charge; you pay in full. It's difficult to play games with a charge card. Without the purchasing limit, one might fear going nuts in the first month or two and spending beyond the ability to pay in full. If that happens, which surprisingly is not that common, it won't happen again. Either the card will be canceled or the cardholder will quickly learn a difficult lesson.

One drawback with a charge card is the lack of choices. American Express, while more popular than Diner's Club, is still not accepted as widely as Visa.

DEBIT CARDS

Debit cards are issued by your bank and are tied to a bank account. Most debit cards double as an ATM card. In fact, banks have gone to great lengths to replace all generic ATM cards with Visa- and MasterCard-branded debit cards. It is to the bank's or credit union's decided advantage to have its customers swiping debit cards all over town. They want to become involved in every consumer purchase, not only the larger ones that consumers have been trained to pay for with a credit card. Debit cards allow banks, credit unions, Visa, and MasterCard to get in on the little purchases too, provided they can train their customers to use the debit card for those smaller purchases.

There are two types of debit transactions, and both are often housed in the same card. Your old ATM card limited use to on-line transactions. That new Visa or MasterCard debit card allows you to operate on-line and off-line.

On-line: On-line transactions are the kind you perform at a cash machine. For an on-line transaction you need your personal identification number (PIN). The funds you tap are electronically transferred from your checking account immediately. On-line services are not free. Use your card at the grocery store, gas station, or an ATM machine that doesn't belong to your bank and you will be hit with 50¢ to $3 per transaction.

Off-line: What's new and growing fast are the off-line transactions. These feel like credit card sales and don't require PINs. The store clerk may not even know you are using a debit card. The total of the purchase will be subtracted from your checking account within a few days. Typically, you won't pay a fee for the transaction although the merchant is required to kick back money to the bank, typically 3 percent of the transaction amount.

Banks are pushing the use of debit cards because the transactions are cheap to process. It costs a bank five times more to process a paper check than a debit-card transaction. If banks succeed even partially in converting customers to debit cards, they'll reap huge profits on overhead savings alone.

Merchants love debit cards too. Even though they pay a fee every time that card is swiped, they do so willingly because they know a customer who shops with plastic impulsively spends more than one using old-fashioned cash or even a checkbook.

A Visa- or MasterCard-branded debit card looks just like a credit card and works like one wherever those cards are accepted. The merchant or retailer does not know the difference. You can purchase an airline ticket with a debit card provided you have the cash in the bank to cover the purchase. A debit card will also work to rent a car at most places, with this specific warning: The agency is going to place a "hold" on the account for at least $500. This means you will not be able to spend your checking account below that point until your rental car tab is settled. That could ruin your trip and cause a lot of checks to bounce if you've not properly prepared.

A debit card differs in several significant ways from its cousins, the credit and charge cards.

There is no annual charge for a debit card; however, some banks charge various use fees. Be sure to check the details of all charges and fees should you select a debit card as your plastic of choice.

Unlike a credit card or charge card, a debit card does not enjoy the same protection against theft or fraudulent use. On a debit-card incident, you are responsible for a maximum of $50 provided you report the loss or fraudulent charges within two to four days. If you wait longer, you could be responsible for up to $500. If you don't notice anything wrong until after sixty days, the total of your loss would be your responsibility. These provisions seem to vary from card to card, which only adds to the confusion. Check with your own issuer to learn the specifics of your fraud protection, if any.

Using a debit card means an immediate deduction for the purchase amount from your bank account. There is no "float," or grace, period. You lose interest from the moment you make the purchase.

There is a potential hidden danger with a debit card that has the potential of wiping out its benefits: Many banks offer—while some even require—an "overdraft protection" feature when a debit card is attached to a checking account. This provides that in the event the account holder overdraws the account, the overdraft is automatically covered by a draw against a line of credit. Of course the bank makes this sound like a wonderful protection for the account holder. While it will prevent the embarrassment of bouncing a check, it is a sneaky way to incur debt. Most of the accounts do not simply cover the exact amount of the overdraw, but rather, they dump money into the account in increments of, say, $100. Because this is actually a cash advance, interest accrues immediately and at a hefty rate. Plus, the penalty fees for overdraft protection can be significant.

Suppose you have $150 in your checking account. You find a terrific sale the same day you have haircut appointments for the family. You swipe that debit card a couple of times to the tune of $151 for the day. *What's a buck?* you reason (if you even realize what you've done). That is not, however, the way that big computer-in-the-sky looks at your misdeed. Without flinching, your overdraft protection feature sends $100 to your account, and you begin paying interest at that moment on the entire $100, not just the $1 you needed to stay above water. Considering the fees, interest, and the possibility that you'll go ahead and spend the rest of the $100 rather than pay it back immediately, that could be the most expensive $1 you ever spent.

Human nature being what it is, most people will not immediately go through the steps necessary to pay back the entire

$100 at the next deposit. Believe me, financial institutions count heavily on human nature.

I have actually received letters from people who swear they have no unsecured debt, all the while failing to see the $4,000 balance on their overdraft protection account as exactly that: one pile of debt! I can only conclude that "overdraft protection" has some kind of virtuous ring to it, and consumers pride themselves in paying dearly for this kind of insurance.

CHOOSING THE PLASTIC THAT IS RIGHT FOR YOU

Each type of plastic—credit cards, charge cards, and debit cards—has its own pros and cons when it comes to owning one good, all-purpose piece of plastic. When making the decision, you should take into account your current and specific situation.

If you are not yet debt free but are aggressively working on your Rapid Debt-Repayment Plan, you would probably be better off to stick with whatever you have until you become debt free. At that time you can reassess your situation.

A charge card has a decided benefit for the person who carries no debt but feels insecure about inviting that temptation to lurk in the background. If you don't want to deal with the temptation and don't mind paying an annual fee to be freed from it, a charge card might be the best way for you to go.

It is possible to turn any credit card into a charge card provided you exercise the discipline outlined in our credit card rules above. You must repay the entire balance, if any, during the grace period and never incur fees or interest. Exercise this kind of personal discipline and financial maturity, and you will have the best of both worlds: full availability of the benefits of plastic with no annual fee and no interest charges.

There was a time, and not that long ago, when I would have scoffed at the person purposely choosing to pay an annual fee for a charge card. From time to time readers would write and tell me they carry an American Express card and willingly pay for it because it keeps them on the "straight and narrow." That balance must be paid in full every month; there is no other option. My reply was always curt, yet playful: for half the fee I'd be happy to babysit them and apply all the pressure needed to make them pay the balance in full during the grace period if they would switch to a no-fee credit card.

But things have changed drastically in the past few years. Credit card companies have pulled in all the slack. While in the past one could be even fifteen days late with a full-balance payment and not incur penalties, nowadays such a slip up could result in a $29 late fee, interest on the full amount, and possibly a repeat performance next month if the balance is subject to the two-cycle billing method. Even the most straight-shooting consumer is human. Things happen. It is very easy to slip up and end up paying far more than the $55 annual fee on a charge card.

So, I admit to having a change of heart. I believe that for many people the freedom from worry of a slip up might just warrant the fee required for a charge card. It certainly eliminates many hassles.

Debit cards are by far my least favorite of the types of plastic available. First, they have limitations when it comes to the purpose for which you need the plastic in the first place, namely renting a car. The fraud protection is, in my opinion, shaky. But beyond that there is the temptation to use a debit card with a certain level of abandon—to purchase everything under the sun by swiping instead of writing a check or using cash. It becomes far too easy and is a sneaky way to empty

your bank account more quickly than you would if you actually
had to write out the check and think about what you're doing.
I would rather see you use a credit card or charge card as outlined above than to choose a debit card.

OBTAINING YOUR CARD

The following information should help you locate whatever
type of card you choose.

Credit cards: To find a current list of no-fee and low-interest credit cards currently available, visit the Internet site of
Ram Research, www.cardtrak.com, and click on "No Fee." You
will also find a list of currently available low-interest cards.

Charge cards: American Express Green Card, $55 a year,
800-THE-CARD, www.americanexpress.com; Diners Club,
$80 a year, 800-2-DINERS, www.citibank.com/dinersus.
Recommendation: If you go with a charge card, select the
green American Express. Don't let your ego lead you astray
into gold or platinum status. For no additional benefit you will
have to pay a much higher annual fee.

Debit cards: Contact your bank or credit union if you do not
already have a Visa- or MasterCard-branded debit card but
have decided this is the best choice for you. Treat your debit
card with all the respect of a credit or charge card, and you
will not fall into the temptation of seeing it as easy access to
your cash in the bank.

⇐

## Chapter Thirteen

Express Lane from the Frying Pan into the Fire

DEBT-CONSOLIDATION LOANS

Consolidation won't make your debts magically disappear, but it can help you get a handle on them if you use it in the right way.

Gerri Detweiler

Consolidating debts is being widely touted these days as a life preserver for those who are drowning in debt. Here is the way debt consolidation is supposed to work: You add up the total of all your small consumer debts (credit card accounts, installment and personal loans) and pay them off with the proceeds of a new loan—either a new credit card or a home equity loan—that has a lower interest rate and a monthly payment that is less than the total of the previous payments.

In theory, debt consolidation is a terrific solution for a burdensome debt situation because it shortens the time you stay in debt and reduces the associated costs. In practice, debt consolidation offers an express lane from the frying pan into the fire.

Debt consolidation does not refer to a single type of loan but rather to any plan whereby the lender hands you a lump sum of money to pay off as one large loan instead of all the smaller ones. A debt-consolidation loan can be either secured or unsecured. It could be a new credit card onto which you transfer all the outstanding balances from all your other credit cards; a home equity loan (see chap. 15); a loan from a retirement account, such as a 401(k); a new loan from a finance company; or a personal loan from a friend or family member.

Debt consolidation is not a panacea. On the contrary, it often represents a much more costly and eventually difficult situation than the problem it was supposed to relieve.

I am not at all thrilled with the whole idea of debt consolidation for the following reasons:

Debt consolidation represents a detour. Of course there are occasional exceptions as we will see later, but for the most part debt consolidation represents at best a lateral move. It doesn't pay down debt but only moves it around. Just because it makes your debt situation more comfortable doesn't put you any closer to getting rid of the debt. Many times it does just the opposite—it reduces the payment but extends the payback time so far into the future that the debt grows considerably in the process.

Michele recently wrote with a question on debt consolidation. It seems she and her husband have a $25,000 second mortgage at 15 percent interest and a $3,900 signature loan at 23 percent with the same household finance company. She explained that the interest rates are so high because when they took these loans several years ago their credit history was, shall we say, less than pristine.

She went on to say that the lender had approached them with a preapproved offer to combine both loans into one at a fixed rate of 13 percent, extending the payoff time to 20 years. Of course they were willing to increase the loan to give themselves a little breathing room or take that well-deserved vacation or add on to the house. She wanted to know if this was a good deal, since the monthly payment would drop considerably.

Before I even looked at a single number, I had my suspicions. I don't believe there is a lender on the face of the earth who would approach a current customer with an offer for a new loan deal that wasn't in the financial interest of the lender. What lender would volunteer to rewrite or consolidate debt if it only benefited the borrower?

That fact alone should be a clear signal that someone is about to go for a ride. Then add on the fact that they want to lend even more money to this family, and you can see the proverbial handwriting on the wall.

Reaching into the Tool Chest at my website (shameless plug, www.debtproofliving.com) and pulling out the Loan Comparison Calculator, I was able to come up with comparative figures the lender didn't happen to mention to Michele.

I learned that given her current loans and payment schedule, she would pay $31,951 in interest on the second mortgage and $1,264 in interest on the signature loan, or a total of $33,215. The proposed consolidation loan, on the other hand, would, over 20 years, require interest of $52,360.

The lender stands to increase his position by more than $19,000 in this deal. Clearly, if Michele were to fall for this, she would be taking a major detour on her journey to becoming debt free by tapping into her home's equity and paying even more interest.

Debt consolidation prevents personal growth. When we keep putting Band-Aids on difficult financial situations, it is nearly impossible to learn the tough lessons about what got us to this point in the first place. For example, if you have ten credit cards, all of which are maxed out, and you transfer those balances to a new credit card that promises a lower monthly payment, you have in fact told yourself that new debt is the solution for old debt. That's wrong. The solution for old debt is first to figure what prompted the situation to escalate to this point and then do whatever it takes to repay the debt— not simply move it around to a more comfortable position.

The doubling effect. If you've ever lost ten pounds and gained back twenty, you'll easily recognize this danger.

Consolidation sounds good in theory: Transfer all of your credit balances with high interest rates to a single new credit card with a lower rate of interest. Your one monthly payment is now lower than the total of all your individual credit card payments.

However, this is when the trouble begins.

If you are like most people, you look at the credit cards that now have zero balances and you feel a certain sense of delight. You're quite proud of yourself because it feels like you paid the debts (you didn't really, but you enjoy pretending). You know for sure that you will never use those cards again (yeah, right), but do you close the accounts? No. You think that just in case of some unforeseen emergency it would be nice to have the financial cushion these credit lines represent. You also reason that if you do close them and then end up needing them in the future you'll have to reapply and go through that needless hassle. (I know you quite well, don't I? That's because I know myself.)

You may even feel a bit like a savvy financial counselor as you instruct yourself to put the cards in a safe place where the balances will all remain at zero.

The truth is, regardless if those cards are in your wallet or stashed in the bottom of a vault in another city, that available credit will haunt you. In the beginning you'll be terrified that you will find a reason to use some of it. Unfortunately, the feeling will go away quickly.

Before you know it, an emergency will show up, and that will be the beginning of the end. It is a strange thing how the availability of credit creates emergencies. And it does so in record time, particularly if you don't have clear and concise personal criteria in place for what constitutes an emergency.

Statistics indicate that the person who does the credit-card-balance-transfer thing—or takes a home equity loan to pay off all the credit card balances—will manage within two years to get those credit card balances back up to their all-time high. Then you have double the debt and twice the trouble— the credit card balances *and* the debt-consolidation loan to contend with.

When looking at a debt-consolidation loan, you cannot place all your attention on the monthly payment. It is conceivable and quite likely that while the monthly payment is less, the interest rate will be higher and the payoff time longer. You must look at the big picture, comparing the total amount of interest to be paid as well as all terms and conditions.

So, is there ever a time when a debt-consolidation loan would be in order? Theoretically, yes. However, it is becoming more and more difficult to make it work—not only because of our weak human nature but because of the credit industry as well. By the looks of the average person's mailbox, low-interest credit card deals are quite plentiful. But don't be fooled; carefully read all the terms and peruse each and every bit of fine print before you decide to apply.

Even the low-interest, fixed-rate cards are not all they appear to be. First, the interest rate may be fixed, but for only a specific period of time. What happens at the end of the first year? If the rate climbs significantly or then becomes a variable rate tied to some index, watch out. Other offerings have very attractive interest rates and terms, but you need to pay careful attention to their penalties for paying late. Many deals provide that if you are late even one time during the introductory period (and that means missing the deadline by even five minutes), the rate immediately shoots up five or six percentage points. If you make that mistake twice, the rate on some of the more popular deals can go to 22.99 percent or higher. Clearly that kind of deal makes a beneficial consolidation attempt nearly impossible.

If you are able to find a better deal and you can qualify to consolidate your debts to a less costly account—and you've done your homework and understand every aspect of the deal—make sure you not only cut up all the other credit cards you paid off, but call the companies and close the accounts as well. That will immediately put to rest the idea of seeing those lines of credit as available to you, and it will help to clean up your credit report. Remember that in some cases, like qualifying for a real estate loan, available credit is looked upon as a negative (see chap. 11).

DEBT CONSOLIDATION SAFETY RULES

1. Do not tap into appreciating resources like home equity or a retirement plan to consolidate or pay off consumer debt. It is not wise to use appreciating assets (your home equity and retirement plan are both growing in value) to pay for depreciating goods and services.

2. If you can successfully switch your credit card balances to a lower interest credit card, keep paying the most you can each month. Never allow yourself to see the minimum payment as appropriate.

3. Completely close the paid-off accounts. Simply cutting the card is not good enough. You must call the company with your instructions to close the account and follow up in writing. Do not consider the matter closed until you receive written confirmation.

4. Do nothing to add to your total debt load. Used properly, a debt-consolidation loan should lighten your debt load, not increase it. It should put you in a more favorable position, not further behind.

In most situations, debt consolidation cannot live up to its promises. So instead of looking for shortcuts that may well turn out to be costly detours, stop using the plastic, get busy putting together your Rapid Debt-Repayment Plan (see chap. 7), and stop thinking of new sources of debt as the solution for existing debts.

Debt consolidation should be considered only by financially mature and highly disciplined persons. Curiously, financially mature and highly disciplined people don't often find themselves in need of debt consolidation in the first place.

## Chapter Fourteen

A Home of Our Own

MORTGAGE LOANS

Home ownership is a state of mind. It's your piece of the earth. It's where a family's toes grow roots.

Jane Bryant Quinn

Home ownership is more than a financial decision. Sure those monthly payments represent forced savings, and of course you anticipate that over time your home will gain value and produce a profit. But it is definitely more than that—much more.

Home ownership is a state of mind. It is a place where you can enter, close the door, and know that all others must wait for an invitation. It's a security blanket between you and a lease agreement. Home ownership represents that one place on earth you can call your own, where your kids can grow their roots. It's probably your only hope for a rent-free retirement where no one will be able to take your home away from you.

Regardless of the way property values rise or fall, if you ever wonder if you would be better off just renting a place so

the landlord can take care of everything, remember this:
Mortgage payments come to an end, but rent goes on forever.

Home ownership is a good thing and would be out of reach
for 99.99 percent of the ordinary people in this country were it
not for the home mortgage.

From its inception, the home mortgage was designed in
such a way that paying it off would fall just slightly ahead of
retirement. Still, to this day, it is reasonable to believe that
thirty years is time enough to repay one's home mortgage. Yes,
one would think.

HOME OWNERSHIP VS. MORTGAGE OWNERSHIP

Something changed in the fifty years between 1929, when
Bill and Agnes McAulay refused to buy a car until their mortgage was paid in full, and 1999, when Sharon and Bill Farris
bought their first home. Not only are the Farrises stretching
beyond reason simply to make their monthly mortgage payments on time, they hold absolutely no hope of living long
enough to pay it off. What changed between then and now is
our definition of home ownership.

To Bill and Agnes, owning their home meant owning their
home. To Sharon and Bill, owning their home means owning a
mortgage on their home. Owning a home used to mean having
a paid-in-full note and an unclouded title. It meant making
significant sacrifices until the larger goal was reached. Now it
means 360 payments, wondering if and when to refinance,
unbelievable amounts of interest, home equity lines of credit,
and second mortgages. Then, just when the equity starts
building and the payments become not only manageable but
comfortable, homeownership invariably means trading into
something bigger and better and, as a result, picking up a
fresh new batch of even larger payments.

The difference between owning a home eventually and owning a mortgage depends on your way of thinking. If you start planning to reach the goal of owning your home outright, you can do it. But you're going to have to take things into your own hands. You're going to have to run the show.

AVOID PREPAYMENT PENALTIES

Whenever you are shopping for a mortgage of any type, you want to make sure it is not subject to a prepayment penalty. Many years ago it was not uncommon for a mortgage to carry some kind of stiff financial penalty if the borrower paid it off more quickly than originally prescribed. Nowadays, however, prepayment penalties have mostly disappeared from home mortgages—except in the case of the 125 percent loans and other shyster-type deals.

PREPAY THE PRINCIPAL

The key to rapidly repaying your mortgage is to prepay the principal. Each month, you have a required payment to make. Much of that payment is interest; only a small amount is principal. That's why you can make $896-monthly payments on a $125,000, 7.75 percent, 30-year mortgage for two and a half years and still owe $122,000. You've paid more than $25,000 but reduced your debt by only $3,000. When you prepay the principal ahead of schedule—even by a little bit—it affects dramatically the eventual total cost of the mortgage.

There are a couple of very painless ways you can do this. The tactics will net you a tremendous amount of interest savings and bring your mortgage-free day much closer. However, beware of the following one that works but doesn't make good sense.

The Biweekly Mortgage Scam

This is the plan that in theory is great, but practically speaking doesn't work well enough to get all excited about it.

Years ago, some very smart person figured out that if you paid one-half of your mortgage every two weeks instead of the whole thing once a month, in a year's time you would end up paying one complete extra payment in that year. You see, if you make one payment a month, you make 12 in a year. But if you make one every other week, biweekly, you will make 26 one-half payments in a year or the equivalent of 13 monthly payments. So far, so good—this is a terrific theory.

A problem arose, however, when mortgage companies were not set up to deal with half payments and a biweekly payment schedule—nor were they required to—the way that credit card companies receive and process any amount at any time. Some banks would return the partial payments as "unprocessable," while others would just hold the half payment pending the arrival of enough money to make a full payment as required by the mortgage documents.

The desire of consumers to participate in this trendy new fast-pay method, combined with the entrepreneurial spirit, produced middleman companies who began selling the biweekly mortgage theory. Simply put, this middle company would collect the half payments for a fee and then see that the equivalent of 26 half payments were sent to the customer's mortgage holder each year.

Eventually, many lenders, GE Capital for instance, saw the demand for this alternative payment schedule and the money to be made by allowing customers to make biweekly payments. I imagine they didn't like the idea of a middleman company collecting all that gravy. So in personalized letters that included the homeowners' potential savings, some banks and mortgage companies tried to get customers to sign up for a special program that would convert the monthly payment schedule to biweekly.

In the case of GE Capital, one of the nation's largest mortgage holders, there was a stipulation that the borrowers would allow the lender to deduct the equivalent of one-half payment from their checking account every two weeks for a one-time set-up fee of $340 plus a $2.50 service charge for every withdrawal.

Even late-night television infomercials showed up hawking multilevel, biweekly conversion network marketing schemes—but presenting them as a complicated issue the typical homeowner was not qualified to handle.

Why did so many consumers fall for these biweekly servicing schemes? Marketing pitches can be powerful persuaders, and many people bought into the idea of simplicity, savings, and service. Becoming accountable to a middleman disciplined them to make those biweekly payments.

Marc Eisenson, mortgage prepayment guru, first pointed out to me just how ridiculous it is to pay even a cent of one's hard-earned money for the privilege of a special prepayment plan of any sort. It is, he insists, a complete waste of money, and mortgage companies pushing for the for-a-fee service should be ashamed of themselves.

Eisenson's alternative plan was brilliant and something every mortgage owner should consider seriously.

The Do-It-Yourself Biweekly Payment Program

First, divide your monthly mortgage payment by 12. Example: Your mortgage payment of $600 divided by 12 equals $50. Every month, send $50 along with your regular monthly payment of $600. As long as you are paying a full payment or more, the mortgage company has to accept and process the entire amount. As a precautionary measure, I suggest that the additional amount be written in a separate check with "Principal Prepayment Only" clearly written in the memo area on the face of the check along with your account number. Now there will be no question as to your desire for the disposition of this prepayment amount.

If you fear you are not disciplined enough to make this additional partial payment each month, just authorize your lender automatically to withdraw it from your checking account once a month. Eisenson says that virtually every lender will do an electronic transfer for free, but you have to ask.

With this alternative biweekly payment schedule, you will pay the equivalent of 13 monthly payments each year because you are paying that extra one at a rate of 1/12 each month.

If you are the type who needs proof, check out the figures below. The power of principal prepayment never ceases to amaze me. Every dollar you invest into the prepayment of your mortgage is a dollar well invested, simply because it represents a guaranteed return on investment. No investment is as sure as a repaid debt.

			INVEST IN YOUR MORTGAGE FOR A GUARANTEED RETURN TERMS: $100,000 PRINCIPAL, 8% INTEREST, 30 YEARS. MONTHLY PAYMENTS: $733			
Principal	Fixed Interest Rate	Monthly Principal Prepayment	Total Interest over Term	Number of Payments	Interest Savings	Payoff Time Reduced by
$100,000	8%	$0	$164,610	360	$0	0 years
$100,000	8%	$20	$144,815	325	$19,345	3 years
$100,000	8%	$50	$124,249	287	$39,911	6 years
$100,000	8%	$100	$101,696	242	$62,464	9.8 years
$100,000	8%	$200	$ 75,891	189	$88,269	14 years

Now if that $340 or $375 initial fee (whatever your mortgage company charges to convert to a biweekly payment
schedule) is something you really want to pay, pay it to yourself. Jump-start your new payment plan with an initial prepayment plus that amount. Now every dime of it will go toward
your account and not the bottom line of a middleman or mortgage company. And that $2.50 a month service fee you won't
be paying? Add it to your prepayment check just as if you still
believe that $2.50 is a very reasonable fee for such a beneficial
service. With this method, every cent you prepay counts and
will come back to bless you in the future.

The tremendous savings of interest and hastening of one's
mortgage payoff date results from paying the equivalent of a
thirteenth payment each year. Your mortgage company will
not accept less than a full payment at any one time, but they
will accept a payment that is greater than what you've agreed
to pay each month. That is the key—and the reason you never
want a mortgage with a prepayment penalty.

An important feature of this do-it-yourself mortgage prepayment plan is flexibility. Let's say your company is part of
a leveraged buyout, and you find yourself in the unemployment line. Of course you will have your Contingency Fund
and Freedom Account in place, so you will not panic.
However, it might be in your best interest to pull back on
every optional expense and carefully conserve your funds. If
you have agreed to a formal biweekly conversion of your
mortgage, you are pretty much stuck. You might be able to go
back to monthly payments, but that's a hassle, and it will
undoubtedly result in an "unconversion" fee. Besides, this
situation could be temporary, meaning you'd want the option
to return to the highly beneficial biweekly plan at a later
date.

Administering your own prepayment plan, however, lets you retain the option of going back to monthly payments any time you want.

You also retain the flexibility to prepay much more than just 1/12 of a payment each month. Say you receive a dividend payment or some other type of unexpected amount. You can choose to add that to your mortgage prepayment check. No amount too small, no amount too large, and every cent of it will go toward your future. You could even calculate what the payment would be if your loan was amortized over 15 years rather than 30, increase your payments accordingly, and then reap all the benefits of a 15-year mortgage. But again, you could go back to the 30-year schedule if necessary without seeking permission or going through any kind of conversion process.

REFINANCING YOUR MORTGAGE

SHOULD YOU REFINANCE?

Mortgage interest rates are, as of this writing, relatively low—but higher than they were a year ago. Should you refinance? That depends on a couple of rules of thumb most experts rely upon.

Test #1: Will you reduce your annual interest rate by at least 2 percent?

Test #2: Do you plan to stay in the house long enough to recoup the costs of refinancing?

The key is to figure out the amount of time it will take to pay for all your up-front costs by the lower payments. Obviously, if the period is longer than you plan to own the house, refinancing doesn't pay. If it is exactly the same, the hassle of refinancing loses some of its appeal. But if you can recoup in two years or less, refinancing could be the way to hasten the day you turn from mortgage holder to homeowner.

Refinancing costs can be considerable. They include the application fee, title search and title insurance, points (one "point" is equal to 1 percent of the loan), appraisal fee, attorney or escrow fees, and possibly a prepayment penalty on your present loan.

Let's say that by refinancing you can reduce your monthly payment by $100, and it's going to cost you $4,200 in fees to do that. Divide $4,200 by $100 and it equals 42. It will take 42 months to recoup the costs of refinancing. If you stay in the house for at least 42 months, these costs will be recovered. In this example, refinancing would seem to make sense, but only if you have every intention of staying there at least four more years.

Another fact to consider is the type of mortgage you have presently. If you have an adjustable-rate mortgage (ARM), refinancing into a fixed-rate loan also makes a lot of sense. While interest rates are presently low, no one can predict where they will go in the future. Getting into a low fixed-rate mortgage now in order to lock in a low rate for the life of your loan could be highly advisable.

WHERE TO START

The competition is keen among mortgage lenders these days, so the best way to find a good refinancing deal is to get out there and shop.

The most logical place to start shopping for a new mortgage is your present lender. If you've enjoyed a long, mutually beneficial relationship with them, you may be able to cut through a lot of the red tape, even some of the refinancing fees.

As you shop, keep this in mind: Lenders are in competition mode, and some are showing a bit of creativity in order to get folks to agree to their programs. Some are willing to negotiate the fees, waive points, and do all kinds of creative things to keep your up-front costs down. The tradeoff? Likely you'll be given a higher interest rate. You have to run the numbers to see if that's a good deal or not.

If you plan to be in your house for a short time, you want to find a loan with the lowest fees possible. However, if you plan to be there for three to five years, you'd probably be better off paying points in exchange for the lower interest rate.

Once you have several numbers to compare and if you have Internet access, plug them into our Mortgage Refinance Calculator at www.cheapskatemonthly.com. You can do various "what-if" calculations and run through a variety of different scenarios.

It is important to note, however, that the mortgage lenders you talk to will be able to qualify you far better than any computer program. Lenders have the ability to be flexible when it comes to qualification and to take your individual circumstances into account.

Here's another rapid prepayment strategy to consider in the event you do refinance for a lower rate resulting in a lower payment: Go ahead and refinance, but do not take out any equity. Continue making your old, higher monthly payments. You'll pay that new mortgage off even more rapidly and avoid paying a lot of interest.

## Chapter Fifteen

The New Way to Hock the Farm

HOME EQUITY LOANS

Home equity loans are quite dangerous because you can lose your house for nonpayment. They should have the top priority for repayment, even ahead of other consumer debt.

Austin Pryor

I f anyone had told the typical homeowner in the 1940s that second mortgages—then viewed as a major cause of human misery and financial ruin—would one day be a hip way to pay off credit card debt, send Junior to college, or take the family on a Caribbean cruise, they would have been too stunned to respond. But that is exactly what has happened.

This type of loan got a spiffy new name in the 1980s—the home equity loan (HEL)—and it rocketed in popularity when it became the only game in town for the consumer seeking tax-deductible interest payments. Unfortunately, a second mortgage by any other name is still a second mortgage.

Locked up in your house is a beautiful pot of tax-free money, reachable only if you move. This money represents all the profits you've ever made on the homes you've owned.

Every time you sold a home, you probably rolled those profits over, tax deferred.

A home equity loan does not let you access your money in the same way you could if you sold and moved. It simply grants you the temporary *use* of these funds. Essentially, an HEL allows you to rent your money, placing you under heavy-duty restrictions and requirements for the privilege.

TYPES OF HOME EQUITY LOANS

Home equity deals come in two varieties: loans and lines. In either case the homeowner is allowed to borrow up to 80 percent of the home's current market value minus the balance on the mortgage.

The home equity loan is the traditional second mortgage. It generally comes with a fixed interest rate, and you get all the money in one lump sum to be repaid over 5 to 15 years.

The home equity line of credit is the most dangerous of the two. Typically the line of credit is open-ended, meaning that the amount available floats with the then-current market value of your home. As your equity increases, so does the amount of money you can borrow against it. Once the loan is approved, the borrower receives the equivalent of a checkbook, not the proceeds of the loan. You simply—the simplicity being one of the main problems with the line of credit—write a check to tap into the equity. You then pay interest on only the portion you have drawn out, not the entire amount available.

In theory, the home equity line of credit sounds too good to be true—a way you can have your cake (own the property) and eat it too (spend the equity). In reality, it offers the same temptations as a dozen low-interest credit cards. Both closed- and open-ended home equity loans still let you ruin your financial life—just more slowly and, some financial-advisor types might argue, more intelligently than with credit cards.

I am generally opposed to both types of home equity loans, but especially to the line-of-credit variety. First, it feeds the myth that the equity in your home is a liquid asset. Having those HEL funds so readily available (essentially you are walking around with the sum total of your home's equity in your pocket—calling out to you the way money has a way of doing) makes it feel as if this is your money and you can spend it any way you please. A home equity line of credit brings new meaning to the idea of money "burning a hole in your pocket." Having the funds at your fingertips has a haunting effect—like a monster that is always staring at you.

If you resist, you might begin to fear that your spouse will find something to spend it on instead of you; you'll quickly lose control and go through the entire wad in a week and a half. If you are the one who cannot rest as long as all the money is there to be spent, your spouse might be the one filled with paranoia.

When eventually you give in and spend it (and you will, trust me), even if it is for the most reasonable and noble cause, the vicious cycle will have begun. You make regular payments, but because nearly all of it goes to pay the interest, you don't make a dent in the principal. Then when those unrelenting payments become a financial strain on what used to be your barely-making-ends-meet-every-month situation, the temptation to tap further into the equity will be there staring in your face.

The equity in your home is one of your most precious assets. For most of us, it is the only appreciating asset we have now or possibly will ever have in the future. Borrowing against your home's equity to pay down credit card balances, finance a fabulous family vacation, or purchase new furniture may not seem like a big deal if you are young and believe you have all kinds of time to prepare for retirement. But when you tap into your home's equity, you are not only reducing its overall value, you are severely retarding—and in the case of the line of credit, wiping out completely—that important feature called *compounding growth*. You are, in essence, killing the one financial asset that is actually growing.

Spending the equity in your home as quickly as it appears essentially eliminates the prospect of ever owning your home outright, mortgage free. It guarantees you will have mortgage payments or rent for the rest of your life. If you use that equity to pay for things early on in your life, it and all of the offspring it should have reproduced are not going to be there when you deserve a rent-free retirement. When you reach into your home's equity, you are, in fact, tearing a hole in your safety net. Never underestimate the worth of a rent-free retirement.

Unfortunately, many people are drawn to the concept of a home equity loan because the tax-deductibility of the interest has a righteous ring to it. But let's face it: this option qualifies as secured debt (see chap. 2) and shoves this kind of loan into the semi-intelligent category. What's more, the benefit of tax-deductible interest is highly overrated.

Say you owe $1,000 on your home equity line of credit and your interest rate is 10 percent. If you pay it off in one year, you will also pay $100 in interest. If you are in the 28 percent tax bracket, you will save $28 (28 percent of $100) at tax time if you itemize your deductions. So after you factor in your tax savings, the amount of interest you actually paid was just $72. The point is, you still had to pay the $72. Many equity borrowers assume that because the interest is tax-deductible for them, the tax savings not only wipes out the effect of paying interest, it in some way rewards them with cash back.

Here's another way to look at it: The after-tax interest rate on the 10 percent home equity line of credit was merely reduced to 7.2 percent. Wow.

THE HOME EQUITY LOAN SALES PITCH

WHAT LENDERS WANT YOU TO KNOW

If you have eyes toward a home equity loan, the lender is going to do all he can to convince you that the line-of-credit type is far more virtuous than the straight second-mortgage variety for the following reasons:

It is flexible. You draw down as much or as little of the line as you want and pay interest only on the amount you actually use.

You have easy access. You have either a checkbook or an ATM card that allows you to mainline the equity in your home.

The interest rate is lower. Compared to the interest rate and fees involved in a credit card account, the interest on a home equity line of credit is significantly lower. Because of its variable-rate feature, it is also lower than its fixed-rate home equity loan cousin.

WHAT LENDERS DON'T WANT YOU TO KNOW

What the lender will fail to point out are the negatives that come packaged with a home equity line of credit:

The temptation. No matter how you slice it, a line of credit has "easy money" written all over it. Just knowing all the money is available brings decorators, travel agents, and car dealers out of the woodwork.

Lightweight repayment. Home equity lenders are particularly anxious for repayment to be done at a leisurely pace and over a long period of time. They don't want you to repay too quickly or they lose their passive income stream. A home equity line borrower becomes quite a golden-egg-laying goose.

Variable interest rate. This may seem like a nice feature when interest rates are low, but what happens when the cycle takes a turn and inflation kicks in? Remember, when the rate increases (and you must assume that it will), the entire amount you owe will be subject to the increased rate, not just the amount you withdraw in the future.

Annual fees. While a home equity loan does not have annual fees (all fees, if any, are part of the origination costs), a home equity line of credit is subject to an annual fee of $50 to $150. This fee is not included in the annual percentage rate and might not seem like such a big deal—until you multiply by the number of years you will have that line available; then it becomes quite a significant number.

USING A HOME EQUITY LOAN

While home equity loans are not ideal (what kind of debt is?), I am not entirely opposed to them. However, their purpose is very limited. Following the principles that set intelligent borrowing apart from debt, the proceeds of a home equity loan should be used only to create or add to an appreciating asset. That means putting the funds right back into the home—to improve, renovate, or add to it. This way the home equity loan becomes a financial investment.

There are also times, unfortunately, when financial situations become so tenuous that one's home equity is the last hope before a trip to the bankruptcy attorney. But realistically, if things are that bad, getting the loan will be difficult, if not impossible. The fees and interest rate will be tremendous, and your efforts might only delay the inevitable, not prevent it. In such an extreme case, it seems to me that selling the home would be the better option—thereby releasing the equity, if any, and using it to repay creditors in the hopes of getting back to point zero and starting over.

UNETHICAL HOME EQUITY LOANS

There is one type of home equity loan that you should avoid at all costs. Some call it the 125 percent loan; others, like myself, call it just about the most ridiculous thing to come down the home mortgage pike.

Perhaps you have seen the compelling commercials on late-night television. Invariably some ex-athlete is hawking this no-problem solution to any financial situation. Their pitch is that they will not only lend you the full market value of your home, they'll go one better and lend you more than it is worth! I guess we're supposed to see this as a chance to beat the system or get away with something that is too good to be true.

The problems with such a ridiculous kind of loan are many. Here are the most glaring:

Fees. First of all you should know that finding out the details of these potential loans is not easy. I made several calls both as an investigator and as a potential customer. I could not get any loan officers (and I use that term loosely) to state the interest rate or the fees involved. They will deal with you only after you have filled out a loan application and given them permission to pull your credit report.

Therefore I had to get this information from people who fell for the pitch and now live to regret it. Interest rates on these loans are outrageous, often 5 to 10 percentage points more than the going rate. But the killer is the loan origination fee. I have had reports of the up-front fee being as high as 15 percentage points of the loan amount.

Prepayment penalty. These outrageous loans almost always carry a very stiff prepayment penalty, meaning that if you attempt to accelerate the payment of the amount borrowed you are hit with a huge penalty. This pretty much wipes out the possibility of selling the property, refinancing, or paying the home equity loan off earlier than agreed to in the beginning.

Lender disappearance. This is probably the most curious part of these deals. The lender is quite friendly in the beginning—and so available. But try to speak to someone— anyone—once the deal is done? Good luck. It's not going to happen; nor will your letters get a response.

In my opinion, these companies have just one thing in mind: They want your property. The intention is to take advantage of a miserable situation (these loans appeal only to those who can least afford them), fleece you of every dime up front, grab all the interest they can from you in the beginning while you are still hanging on by your fingernails, and then simply hang a foreclosure notice on your front door when you fall behind. And believe me, that friendly ex-jock salesman, who made you feel so special and privileged while assuring you he wanted to make your life better, will have disappeared into the sunset.

For most of us the equity in our homes is the biggest and best investment we will ever know. Steering clear of any type of growth-stunting home equity loan is just about the best way to protect this investment so it can thrive undisturbed.

Chapter Sixteen

Don't Get Taken for a Ride
BUY OR LEASE A CAR

*Buying a good late-model, low-mileage, used car
instead of a new one can go a long way toward keeping
your driving costs down.*

Mark Eskeldson

The biggest problem with automobiles is not the vehicles themselves but the emotions and egos of the people who drive them.

It used to be that people thought of a car as a mode of transportation. They spent about two months' salary to buy one, and if they didn't pay cash, they financed it over eighteen months—tops.

But somewhere along the line things changed. Cars became an outward expression of self-worth, a status symbol. Now people spend a fortune for a car—agreeing to car payments for an eternity and then turning around and buying another car every few years just to keep the image thing going. Then they wonder why they can't afford a house and why the kids go to college on student loans.

As long as you believe that you are what you drive and that
no matter what, you deserve to drive the car you can afford to
want, you will probably remain financially enslaved by automobile ownership.

If, on the other hand, you are willing to consider that your
car is just a tool of convenience to get you from here to there
safely and comfortably, then we have something to talk about.

BUYING A NEW CAR

There are only two reasons I know of that you might consider buying a new car.

1. You can pay for it with cash, and you intend to drive it
    until the wheels fall off.
2. You own a business, and for reasons beyond the scope
    of this book, your accountant has recommended this
    kind of business expense.

I am quite confident that if you qualify for reason number
one, you will never exercise it. There's something peculiar
about finally saving up that much money and then not wanting
to drop it all in one place—especially on something as foolish as
a brand-new car. Nevertheless, if you can pay cash for a brand-
new car and that doesn't induce painful twitching, bless you.

My opinion is that if you are serious about debt-proofing
your life and maximizing each of the dollars that flows into
your life, you should not short-circuit that endeavor by buying
a new car.

Marc Eisenson, publisher of *The Pocket Change Investor,*
agrees on this matter and has a clever way of explaining why:

Say you want to buy a brand-new $18,000 car,
and you've done battle to "win" a 10 percent price
reduction, which would bring it down to $16,200.
You decide it pays to pocket a $1,000 rebate from

the manufacturer. So that $18,000 buggy would cost you $15,200. Right?

Wrong! Let's assume you finance 90 percent ($13,680) at 7.5 percent interest for three years. That'll add $1,639 in interest to the $15,200, for a total cost of $16,839. Right?

Wrong! Even if you disregard your new car's sales tax, registration, and insurance (which will add up to way more than pocket change), there's still income tax to factor in. If you're in the 28 percent federal tax bracket, you'd need to gross over $23,000 to pay for this horseless carriage. That's over 50 percent higher than the $15,200 rock-bottom price you negotiated, and the equivalent of almost nine months of hard labor for someone earning $30,000 a year.

And that's without adding in the cost of state and local taxes, to say nothing of Social Security. Do you really want to spend the better part of a year working—not for food, clothing, or shelter—but just to pay for the privilege of parking that car in your driveway?

Get ready for the final insult: Your shiny new car will lose about 20 percent of its market value the minute you drive it off the lot.

Is a new car worth more than a year of your life? The decision's yours. Me? I'd rather buy the cream puff you're about to trade in.[1]

LEASING A NEW CAR

In the 1980s, as new car prices crept higher and higher, new car sales began to slip. Dealers saw buyers trading in their cars for new ones every seven to eight years, not every three to four years as they had been in the good old days of the auto industry. Another problem: People couldn't afford the payments on the more expensive new cars.

Automakers had to try something (I can only assume cutting prices didn't cross their collective mind) to get people to buy more new cars, more often. The solution: auto leasing. Before this time, auto leasing was limited to businesses that leased cars in fleets and to the very wealthy. So when major automakers embraced the idea as a way of getting around the annoying affordability problem most people had, they easily convinced the masses that leasing was better than buying.

The auto industry's plan was that they would give people two- to three-year leases, require customers to turn in the cars at lease end, and then convince them to turn around and lease another new car. They used low monthly payments as the bait, and in no time at all, automobile leasing became more popular than buying.

The line was that leasing was cheaper than buying, that when you lease "you only pay for the part of the car you use instead of the whole car." That was all marketing hype.

In theory, leasing should not have been a bad deal for someone who planned to buy a new car every two to three years, but something went wrong. Because dealers were not held to the same laws that regulate automobile sales, they failed to disclose actual prices and interest rates in writing. Leasing scams became the normal way to do business, and customers were none the wiser.

In recent years, laws have been enacted to tighten up on leasing so as to eliminate the scams and customer rip-offs. It has helped, but only slightly. The biggest problem is that customers do not understand leasing, so they cannot scrutinize the facts and figures; plus, the salespeople who get paid to tell customers how wonderful leasing is don't understand either. A salesperson has an ethical and legal obligation to disclose adequately in writing and explain to the customer the cap cost (purchase price), cap reduction, interest rate, trade-in, residual, monthly payment, excess mileage charge, termination penalty, acquisition and disposition fees (if any), and the total due at signing.

Over the years, I have studied the pros and cons of leasing a new automobile. Invariably the arguments in favor come from those who have some tie to the automobile industry, while other independent experts seem to agree that leasing an automobile is mostly not a very wise move. I have based my conclusions on both research and personal experience.

As attractive or sensible as a leasing transaction might appear, I can tell you that in reality leasing cars really stinks.

We got onto the auto leasing treadmill that day in 1976 when we drove a brand new AMC Pacer station wagon from the car lot, complete with windows of greenhouse proportion and a very complicated lease agreement. (I don't know which was worse—that we executed the lease or made that particular choice in cars.)

Stupidly, we determined leasing was the only alternative given our particular set of circumstances. We had no cash (the insurance proceeds from the accident that totaled our car somehow evaporated into thin air), and used cars were simply beneath our dignity.

We justified the transaction by saying we'd start saving right away so we could buy the car at the end of the lease. After all, this was our dream car. We'd drive it forever. And if you believe that, you're too young to remember the AMC Pacer.

Being a lease and all, there was no easy way to know exactly what we'd be paying for the car. But it didn't really matter. American Motors was nice enough to let us make the deal, and the specific details were unimportant.

Leasing a car was a pretty cool way to get what we wanted without spending any money. So cool, in fact, we repeated the process two years later. The next deal was unbelievably accommodating. The salesmen calculated the difference between what we owed (a lot) and the value (by this time very little—remember, AMC Pacer) of the dream-car-turned-embarrassment. He rolled that amount over into a new lease, mercifully took the Pacer off our hands, and let us drive away in a much more socially acceptable new car. So slick. So easy.

That leasing cycle continued to pick up speed right through three brand new Mazdas, a BMW, a Cadillac, a Nissan, and a minivan. Believe me, we brought new meaning to the term *rollover*. And the lease payments? They grew and grew, making the very thought of ever paying off an auto lease some kind of impossible dream.

We did manage to break that eighteen-year cycle when, with precious cash—saved over a period of time and with a great deal more dignity than it took to sign any of those leases—we bought a nine-year-old car and paid for it in full. We looked the other way with shame as we bought our way out of the last two leased cars. Finally the cycle was broken (see chap. 9), but not without a great deal of pain and regret.

I don't care what anyone says about the way a lease is supposed to work. In reality, you do nothing more than pay a boatload of money to rent a car. You own nothing, and at the end of the lease, you are horribly penalized if the car shows any signs that you might have actually driven it.

Taking everything into consideration, leasing is not more cost effective than owning. It is, in my opinion, the worst and most expensive way you can drive an automobile.

THE CHEAPEST WAY TO DRIVE A CAR

If you're going to get the cost of driving a car down, you have to avoid that big depreciation hit on the front end. Next, you must keep the cost of repairs and maintenance at bay. Even if you get it as a gift, an old clunker could become very expensive when you consider repairs, maintenance, and the cost to fuel the gas guzzler.

The cheapest way to drive a car is to pay cash for a two- or three-year-old, well-maintained, low-mileage automobile that the automobile insurance industry has designated as neither highly desirable nor a sports car. (Both highly desirable autos and sports cars are very expensive to insure.) In this way you can expect to pay 35 to 50 percent of the car's original price. Now you have the best of all worlds: low purchase price going in because the first owner paid for that big chunk of depreciation, low maintenance expenses, low insurance, and no financing charges. If you keep the car for about five years before you repeat the process, you will have experienced the cheapest way to drive a car.

One of the best places to find this ideal car is—believe it or not—within the automobile leasing market. Leasing companies sell cars that come back at the close of a lease. That's routine. Car rental companies also sell cars when they reach 15,000 to 20,000 miles. Many of these cars come with warranties. Of course, you need to take all of the precautions recommended when buying a used car.

TIPS FOR BUYING A USED CAR

1. Research market values before you go shopping.

2. Call your insurance company first to find out if the model you're considering is either at high risk to be stolen or considered a sports car. If the answer to either is yes, keep looking.

3. Pay to have a reputable mechanic do a thorough inspection of the car before you finalize the deal. If only minor problems exist, use them to negotiate a lower price.

4. If buying from a dealer, assume the price is marked up by $2,000 to $3,000. There's lots of room to negotiate.

5. If the dealer will not allow you to take the car to your independent mechanic for a thorough inspection, insist on a free bumper-to-bumper six-month warranty.

GETTING OFF A BAD TRACK

If you're stuck with a bad lease or haven't the cash to buy a used car, what are you supposed to do? Start planning. No matter how difficult or unfortunate your present automobile situation, you can get out. It will take time, but it is possible. You can do it.

Let's say you are two years into a three-year lease. First, you need to reread your documents. Find out exactly where you are with regard to your residual value (how much they will say the car is worth when the lease is completed) and the current market value for this car. Read to see if you have any early termination rights. Run the numbers. You may have the right to sell the car now and settle the lease out that way. If there is no hope of getting out of it, just live it out. But start today to stash cash so you'll have an alternative to leasing again when this deal is finally over.

If you have two cars, consider getting rid of one of them and then begin immediately to save what you would've spent on it for payments, insurance, operation, and maintenance. Oh, I know, there are a million reasons why you need two cars, but you'd be amazed at what you can do when you are truly motivated. I never dreamed Harold and I could share one car, but we decided to try it, just for a while. That was five years ago, and I don't see us ever going back to two cars.

HOW TO BUY A CAR FOR ALL CASH

Even if you have no money set aside to pay for a car, there is no reason you cannot pay all cash for a car someday soon. I came up with this plan when I got a letter from a young woman who informed me that she had no money but was going to lease a car because she knew she could afford the monthly payments.

My challenge to her: Prove it! For the next six months keep the clunker car you have now and make those $389 dollar monthly lease payments . . . to yourself!

On the first day of every month, write out that check and prove it to yourself that this is doable and even comfortable. If at the end of six months you have faithfully made the payments you know you are able to make, you will have $2,334 in cash. Take that money and whatever you can get for your clunker and buy the very best used car you can find for all cash (no financing). Keep making your $389 payments to the Bank of Me. At the end of a year, you will have saved $4,668. Sell the car you bought a year ago (let's say you can get $2,000 for it), add that to your car fund, and buy the best used car you can find for $6,668. Keep making your monthly payments to yourself. One year later, sell the car you're driving for $6,000, add that to the $4,668 you've saved in the year, and buy the best used car you can find for $10,668. Do this every year, and in about three years you will have enough cash to buy a brand new car for all cash, if you think that is a wise choice. Otherwise you can just keep parlaying your money into the best used cars you can find.

The reason this works so dramatically is that you are paying no interest. All of your $389 "payment" is credited to your benefit, not paid out in interest to a finance or leasing company. And for a bonus—my example doesn't even address the interest you will earn on the car payments you make to yourself.

An automobile is one of life's big-ticket items that carries that annoying depreciation characteristic. No matter how you slice it, it is a losing proposition. However, paying cash for a late model, low-mileage, low-maintenance car goes a long way to ease the pain.

⌒

---

1. Reprinted with permission *The Pocket Change Investor*, 14, Good Advice Press, P.O. Box 78, Elizaville, NY 12523.

## Chapter Seventeen

Every Honest Driver's Toll Bridge

AUTOMOBILE INSURANCE

The only thing in the world that can make riding the bus look good to a teenager is a quote for auto insurance.

Stephen M. Pollan

Just when you think you have won automobile ownership battle and you are driving a car the cheapest way possible, you get the bad news: It is going to cost more to insure that car than it did to buy it.

Automobile insurance is very expensive because it is based on the insurance company's risk and the chances that eventually you will have a claim. Those chances are, by the way, very high—and higher still if you add a youthful driver to the picture.

The high cost of auto insurance can be blamed on many factors. Today's cars are much more expensive to repair, there are many more inexperienced and youthful drivers on the road, road rage has become a popular way for drivers to vent their tempers, auto theft is at an all-time high, and litigation and huge settlements have become much too common.

All of these things contribute to high insurance rates. When you add the fact that the industry is run tightly and regulated heavily, honest drivers often assume they have no choices.

If you own a car or have a license to drive one, there is no circumstance under which you can be without automobile insurance. In some states it is illegal not to be insured, but it is stupid in all states. The laws of your state, the requirements of the lender (if you borrowed to buy your car), or those of the lessor (if you are leasing) specify the minimum coverage required.

The purpose of this chapter is to help you figure out how to get the insurance you need for the least amount of money possible. The way you do that is to trim your coverage to the essentials, determine your specific requirements as dictated by your personal situation, and then shop around for the best deal. While the coverage from one company to the next is much the same, rates vary widely among insurers.

Fault or No-Fault Insurance

It would be nice if every state had the same laws and regulations for auto insurance. But, alas, they do not. Some states are "fault" states. What that means generally is that the party who was at fault in the accident (or his insurance company if he has coverage) pays the costs associated with the accident. If fault was shared in a "fault" state, then both parties share the costs proportionately.

If it is a "no-fault" state, each person (or his insurer), regardless of fault, is responsible for his own damages and injuries.

THE SPECIFICS OF INSURANCE COVERAGE

If you have never read your auto insurance policy in its entirety, I wouldn't be surprised. It is not the most stimulating read. It does, however, spell out specifically for what you are paying. It doesn't explain it, but it does spell it out. There is a slight possibility that you are paying for coverage you do not need. How could that happen? Remember, the insurance agent who sold it to you receives a sales commission based on the premiums that you pay. Any more questions?

While your specific needs and requirements will depend on the laws and regulations of your state, the following is the kind of coverage you need.

Liability for bodily injury. This pays if you hurt someone in an accident that is your fault. This includes people in your car, in the other car, and pedestrians. You could be sued, and that opens the possibility of a high judgment depending on the circumstance. The injured parties are going to come after you for medical bills, loss of wages, and pain and suffering, and the result could be huge. You want coverage in this category to cover your net worth (the difference between what you own and what you owe). The more wealthy you are, the more coverage you need, but don't go nuts. Typically the judgment would not exceed your worth, so let that be your guiding light.

Liability for property damage. This pays if you damage another person's property. This could be his car or something tangible that you ran into that would be considered property. The minimum coverage you need is the fair market value of the average car in your area. If you worry you might hit something expensive, add coverage accordingly.

Medical payment coverage. This covers the medical and funeral bills for anyone injured in your car regardless of whose fault it was. Even if a family member is injured as a pedestrian or as the passenger in someone else's car where your car is not involved, your medical payment coverage will pay the bills beyond health insurance coverage the family member may have. Medical payment coverage is actually secondary insurance and explains why you don't need to carry large amounts. Experts suggest you should carry just an amount equal to your health insurance deductible, or about $2,000 per person.

Personal injury protection. This covers your medical bills and lost wages not covered in the liability for bodily injury section of your policy when the accident is your fault. If this is the case, you will probably look to your health insurance for primary coverage of your medical expenses. How much personal injury protection you carry may depend on the regulations in your state. It is interesting to note that New York requires the first $50,000 in bills for your own medical care for injuries from an auto accident be paid by your no-fault auto insurance policy rather than your health insurance policy. It also puts limits on how much doctors and therapists can charge to treat your injuries.

Think of personal injury protection coverage as back-up insurance to your health insurance in which case you won't need to carry a great deal.

Collision coverage. This covers the damage to your car even if the accident is your fault. The price of your collision coverage is determined by the size of your deductible (the amount of any claim you are willing to pay first before the insurance kicks in—anywhere from $100 to $1000). Collision insurance is typically quite pricey. You can achieve significant discounts, however, if you are willing to increase your deductible. The higher the deductible, the lower the premium. It is difficult, if not impossible, except in very rare cases, to get the insurance company to write collision coverage for more than the car's fair market value. This is why it is not advisable to pay for collision insurance on an old clunker that has a fair market value of less than about $2,000. Even if your car is totaled, you will not recover more than its fair market value regardless of how valuable the car was to you or how much you dumped into the pot in the form of collision premiums. In this case you would be better advised to drop the collision portion of your policy and save that amount instead in your Freedom Account for the purchase of another car.

Comprehensive coverage. This pays for damage not caused by another vehicle but rather by random acts of damage. This might include fire, hail, vandalism, grand theft auto, even damage to the upholstery by a pet overcome by a case of the munchies. This portion of your policy also carries a separate deductible, and like collision coverage, the higher the deductible, the cheaper the premiums.

Windshield coverage. This coverage pays for the replacement of a damaged windshield regardless of the reason and without deductibility. This coverage is typically very cheap and quite worth the price.

Towing and service reimbursement. This covers the cost of having your car towed after an accident or breakdown. While advisable, you would be better served to join AAA because the rates will be cheaper, and you'll get better service plus a load of additional benefits such as excellent maps, trip planning, and traveler's checks for no fee. In some states AAA can also handle your Department of Motor Vehicles transactions such as accepting annual auto registration fees.

Rental car reimbursement. For a very small annual premium of $5 to $20, you can get a daily stipend to pay for a rental car if your have an accident or your car breaks down. If

you need your car for business, this is an advisable coverage.
If not, it's pretty much a toss-up given how much you need
your car on a daily basis.

Uninsured and underinsured motorist coverage. Many
states require this coverage; other do not. This covers the cost
of your own injuries if it's the other guy's fault and he has no
insurance or is inadequately covered, meaning your injuries
exceed his coverage. If you have good life insurance, disability
insurance, and health insurance, this coverage could be
needless duplication. If you don't have those other types of
protection or those policies are fraught with exclusions, take
this coverage and don't scrimp.

Umbrella insurance. Even if you are not ready for this coverage now, given your decision to debt-proof your life, you will
be soon enough—so listen up. Umbrella insurance is a large liability policy that covers liability judgments that exceed the limits of your auto and homeowner's policies. You would only want
to do this if you're . . . well . . . rich. If you are or become fairly
affluent and have, for example, $700,000 in assets, you can buy
a one-million dollar umbrella policy for less than $75 to $200 a
year (depending on the number of cars you own) to add to the
$300,000 you have on your home or car. Typically you have to
carry $300,000 worth of liability on your basic policies.

Umbrella coverage can be quite versatile defending you
not only against claims of damage or personal injury but
against libel (unless you are a professional writer), slander,
false arrest, invasion of privacy, and similar charges that can
ruin your day.

HOW TO REDUCE THE COSTS

Drive defensively. I cannot stress enough the importance of
driving in such a way as to prevent auto insurance claims.

These days, with so many drivers on the highway (many of whom are under the influence of something and/or uninsured), you have to drive for five people: yourself, the guy talking on the telephone in front of you, that teenager rockin' to the beat of his stereo behind you, the young mother with three squirming toddlers to the right, and that octogenarian on the left. A clean driving record and an accident-free history (even accidents in which you were not to blame can go against you as it appears you are "accident prone") are the best ways to keep your premiums at rock bottom. Work on a pristine record. If you can stay citation and accident free, you will reap the benefits financially because you will qualify for lower rates. But every driver on your policy must be in this excellent driving behavior mode. Work out a monetary reward system for your teens who by their driving behavior keep your rates low. I'd rather give my kids the money any day than the insurance company and as a bonus develop safe and reliable drivers.

Compare prices. Rates vary widely, so get several quotes. Call GEICO, a company that deals through the mail and over the phone and has no agents (800-841-3000). If you and the others on your policy have excellent driving records, you can save a bundle with this well-respected company. If you or one of your relatives is or has been in the military, you might qualify to purchase auto insurance through USAA (800-531-8080). USAA's prices are impressive, so it would be worth your while to think about this for a few minutes. If in doubt, give them a call. They'll let you know if you qualify. Look in the Yellow Pages for State Farm, Allstate, and Nationwide Mutual. These companies use agents, so call one in your local area and get a quote. In your quest to reduce your annual premium, don't count out your current insurance agent quite yet. Show him the quotes you have gathered and find out what he can do for you. It's amazing what a little competition and the threat of losing a customer can turn up.

Drive a cheap car. The premiums you pay are based on how much it would cost to repair or replace your vehicle. Therefore, the premiums on an older or less fancy car will be significantly less. Before you buy a car, always call your insurance agent first to see which of those cars you are considering is cheaper to repair and the least desirable, meaning the chances of having it stolen are reduced. Now you know which models will produce lower insurance premiums and which ones to stay away from.

Don't buy from the lender. Many times the lender, if you have a loan, or lessor, if you are leasing, will offer you automobile insurance. It sounds convenient and you might be tempted to say yes—unless you know that it is about the most expensive way to go. (And now you do.) Do your homework as outlined above, and you will be rewarded.

Get a discount. Many companies give significant discounts on automobile insurance if the company also carries your homeowner or other types of insurance. Some companies give significant discounts for students with excellent grades. If all of you have pristine driving records, you will also notice some handsome discounts. If you are a nonsmoker and a nondrinker, most companies will reward your clean living with yet another discount. If you have a security device on your car, keep it in the garage, drive it only for pleasure—speak up and let the company know. All of these things reduce your exposure to a claim and translate into lower premiums.

Pay the premium annually. Many companies these days offer monthly, quarterly, and biannual payment plans. And they charge extra for that little service. Do everything you can to pay the entire year's premium at one time and you'll save some dough. This will be very doable once you have your Freedom Account up and funded.

Go to reform school. If you are nailed for a moving violation, by all means attend traffic school if available. By attending about eight hours of classroom instruction, most states will allow the ticket to be removed from your record. Traffic school is even offered over the Internet. You'll probably have to pay for the ticket and the cost of traffic school (it will vary from state to state), but that is nothing compared to how much your insurance rates will go up if you simply pay the ticket and don't go to traffic school. Where I live, you can go to traffic school only once every two years, so it is certainly not a panacea.

Raise the deductibles. If you carry collision and/or comprehensive coverage, raise your deductibles to get significantly lower premiums. But before you do that, establish a subaccount in your Freedom Account to accumulate the higher deductibles. Now if you need them, they are all in place. If you don't need them, you have a larger stash that brings you just a modicum of additional peace of mind.

Move. If you live in an area where the insurance rates are especially high, consider moving to another zip code where the rates are lower. Your insurance agent can give you the lowdown on lower rates. This just might be the excuse you need to leave the big city and move to the country as you've always dreamed.

A Few Tips about Making Claims

Unfortunately, the real proof of whether you have the right kind and the right amount of automobile insurance is found in filing a claim. While I hope you will never need that kind of proof, let me offer a few suggestions in case that day arrives.

If you are involved in an accident that is not your fault, but the other party is insured by a deadbeat company that appears to be noncooperative, you don't have to wait around if you carry collision insurance. Call your agent immediately. Your insurance will pay to have your car repaired to your satisfaction (less your deductible in some states) while they go after the other party for reimbursement. Make sure you keep following up until you get full reimbursement of your deductible. It could take some time, and for this reason many people forget and never do receive their deductible. You would only be liable to pay the deductible if the accident was your fault (I'm speaking of how it works in a "fault" state).

If your car is stolen or totaled, the insurer is supposed to pay fair market value. Unfortunately, fair market value is a nebulous term. For us, when our 1986 Chevrolet El Camino was stolen, stripped, and left like a fish carcass to dry up in the summer heat, we felt fair market value should mean the amount of money it would cost us to buy another 1986 El Camino complete with the brand-new engine and brand-new interior that were less than a year old. We learned that the insurance company interprets fair market value as what the average 1986 Chevrolet El Camino was going for in the local classified ads. Unfortunately, there aren't many of those around, and the prices ranged anywhere from $1,500 to $10,000 depending on the condition and restoration.

We were not at all happy with the amount the insurance company said they were mailing us in full payment of the claim. Clearly, they forgot to look in the paper or on the local used car lots. Their offer was simply too low. So we asserted our car's actual value with documentation of similar vehicles being offered in the area. We haggled back and forth, and they finally agreed to a number that was better, although it still didn't come close to mitigating our loss.

While your automobile insurance will not replace or cover the items in your car that are destroyed or stolen, your homeowner's or renter's policy may.

If you feel your insurance company is not playing fairly with you, assert some muscle. Go on the offensive. Complain to the manager of the company. Write a letter to the state commissioner of insurance and send a copy to the president of the company, perhaps even to your local consumer office or Better Business Bureau.

As with the other types of insurance you must carry, automobile insurance is one of those that you absolutely have to have but pray you'll never need to use.

## Chapter Eighteen

The Money on Your Life

LIFE INSURANCE

One pays for everything, the trick is not to pay too much of anything for anything.

John Steinbeck

Life insurance. Ugh. We need it and then hope we won't. Pay for it but haven't a clue what we've got or if it's right. As a result, a good many of us are wasting money that could be put to much better use.

Life insurance should not be seen as life insurance at all. It is income insurance. And it's not for you; it's for those you'll leave behind.

The purpose of life insurance is to replace your income for those who would be left in the lurch if you were to die and that income disappeared from their lives. Life insurance protects your survivors who are dependent on you for their sole support from the premature and permanent loss of your income.

One of the worst financial decisions Harold and I ever made came while sitting at our kitchen table late one night.

That's when we turned off our brains and surrendered our judgment to someone with the title "estate planner." Our friend Tracy, an insurance professional herself, recommended that we meet with him. It felt prosperous for someone to suggest we needed an estate planner.

This guy, with all the sleaze of a used-car dealer and the guilt-inducing charm of a funeral director, sat at our table for hours using words and jargon completely foreign to us. He had fancy graphs and charts with all the indicators pointed straight up.

He all but guaranteed that without his intervention there was no way we would ever have an estate to plan, and that lucky for us he happened to have the papers right there in his briefcase—right next to the bathroom scale and blood pressure cuff. We were so tired and anxious to get rid of him, we went through the motions and signed the papers believing he wouldn't suggest something that would not be right for us.

That brilliant move ended up costing us a fortune. For years we sent close to $600 a month—often going into debt to manage it—to some insurance company for two life insurance policies about which we knew zilch. But we continued to believe that this "estate planner" knew best, so we didn't question his motives or advice. Of course, when we eventually wised up and cancelled the policies, there was no recoverable cash value. On a positive note, I see this man and his universal-life policies as one of the catalysts that kicked me into self-education mode, and for that I am grateful.

TYPES OF LIFE INSURANCE

Life insurance comes in two basic flavors. The plain vanilla version is term insurance. Think of it as pure insurance. The tutti-frutti variety is whole-life insurance. It's the hot, glitzy, and—in my humble opinion—dangerous product. Whole-life insurance is the one that sometimes gets even the savviest consumers in over their heads and still underinsured.

TERM INSURANCE

You pay the premiums and the insurance stays in force as long as you pay. If you die when the policy is in force, a set amount of money is paid to your beneficiary. Term insurance includes no cash build up or savings. Plain vanilla insurance, it is relatively cheap.

There are ways that term insurance is packaged: annually renewable term and level-premium term (sometimes called reentry term).

The premiums on an annually renewable term policy start out low and increase some every few years. The benefit of annually renewable term is that the insurer cannot cancel your coverage or increase the premium due to any health issues. Once you pass the first medical exam, you never take another, and you can keep renewing until a maximum age of about seventy. This is fine, because by that age you will have an investment portfolio and retirement plan in place to cover anyone who is still dependent on your income. You will not likely need life insurance.

The premiums on level-premium term policies start out somewhat higher but are fixed for ten years or more. There is no renewing process and additional medical exams are not required during the term. You will likely pay less for level-premium term than annually renewable term over the course of ten or twenty years. The difference, however, is that with level-premium term policies you will have to requalify through a medical examination if you want to renew. You won't be denied insurance based on that exam, but the premiums could go up significantly.

WHOLE-LIFE INSURANCE

This is term insurance with a savings account attached to it. The longer you are in the plan, the more savings you will have. When this type of insurance is presented, there are always very attractive illustrations of the growth on the savings side. Beware, because the savings advantages are always inflated, never guaranteed, and rarely fully understood by the person explaining them to you. The same amount of coverage will cost three to four times as much if you buy whole-life than if you buy pure term. That is the reason many people who carry whole-life are underinsured. They are spending all they can but not getting their money's worth when it comes to the reason for the policy in the first place.

All other types of life insurance are variations of whole-life.

INSURANCE MISTAKES

I have compiled, for your life insurance reading pleasure, ten easy-to-understand life insurance mistakes and how to avoid them.

Mistake 1: Buying life insurance as an investment. Life insurance is designed to replace your income stream if you die so that your dependents will be able to maintain a normal standard of living in your absence for a reasonable period of time until they can change their lives to fit their new economic circumstances. Life insurance is not designed to fund your retirement or pay for your kids' college educations.

The single worst reason to buy life insurance is as an investment or a forced savings plan. Insurance companies have a great reputation as insurers but as investors they are anything but sterling. That means the only kind of life insurance you should consider is term. Forget about anything with whole, universal, or variable life in the title. It makes for great marketing brochures and fancy graphs but cannot measure up as a great investment when put to the test.

Mistake 2: Buying life insurance you don't need. Skip insurance such as life insurance for your children (a smart move only if your child is a movie star and you depend on his or her earning power); credit life insurance offered as an option when you take out a loan (a good buy only if you are elderly or terminally ill); or flight insurance (never a good buy).

Don't buy mortgage insurance that pays off your outstanding mortgage in the event of your death. There are lots of reasons why that is a poor buy; the biggest one is that the premium does not reflect the fact that your outstanding balance is always in a descending mode. Also, in the event of your passing, your spouse will have no choice but to allow the proceeds (which will not be one penny more than the current outstanding principal balance) from the mortgage insurance to pay off that loan—even if that move is not in his or her best interest. If your mortgage is at a very low rate and the payment is manageable, insurance proceeds might be better invested or applied to another area, but with mortgage insurance your survivors will have no choice. You'd be better off to use that same money you'd spend on mortgage insurance premiums to purchase plain term insurance. You'll give your survivors better options.

Do not buy credit card life insurance that will pay off your outstanding credit card debts in the event of your demise. Many credit card companies push this and push it hard. They try to get you to agree to a monthly charge to your account, and of course they come up with all kinds of slick marketing jargon to close the deal. I have, in fact, seen some credit card offers that automatically activate this as if it is required.

First of all, you shouldn't have any credit card debt, and if you do, you should be doing everything you can to clean the slate. This insurance is expensive. As a typical example, if you have a $2,000 balance, it costs $13 a month. For $156 a year, a thirty-five-year-old male could buy $200,000 worth of term insurance or enough to pay off that $2,000 credit card bill one hundred times!

Mistake 3: Allowing a commissioned salesperson to advise you on the type and amount of insurance to buy. Face it, the insurance industry—in general designed to overwhelm, perplex, and bewilder—thrives on its ability to confuse the customer. If you don't believe me, pour yourself a nice cup of coffee and spend a few hours reading a life insurance policy. Even the people who sell life insurance don't always understand how their products work. First, you must determine the amount of coverage you need, then the type of policy that is appropriate, and finally, the source from which to buy it. Don't rely solely on someone else to figure out how much life insurance you need or to tell you where you should buy it, especially someone who has a decided conflict of interest because he or she will be making a commission based on your decision.

Buying term life insurance is a simple purchase—one you can do yourself.

Mistake 4: Buying whole-life insurance because "the cash value of your policies is your savings." If you believe that a life insurance policy is the proper place for you to keep your savings, did you know that if you take your savings, you lose your insurance? If you die, the company keeps your savings? If you need money, it costs you 4 to 8 percent interest to borrow your own money? Here's the deal with the cash values: If you die, the company uses those savings to pay part of your death benefit.

Why would you pay interest to use your own money? Imagine a bank that charged you interest to withdraw money from your checking or savings account. Would you bank there? Then don't bank with a cash value (whole life) policy.

Mistake 5: Not buying enough life insurance if you determine you need it or buying too much. While many experts give rules of thumb on how much insurance you need (eight-, six-, three-times your annual income), none of them is accurate because so much depends on how old you are, whether you have children, what your spouse earns, and how much money you've saved. Every situation is unique. Six times is about average.

Start your estimate with enough coverage to replace the insured's income (or equivalent contribution in the case of a stay-at-home mother whose many duties would have to be hired in the form of nanny, housekeeper, laundress, cook, social planner, chauffeur—you get my drift) for three years. Your intent is to ease the transition, not set your survivors up for the rest of their lives so they never have to make the necessary adjustments. Of course, if you are self-employed and your unexpected departure from the company would prove an economic hardship, you need to take this into account.

As your life circumstances change, adjust your life insurance accordingly. As your children grow and leave home and your net worth increases, you will come to the place where you no longer require life insurance coverage because you have investments and assets to cover the requirements you have determined.

Mistake 6: Assuming that because you have already purchased whole-life insurance you're stuck with it. No way. Let's say you bought that whole-life policy at age thirty-five and you're paying about $1,000 a year for $100,000 in coverage.

You can convert that policy to a term policy and instruct the company to use the cash value that would otherwise be returned to you to prepay the premiums until that cash runs out. Then you would begin making the premium payments. Or using the resources and suggested techniques I will give later in this chapter, shop around and save about $800 a year in premiums by switching to term insurance with another company.

Mistake 7: Selecting a company because you've heard of it, it is old and big, and therefore it must be reputable. Major insurance companies were hit in the '90s for misrepresentation and scams, even for selling phony retirement policies. Big money was paid in settlements. Things change, so to protect yourself, you must be informed and take responsibility. Insurance premiums are very serious dollars and should be placed only with highly reputable companies. See the information that follows to learn how to rate a company's strength in the industry.

Mistake 8: Thinking the only way to acquire life insurance is to purchase a policy from a life insurance company. If you are employed full time, the best insurance deal around is probably in your personnel office. Many companies offer life insurance as part of their benefits package, and a certain amount of it is usually free. You may be able to buy even more at your own expense. Dollar for dollar, this supplemental insurance could be the best deal you'll find anywhere. But before you make this decision, go through the exercise that follows so you can make the comparison intelligently. If you leave your job, you can generally convert your group-term coverage, but the cost will be staggering. Your better option would be to hold it only until you can replace it.

Mistake 9: Buying life insurance for children to make sure they will be insurable as adults. Most child-size policies are too small for grown-ups, and when your children need the coverage, chances are they'll qualify on their own.

Mistake 10: Canceling an existing life insurance policy before the replacement policy is in place. No matter how distasteful your current coverage, the last thing you want to do is have any gaps in coverage. You hear horror stories all the time about how the unthinkable happened during that tiny blank place between one policy terminating and the new one taking effect.

WHO NEEDS LIFE INSURANCE?

If you are . . .

. . . young and single with no dependents, forget about life insurance. You just don't need it. You are better advised to get debt free and then build your investments.

. . . older and single with no dependents, you do not need life insurance. If you have life insurance now and could use a little more income instead, cancel it, put the cash value (if any) into savings or investments, and start stashing the money you were paying in premiums.

. . . single with dependents, think: If you die, who will provide for those dependents? Wherever they go, it would be nice for them to show up with enough money so they are not a financial burden to their new family.

. . . a double-income couple with no kids, you probably don't need any life insurance. Each spouse could be self-supporting if the other died. If it takes two incomes to pay the mortgage, consider carrying only enough insurance for that single purpose.

. . . married with children, you need a lot of insurance. If you pass away, your spouse is going to need a lot of dough to raise and educate the kids.

. . . a wife that doesn't work outside the home, you need insurance, but only to the extent that upon your death your husband would not be able to pay from his current income for all the services you now provide.

Michael Minton, in his book *What Is a Wife Worth?*,[1] applied national average wages to the average amounts of time homemakers spend performing their daily tasks, such as household purchaser, maintenance worker, housekeeper, bookkeeper, nurse, dietitian, child psychologist, laundress, chauffeur, and public relations/hostess. The total cost of services provided: $108,049 per year.

. . . retired, you need insurance only if you do not have sufficient savings and your spouse could not live on Social Security and the pension and income you leave behind.

. . . a kid, you don't need life insurance. Stash the money you'd spend on life insurance premiums into a college fund instead.

. . . a college student, you definitely do not need life insurance. Don't waste your or your parents' money. Buy tuition instead.

. . . filthy rich, life insurance may be an estate planning tool that will help your heirs pay the estate taxes in the event of your demise. This may be a very good idea that you should discuss with the appropriate professionals.

SHOPPING FOR INSURANCE

This is going to take a little time, and you will need to expend a bit of diligence. But I guarantee it will be less painful and far more enjoyable than many appointments with agents or brokers. You can do most, if not all, of the work yourself without an agent or a broker.

The method I am about to suggest first involves comparison shopping. You are going to get specific quotes. You are no more taking advantage of a company by asking for a quote without completing an application than you are ripping off a department store when you check the price of an item you're considering. You may find the best bargain by mail order once you've established the playing field. That is not dishonest or unethical. (That should save some of you a postage stamp.)

1. Decide how much life insurance coverage you need and what type of term insurance is best for you. If you do not know, go back, reread this chapter, and then have a heart-to-heart talk with yourself and your spouse, if you have one. It's a simple assignment: how much and what type.

2. Contact at least three free quote services. Below are the phone numbers and/or Internet addresses for seven insurance brokerages that offer free, no-cost and no-obligation insurance quotes. You will be required to give them relevant information, such as your name, age, health rundown, and so on. It is very simple, and most of the time automated.

Basically term insurance costs about the same no matter which company you deal with. The significant price differences you will find are the result of fees, administrative costs, and individual insurer's overhead that are added on. This is why it is important to get several quotes.

Below is a list of companies that will give you quotes for no cost. Some of them will give you the three best quotes they can offer; others will give as many as 150. Using your phone or computer, contact them and then keep track of what you turn up. You would think that each brokerage company's list of quotes would be the same, but not necessarily. Not every brokerage sells every company's product.

InstantQuote	http://www.instantquote.com
MasterQuote	800-337-5433
Quicken InsureMarket	http://www.insuremarket.com

Quickquote	http://www.quickquote.com
Quotesmith	http://www.quotesmith.com
SelectQuote	800-343-1985
TermQuote	800-444-8376

3. Get quotes from direct insurers. These are companies that deal directly with consumers. You do not need to go through an agent or broker, even after all your homework is completed, the way you must if you deal with other companies (more on that to come). However, be aware that these companies have very high standards when it comes to your health and insurability. But their prices may be well worth the effort if you can qualify.

Ameritas	800-552-3553
Charles Schwab/Grt Western	800-542-5433
USAA	800-531-8000 (must have a connection to the military for USAA's life insurance)
Zurich Direct	http://www.zurichdirect.com

4. Say no. Each of the companies from which you get quotes, both brokers and direct insurers, will ask you to fill out an application. It is too soon for that, so decline courteously.

5. Look at all of your bids. Narrow the field to the lowest quotations.

6. Your next task is to find out how your top companies rate within the insurance industry. It is important that you only do business with the highest rated companies. You want to eliminate as much risk as possible that that company with which you are insured will suddenly go out of business. You want them to be just as strong and anxious for your business when the claim is placed as when they made the quote.

There are several companies that rate insurance companies according to their financial strength and reputation. If you have access to the Internet, you can skip the next few paragraphs and get right to the Internet instructions. If you do not, I suggest you contact A. M. Best, one of the most highly regarded rating firms.

Your first call to Best at 908-439-2200 will be to get an ID number for each of the companies you are considering. This call will add $2.50 per minute to your phone bill. That is OK—this is very important, and that charge is quite a bargain. Call 900-420-0400, and using the ID numbers, you can get the most current A. M. Best rating of the insurers that made your cut.

While the Best ratings are highly respected, you should go one step further and run the insurers you are considering through the rating grid of three other rating services. Because each of these will give you only one free quote, ask each for the rating of one of your top three:

Moody's	212-553-0377
Standard & Poor's	212-208-1527
Duff & Phelps	312-368-3157

If you have access to the Internet, you can skip the foregoing and learn all you can about the strength and viability of the companies you are considering for no cost. Go to www.insure.com., where all of your companies can be searched by state, or try www.standardandpoors.com, where companies are listed alphabetically and rated accordingly.

If you do not wish to use the phone and you do not have access to the Internet, you can get this information at your local library in books that list both Standard and Poor's and Moody's ratings. Keep in mind that the information you receive this way may not be as up-to-date as with the other methods.

7. *Make your selection by picking the strongest company with the cheapest rate.* If that turns out to be one of the companies you can deal with directly, make the call and start filling

out the application. If not, call the phone number of the company, and you will be directed to a local insurance agent. Just beware: they will want to switch you into a whole-life product. Stay the course and do not be deterred. You have all the confidence you need to trust your decision and stick to your plan.

⌒

1. Michael M. and Jean Libman Block Minton, *What Is a Wife Worth? The Leading Expert Places a High Dollar Value on Homemaking* (New York: William Morrow, 1983).

## Chapter Nineteen

The Overlooked Safety Net

DISABILITY INSURANCE

A 20-year-old worker stands a nearly 3 in 10 chance of becoming disabled before age 65.

The Social Security Administration

In addition to health and automobile coverage, most people insure their lives so that in the event of their untimely demise—a term that for me always begs the question, Is there such a thing as a timely demise?—those who depend on their income will not be left high and dry.

Term life insurance, the insurance of choice for debt-proof living, is relatively cheap because so many people pay for it who never use it. The insurance companies invest all of those premiums, make an obscene fortune doing so, and end up paying out far less than they take in.

Curiously, less than 15 percent of people who buy life insurance insure something far more important: their ability to earn a living. Face it folks, these days with medical technology what it is, the odds increase every day that a disease or accident that would have killed you even a decade ago will now leave you disabled—alive but unable to work.

Your chances of becoming disabled at a relatively young age, either temporarily or permanently, are far greater than your chances of dying young. Clearly, some would argue (and I would be one), if you cannot afford both life and disability insurance, you should decide in favor of the latter.

The debt-proof living philosophy relies heavily on being prepared for the unforeseen. That's the reason for my emphasis on a Contingency Fund, a Freedom Account, and living without debt. However, none of these provisions is going to carry you through for long periods without an income.

Unfortunately, many of us will need disability income protection sometime before we die. One out of every three people will be incapacitated for ninety days or more before they reach age sixty-five according to the Life Insurance Marketing and Research Association. Without insurance, a disability could spell financial disaster.

A study published in the *Journal of the American Medical Association,* of two thousand seriously ill people, found that although 95 percent had medical insurance, 31 percent still lost everything they owned because of the resulting disability.

Surprisingly, 48 percent of mortgage foreclosures are a result of disability, far more than result from death.

WHY IS IT SO EXPENSIVE?

Disability insurance is far more expensive than term life insurance. In fact, it rivals the more expensive whole life insurance but does not offer the dubious advantage of cash values. No wonder so many people overlook this most important type of insurance.

Disability insurance is relatively expensive because there's a much higher probability you will use it. Insurance companies operate on levels of risk. The greater the chances they will have to make payment on a claim, the higher the premiums.

With life insurance, most people underestimate their life span, so they end up buying insurance they will never use. Or they buy ridiculously expensive insurance such as whole-life or universal-life, and then drop it the minute they go through a financial downturn. That's why insurance companies make out like bandits.

But when it comes to disabilities, people of all ages have equal risks, which means it is more likely that you will need disability insurance at some time during your earning years. If you are in a two-breadwinner household, it is likely you need disability insurance more than life insurance, given how expensive it can be to care for a disabled person.

Disability insurance is not, in my opinion, the luxury item most people consider it to be.

HOW IT WORKS

Standard disability insurance is straightforward. If you are unable to work and disabled as defined by the disability insurance policy, the insurance company replaces a specific percentage of the income you would have earned had you not been disabled.

In the same way that health, auto, and life insurance policies have unique provisions, exclusions, and stipulations, there are all kinds of provisions in a disability policy that you should consider carefully. Generally speaking, the lower the premium, the greater the number of exclusions and stipulations. Consider them carefully, and never buy insurance coverage that you do not fully understand.

WHAT TO LOOK FOR

1. Simple definition. You want a policy that defines disability very simply: a decline in income as a result of sickness or
accident. A policy that gets complicated in this regard will
likely be difficult to nail down when it's time to file a claim.

2. Guaranteed and noncancelable. This type of policy
will have a fixed premium and will stay in effect as long as
your payments are current regardless of health issues or
other variables. Just as the provision states, you have guaranteed coverage and it is not cancelable. Avoid a policy that
carries a provision that it is "class cancelable." That means
a policy is cancelable if an entire class of policies are canceled. If a company were to cancel an entire class of occu-
pations, say truck drivers, and you were one of them, you'd
be out in the cold even if your policy was guaranteed and
noncancelable if it did not carry a further provision that it
was not class cancelable.

3. Addresses pre-existing conditions. Make sure your policy
covers disabilities resulting from pre-existing conditions that
you disclosed at the time of application. If you had a disabling
back condition twenty years ago and have since recovered, you
don't want to find out a new back condition is not covered
because of that pre-existing situation. Make sure that if you
have pre-existing conditions they are clearly stated and the
terms under which they will be covered are spelled out.

4. Waives premiums during disability period. You want to
find a policy that waives the premium completely if you are
disabled for more than, say, ninety days. That means that if
you are disabled, all of your insurance provisions stay in full
effect, except you do not pay those expensive premiums.

5. Insures for your occupation. You want a disability policy
that protects you against your inability to work in your own

occupation. Without this important provision your insurer will not pay you unless you can't work at all.

6. Payment increases. You want a rider on your policy that provides for payment increases to keep up with inflation and with your income. If you bought the policy when you made $25,000 and make $45,000 when you suffer a disability, you want to make sure you are covered at the $45,000 level.

7. Pays until retirement. Some disability policies pay for only a specific period of time, say five or ten years. The best policy is open-ended and continues as long as you are disabled, until retirement age.

8. Option to purchase. If your policy includes an "option to purchase" clause, you will be able to increase your coverage at predetermined times regardless of your health or other factors. This is a good protection that will allow you to adjust in the event the economy experiences hyperinflation. There are riders for disability insurance that automatically adjust them upward to allow for inflation, but they are very expensive. The "option to purchase" clause is a reasonable substitute.

HOW MUCH COVERAGE

I could suggest you look for a policy that will pay 100 percent of your income—and you would look forever and never find it. Disability policies pay a percentage of your current income or an average based on some stated period of time. Of course the lower the percentage, the cheaper the premium, so it is important that you determine your absolute minimum requirement in the event you are unable to earn a living.

Your regular expenses will be reduced somewhat during a disability period simply because you won't be going to work every day. Figure how little you could get by on and then start looking for a policy that will meet that portion of your income.

REDUCE THE COST

One thing you can do to reduce the high cost of disability insurance is to accept a longer waiting period or "elimination period." Some policies kick in, or begin paying benefits, immediately upon a disabling event. Others have a 30-, 60-, 90-, or even 180-day waiting period. It is advisable to take the longer waiting period resulting in a significantly lower premium, and then look to your Contingency Fund or other nest egg to cover the bills during the waiting period.

Even if you feel you are not in a position to take on another expense at this time, start thinking about it. I hope that soon you will change your mind and find this a priority you can no longer ignore. At the very least, find out what a good disability policy would cost. Ask friends or relatives for a referral to an agent or disability insurance carrier.

The most logical place to look for disability insurance is right in your own neighborhood, so to speak. Check to see if your employer offers this as a group benefit. Some employers provide a small amount of coverage as an employee benefit and allow employees to purchase more at their own expense. A call to your human resources department might turn up a very nice surprise, since group coverage of any type of insurance is always much cheaper than an individual policy.

If you bomb out on the employer-provided source, find out if any trade organizations to which you belong—or could if you were convinced they offered you something of benefit—makes group disability insurance available. Ask your friends, both personal and professional, if they might have a recommendation.

If all else fails, start looking at individual coverage. Your current life insurance provider may also offer disability insurance, so make that call without making any commitments. Remember, you are only shopping at this point.

Finally, it couldn't hurt to call USAA Life Insurance Company at 800-531-8000 for a price quote. While some of USAA's products are available only to active and former military officers and their dependents, as of this writing USAA offers its disability insurance directly to the public. And the fact they have no agents helps to lower the premiums.

Now that you have a concrete idea of what disability coverage will cost you, you can look to your present insurance company for a cost comparison.

Chapter Twenty

Medical Bills Can Give You a Heart Attack

HEALTH INSURANCE

Of all the things you can afford to be without,
health insurance is not one of them.

Unknown

When it comes to health insurance, it is quite simple: Either you have it or you don't.

If you have it, you work for a company that provides it as part of your employee benefit package.

If you don't have it, your employer is very small or you are your own employer. As a member of the "have-nots," you have few choices. You can either go broke paying for health insurance or go without and still go broke when faced with medical bills.

HEALTH INSURANCE OPTIONS

If you don't have health insurance, you must find a way on your own to, at the very minimum, insure against major illnesses. Going without any type of health coverage isn't an option. You have no choice.

If it falls to you to provide your health insurance, the options are limited and, unfortunately, expensive. You have three, possibly four, choices:

1. Purchase traditional fee-for-service coverage.
2. Join a health maintenance organization (HMO).
3. Join a preferred provider organization (PPO).
4. Start a Medical Savings Account (MSA).

FEE-FOR-SERVICE PLANS

With this type of health insurance policy, you choose your own doctors and hospitals. After you meet your deductible, the insurance company either pays the reasonable and customary charge, or they pay a predetermined percentage of the total and you pay the rest. Depending on the policy you select, your insurance may or may not pay for prescriptions.

With fee-for-service plans you get three choices of coverage:

1. Hospitalization expenses only
2. Nonhospital expenses only
3. Hospital and nonhospital expenses

The advantage of fee-for-service coverage is that you remain in control. You select the medical providers without limitation. The drawback, however, is that traditional fee-for-service medical insurance is very expensive.

HMOs

Basically, a health maintenance organization (HMO) is a group of health-care providers and facilities who have joined forces in some form or another. You pay a monthly premium plus a flat rate for each visit, something around $10. Rather than having a big choice of doctors, you are assigned to a primary care physician who then refers you to other specialists who are members and to any other of their facilities as needed.

The advantage of an HMO is the cost. It is relatively inexpensive as compared to traditional fee-for-service coverage. The disadvantage is the level of services, the limitations of the group of providers, and their desire to keep costs low. It's in the HMO's best interest to limit their members' use of their services. That, as you might already be aware, presents a huge problem if you are not very healthy.

PPOs

Preferred provider organizations (PPOs) represent something between the ghastly expensive fee-for-service provider and the HMO. The providers remain autonomous, agreeing to a loose association. They agree to treat their members for a reduced fee, and you, as the insured, can either choose to go to one of them and take advantage of that lower fee or choose any other doctor or provider that is not a member and pay full fare. PPOs are more expensive than HMOs, but considerably cheaper than fee-for-service.

MEDICAL SAVINGS ACCOUNTS

Medical savings accounts (MSAs) are so limited in their availability and unproven in scope, I hesitate mentioning them as a possibility. However, if you are self-employed, you might want to check into this.

MSAs are a fairly new thing and actually are an experiment to provide a government-sponsored health-care program for self-employed individuals. MSAs were made available through a pilot program earmarked in the Health Insurance Portability and Accountability Act of 1996.

Very simply, an MSA is an account into which you deposit pretax dollars (from $1,500 to $2,250 for individual coverage,

$3,000 to $4,500 for family coverage), and then claim a yearly tax write-off for the contribution. The money pays for routine medical bills, and when yours exceed the funds available, an underlying health plan kicks in. If you don't use the money for medical care, you get to keep it. Bottom line: you are paying for your medical expenses with pretax dollars and hoping that you'll stay healthy and not need the coverage.

MSAs sound terrific, but the idea has failed to catch on and has been declared all but a marketplace flop, a mechanism that benefits the healthy (at the expense of the sick, who pay higher premiums), and a drain on the federal treasury. The MSA experiment might even be abandoned by the time you read this. I mention it only because it remains an option, and it appears there are some individuals out there who are very pleased with this choice.

If you would like to explore the MSA possibility, get in touch with Golden Rule Insurance Company at 800-444-8990 or visit them at www.goldenrule.com. This company has generated more than half of all the MSAs to date, which is pitifully few considering how many candidates there are.

GETTING THE BEST COVERAGE

There's no doubt that the fee-for-service coverage is what you should shoot for if you can possibly afford it. There are ways to get the best coverage at a reduced fee.

1. Select a very high deductible in exchange for a lower premium. In this way you are actually self-insuring for routine medical expenses for you and your family, but making sure you have coverage for the big, catastrophic possibilities. This is the route I have chosen. Our $2,000 deductible results in a barely affordable monthly premium of about $325, but holds us in good

stead if we have needs beyond $2,000 per person per year.

2. Find your way into some kind of a group. Some providers consider as few as three people to be a group. So if you are self-employed, you, your spouse, and one other could make up that required group. You might qualify for the lower group rates. Check on organizations to which you belong or perhaps could join. Professional associations, trade groups, and other such organizations often offer their members group fee-for-service coverage.

If you cannot afford fee-for-service coverage, the PPO route would be the next advisable one to consider. As a last resort, I would suggest you join an HMO. While it is at the bottom of my list, it is infinitely superior to having no health insurance coverage at all. Not even a died-in-the-wool cheapskate would be so foolish as to go unprotected in these days of staggering medical costs.

Because health insurance is such a regional commodity, you need to look to your specific locale to find quotes for health insurance coverage. Ask friends and family for referrals, look in the Yellow Pages, and start calling to get quotes.

If all else fails, you should seriously consider updating your resume and start job searching. Some corporations offer full health benefits to part-time employees. Remember that your quest is to find a job you'll love in a company large enough to offer health insurance to its employees.

Chapter Twenty-One

The High Price of a Sheepskin

PAYING FOR A COLLEGE EDUCATION

Invest in yourself, in your education.
There's nothing better.

Sylvia Porter

College is expensive but generally worth it if you pay as you go. Paying double, however, by putting the cost of a college education on credit to be paid for over the next twenty-five to thirty years, to me, borders on the unthinkable.

You will recall that in the introduction to part 1, I confessed that I am seriously opinionated about the matter of debt—unsecured, consumer debt. And while I'm certain that has come through in previous chapters, hang on to your hat. You haven't read anything yet.

I do not believe that every person able to pass the entrance exam is entitled to an education at the college or university of his choice. Just because your son is smart enough to be accepted into Harvard, for example, does not mean he is automatically entitled to attend. There is this little matter of being able to afford it. To say otherwise would be as ludicrous as saying that because he is a good driver he's entitled to a drive a Ferrari.

I believe that student debt has the potential to be so destructive to a person's life, it should be avoided at all costs. There, I've said it. Now perhaps I can calm down.

STUDENT LOANS: SECURED OR UNSECURED DEBT?

Few of my colleagues share my position on this matter of student loans and the resultant debt. Many hold the position that student debt is secured by one's future ability to earn a better living. Therefore, it is not unsecured debt. Others simply acquiesce to the student loan system, advising that you borrow all that you can and then find a way to deal with it. I take exception to those positions.

Student debt is simply another form of unsecured debt. It offers no escape route. There is no safety valve that characterizes intelligent borrowing as discussed in chapter 2. With student loans, if things don't work out the way you or your student planned ("I'll get a great job and just pay it all back really fast"), you're stuck. Those loans must be repaid. There will be no mercy.

There was a time—and not that long ago—that I didn't have much of an opinion about student loans, believe it or not. Then I made a trip to Nebraska to speak at a women's conference. Included on my schedule for the weekend was a Friday afternoon session at a local private college to speak to the graduating students about the dangers of consumer debt and strategies to handle their student loans.

The women's conference commenced on Friday morning, and after the first session a young woman came up to me in tears. We found a private corner to talk, and she poured out her heart.

I learned that she graduated from the college to which I would be going later in the day. As a freshman, her plan was to become an elementary schoolteacher, and as such, she felt perfectly justified in taking out the maximum student loan each semester. She didn't think twice about the future ramifications and assumed she'd pay the loans off easily when she landed a good job. She figured they'd never give her loans she wouldn't be able to repay, so she didn't question the system. She was thankful for the provision.

During the four romantic years (it is a lovely, old campus), she fell in love and upon graduation married her college sweetheart—also a graduate from the same college—with aspirations to become an elementary schoolteacher. Her husband-to-be had nearly the same amount of student debt. Upon saying "I do," her debt and his debt became "our debt."

She became pregnant within a very short time. He applied for teaching positions, but opportunities were not forthcoming. To keep food on the table, he took a job at a local factory as they awaited the birth of their first child, and her plans to become a teacher made their way to the back burner.

By the time she and I met, she was pregnant with their third child, and he was still at the factory. She said he'd long since given up his dreams of teaching in favor of staying at the factory in this tiny Nebraska town, mostly by default. His salary barely covered their basic living expenses even though he worked as much overtime as possible. Even so, his take-home pay, based on minimum wage, put them close to the poverty line.

She told me how her loans had been in forbearance, but payments of $400 a month were now past due—money they absolutely did not have nor could they get. His loans would come due some months hence, and together their payments would be close to $900 a month. She wept as she told me there was no way out. She spoke of the strain this was placing on their marriage and the family. They absolutely could not make the payments. She said they'd even considered filing for bankruptcy until they found all of the loans were not dischargeable—even through bankruptcy. She related that the loan counselor informed her there were only two ways the loans could be forgiven: full payment or death.

I'm sure that during their carefree college days both of these young people didn't flinch as they signed for loan after loan after loan. What they didn't allow for in their planning was that life doesn't always turn out as we plan. Things happen. Babies are born; jobs don't pan out. Had they not been saddled by this heavy load of debt, their options would have been greatly increased. I had little to offer this woman by way of hope. I suggested that since she had a spare room and a large yard, she might consider opening a day care center. Lots of hard work? Yes, but possibly a way she could work very hard to repay the debt in record time. She could be with her children and at the same time earn additional funds to repay the debt. I never heard back from her, but to this day her story weighs heavily on my heart.

That afternoon as I addressed the students, I learned that most of the graduating seniors would be leaving school with heavy loads of debt. Few of them had a clue about the terms of the loan repayments. The attitude was that surely the school wouldn't allow them to get into something they wouldn't be able to handle. Many of these students, I learned, had purposely taken loans for more than they really needed so they could buy computers, cars, and pay for ordinary living expenses so they "would have more time to study." One young man was very open about the fact that he used much of his loan proceeds to pay for an off-campus apartment and to buy a car.

After the session, one young lady—she said she thought she had about $30,000 in loans—lingered to chat. I asked about her plans for the future. She hesitated and then said that since she had a double major in multicultural studies and geography she thought she might like to be a travel agent. My blood ran cold. First, I know that travel agents don't make the kind of money required to service $30,000 in unsecured debt. Second, I couldn't imagine anyone spending four years in college, selecting a fairly sophisticated double major, and then being satisfied with a job that requires no higher education. She told me that she decided to come to this particular college because the campus was so beautiful and she knew she'd make lots of friends.

My advice to her was that she see this debt as a top priority in her life—that she buckle down to a very frugal lifestyle and work at least two jobs with the goal in mind to pay the loans in full within the next three years. I followed that advice with, " . . . and whatever you do, don't get married until it is paid." She blushed a bit and then told me she would be getting married just three weeks hence. Yes, her fiancé was a fellow graduate with about the same amount of student debt.

The director of students drove me back to the conference. With two stories fresh in my mind, I couldn't help asking her just how dependent this college is on the student loan system. Her answer shocked me. She said that 85 to 90 percent of all students (or their parents) take out student loans of some type. A denominational church school, she said that many people in the Midwest send their children to this school as an extension of their spiritual training. It is a way they can support their denomination and know that their kids will be in a wholesome environment.

Clearly this particular private college (it costs about $15,000 a year to attend) depends heavily on student loans— as is the case with most of these types of schools, I fear. Without the government loan programs, their student bodies would disappear. I finished that conference with a very heavy heart.

Since my experience in Nebraska, I've received hundreds of letters on this matter of student loans. One came from a young man who prepared to be a chiropractor. I don't know how many years it entailed, but he finished with $160,000 in student loans. He passed his state exams and entered the field only to find that he absolutely hated it. After some time of personal struggle, he admitted that what he really wanted to do was teach school. He is now teaching junior high school, living like a pauper trying to service that huge debt on a teacher's salary.

Another letter sent my stomach into spasms. This man finished law school with nearly $200,000 of student debt. His plans for practicing law (and quickly repaying the debt, of course) were dashed as he failed the bar exam three times and simply gave up.

Still another letter from a young woman told of her heartbreak. The man of her dreams broke their engagement because he simply could not agree to start out their marriage in the hole. She would be bringing nearly $40,000 of student debt with her, and he simply could not handle that.

I've received countless letters from pastors who cannot pay their student loans on their meager salaries. Their secret struggles are nearly more than they can bear. Other letters come from singles, and even some couples, who feel the call of God to be missionaries, but cannot be considered by any mission board because of the huge student loans to which they are obligated.

I could fill hundreds of pages with these kinds of heartbreaking stories rooted in student loans. I do not doubt the fact that for every problematic letter I receive there are countless others for whom student loans have worked out just fine. Unfortunately, I don't hear from those folks. Even so, I have concluded that because life is so uncertain and we cannot foresee the future— nor should we presume upon it. Student loans to pay for education are at the least very risky and at the most terribly ill-advised.

ALTERNATIVES TO STUDENT DEBT

Lest you conclude I am opposed to higher education, let me assure you I am not! While not every person is college material—some are more suited to the job force or to learning a skill at a trade school—I firmly believe that every young person should be encouraged and given the opportunity to seek some type of higher education.

As firmly as I am opposed to student loans, I am convinced it is possible to get an education without going into debt. It takes a lot of work, planning, and even sacrifice, but it can be done. And if an education is important enough to you and your student, you will find a way to do it.

WHO PAYS?

Clearly, parents are required to care and provide for their children for the first eighteen years of life. I am not convinced that includes a college education. Of course this is an individual decision, but let me suggest that that which comes without cost is not often appreciated. I believe that when a young person is required to get involved with the cost of his or her education, it becomes more meaningful and precious.

I had dinner one evening with the dean of women of a prestigious Midwest private university. She told me how easy it is to figure out which students are getting a free ride from their parents and which ones are participating personally in raising the money. The students who are paying some or all of their own way become upset when a professor cancels a class (one such student figured out the hourly rate he was paying for tuition and demanded a prorated refund for canceled classes— and got it), while those who habitually skip classes are there on a free ride. Those students who are contributing to the cost of education are more diligent to study, while the slackers are usually those whose parents are footing the entire cost. It was Elbert Hubbard who said, "You can lead a boy to college, but you cannot make him to think."

I am not suggesting that parents should not help with education costs. I am certain there are situations when paying the entire bill is perfectly warranted. Surely not all situations are the same, but I challenge you to consider that handing anyone an education on a silver platter might not be the best way to go. Tell your kids from an early age that they will have to contribute part of the cost of college—even if that means just the day-to-day living expenses or the costs of transportation and travel. After all, it's the student who's benefiting here. Why shouldn't he or she shoulder at least some—if not more—of the cost?

REALISTIC WAYS TO PAY AS YOU GO

Community colleges. There are fine two-year community or junior colleges in every area of the country. Even if your student is looking for a four-year degree, all of the lower-division prerequisite courses can be taken at the community college level. Then transfer to the college or university of choice for the third and fourth year. Just be sure the classes will earn credits that are transferrable.

State colleges and universities. Many state schools offer an excellent education for a fraction of the cost of a private school provided the student meets the residency requirements. When our oldest son went to a state college, we were astonished to find tuition and all related costs were far less than tuition alone at the private high school from which he graduated.

Living at home. While I agree that the social aspect of college has its benefits, it is not worth going into debt to pay for room and board in a dormitory or all the related costs of renting an apartment.

Sitting out a year or two. As a parent, I understand the fear that if a student doesn't go straight to college after high school he may never make it. I suggest that an equal fear is that he does go to college; however, because he hasn't a clue what he wants to do and therefore lacks direction or motivation, the effort will be completely wasted. Many times, a year or two of dealing with the real world convinces a young person from the inside out that getting an education as the path to a better job is highly desirable. A motivated high-school graduate willing to live frugally at home could in the matter of two years save a tremendous amount of money for college.

Starting when they're babies. Parents choosing to pay for their children's college degrees should start saving when the kids are babies. That is the most painless way to pay for an expensive education. Save regularly and select the investment vehicle for these funds based on the age of the future collegian. Up to age twelve, you can afford to be very aggressive with your college fund. Faithfully put your money away, month after month—good times and bad—into stock mutual funds. Reinvest the dividends and don't worry. Once your child reaches age twelve, leave your mutual fund account alone, but begin depositing your new savings into safer vehicles such as

U.S. Savings Bonds, long-term Certificates of Deposit, and other Treasury securities. As the college years approach, begin transferring the money in the stock mutual funds into the safer havens. Now is the time to make sure the money is safe. You won't have the time necessary to continue reasonably investing this money in the stock market because you will not have recovery time if the market takes a plunge. If those babies don't end up going to college, the funds can be easily transferred into retirement accounts.

Some states now have programs that allow parents to pay for their children's college educations while the kids are still young, thereby providing a hedge against rising costs. Good idea? Perhaps, but be particularly careful before you jump on it. The biggest question: Are the funds fully refundable? Life is uncertain, and should your child decide not to attend college or something else happens in the next eighteen or so years that would preclude him attending school in the state you now call home, you want to make sure you can get that money back, with interest. My advice is, if you have the money, invest it wisely yourself. (If you have at least ten years, you can afford to put it at greater risk to gain maximum growth.) Then when the time for college comes, your options will be plentiful as opposed to what you'll have if you fund the education costs early.

Paying for college with money saved and invested is definitely the cheapest way to go because a great deal of the money you finally send to the college will be made up of interest, dividends, and capital gains. But you have to start early to get those benefits.

Current income. Spending current income—either the parents', the student's, or a combination of both—is a more costly way to go. This will definitely require a change in lifestyle and considerable sacrifice. But when you're finished, you're really finished. That sheepskin will be paid for in full. Achieving that goal is definitely worth the sacrifices required.

Working for the school. Many private colleges give an excellent discount to the children of college employees. There are lots of jobs on a big campus other than teaching positions. Check it out. You never know what you might find out. One school I know of offers free tuition to the family members of school employees.

Pastors and missionaries. Many church-affiliated colleges and universities offer significant discounts to the children of pastors and missionaries. If you fall into one of those categories (or feel a change of profession coming on), make inquiries.

Grants. A grant is a flat-out gift. It is free money, and there is no requirement to repay. The most common is the Pell Grant, money from the federal government to assist low-income undergraduates. But don't get too excited. The amount of grant will be small, at best, and will be determined by the family income. It could be as little as $200 or as much as $2,500. If the student is a "displaced homemaker" (a woman who has left the workplace to rear children and is single as a result of either divorce or death and requires training to return to the workplace) or a "dislocated worker" (anyone fired or laid off due to downsizing or a self-employed person whose business failed because of a turn in the economy), that grant applicant will receive preferential treatment. The Supplemental Educational Opportunity Grant (SEOG) is available for very low-income undergraduate students and ranges from $200 to $4,000 per year. Many states have grant programs for students who go to state colleges or universities. Many colleges have their own grants available based on need.

Work-study programs. A federal program, work-study, provides on-campus jobs for students. The college administers the jobs and supervises the workers. Once the student is granted an award, he must work until that award is earned. There is no requirement to pay the money back even if the student does not graduate.

Corporate benefit. Many large corporations have an education reimbursement program for employees who qualify. This can be an excellent way for a student to get a great deal of their college costs paid for. Those seeking graduate degrees might consider a job change to a corporation with such a program before enrolling in graduate school.

Military. For those young people wishing to serve in the military, an excellent education could be a decided benefit. The military will put you through medical school, for instance, if you enter as an officer and agree to stay for a period of time upon completing your residency.

Senior citizens. Many states have college programs for seniors. In Ohio, for example, any senior citizen can go to a state college or university for no cost. The only requirement is that there be an opening in the class once all paying students have registered. Classes can be taken for full credit or audited for no credit. Ohio's seniors have the opportunity to take a single class now and then or earn a degree—even a master's and doctorate. To find out if your state has any such program, call your state's department of education and ask about programs for seniors.

No-need scholarships. There are jillions of scholarships available that are not based on need but rather on ability or one's ethnic heritage—many of which go unawarded every year. You can find exhaustive lists in the reference section of your library. An organization that's been around for 20 years, the National Scholarship Research Service, will assist you in finding scholarships for which you or your student might qualify. You can go to their website—www.800headstart.com—and conduct your own search for no fee, or for $185 they will do all the work for you, keep you informed on a quarterly basis, and even submit your student's information to foundations and organizations for consideration. You can contact them at 707-546-6777, NSRS 5577 Skylane Boulevard, Suite 6A, Santa Rosa, California 95403.

APPLYING FOR FINANCIAL AID

Financial aid is a term the educational system uses to refer to grants, loans, work-study, and scholarships. Even if you desire to pay cash rather than accepting loans, you might want to go through the financial aid process to learn if your student might be eligible for grants or other aid. You need to apply for financial aid at least one year in advance. I suggest that you take a couple of aspirin before getting started.

The first step is to get a financial aid form from the college (or high school guidance office). It is called the Free Application for Federal Student Aid (FAFSA).

Fill it in and mail it. Be warned: it can be a grueling process, made somewhat less painful because now you can apply online at http://www.ed.gov/finaid.html. The processing center will analyze your financial capability to determine what you can afford to pay.

Even if you feel your student is an independent adult who is on his own and responsible for his own education, the government may not, unless he'll be twenty-four by December 31 of the year the aid will be granted. If not, the family income will be considered to determine if there is sufficient need for financial aid regardless of your protests to the contrary.

Your student's high school guidance counselor will be able
to assist you with starting the financial-aid and work-study
balls rolling. Much of your research can be done on the
Internet as well. Learn the address of an amazing website:
www.fastweb.com. I know it sounds impossible, but provided
your student will part with a bit of personal information, you
can search more than four hundred thousand sources of
money for college at this site. You will also find links to other
important information, such as calculators that will help you
figure out the true cost of what's ahead. It is amazing what the
Internet has done to get information into the right hands. Even
if your teens are still in high school, it is never too soon to
begin learning all you can about this multifaceted subject of
funding a college education. You and your student want to
avoid as many surprises as possible.

A friend, Carol Anne, had a rude awakening while going
through this financial aid process when her daughter enrolled
at a large private university. She went through the long and
arduous process only to be informed that her daughter was eligible for aid for all but $5,000 of her first year's costs. Her
daughter, a brilliant and highly motivated journalism student,
decided to go after every possible scholarship to make up the
$5,000 gap. Sure enough, she was selected as the national
champion for a journalism scholarship to the college of her
choice in the amount of—you guessed it—$5,000. How
shocked they were to be informed by the college that her
financial aid would be reduced dollar for dollar by any scholarship she won on the outside. The college said it wasn't their
fault. They are required to adhere to federal regulations that
require all sources of income be taken into consideration. They
saw the scholarship as a new source of income.

IF YOU MUST TAKE A LOAN

Knowing that all situations are not ideal, I concede that there may be times when there is no way to avoid some kind of student loan funding. Believe me, that is not an admission I enjoy making, but I find it sadly realistic. If you as the parents, or your student, end up going into debt to fund a college education, do it as intelligently as possible.

First, take the very minimum amount you can possibly get away with. Do not accept more than you need so you can:

- invest the excess (this one always amazes me)
- buy a computer (use the ones in the library)
- buy a car (can you say "public transportation"?)
- live off campus (dormitory living is an education in itself)
- do anything else that is not absolutely necessary and will be paid directly to the school (like spring break at Daytona Beach)

Know at all times exactly how much you have borrowed, the interest rate, the exact terms, and when the payments will commence. Start repaying at the first moment possible and pay more than is required. Don't push the limit, consolidate, or rewrite the loans extending the period of time. Never default.

A WORD OF ADVICE FOR COLLEGE STUDENTS

Your college years will definitely be among the best of your life. Make the most of your very expensive education. Don't select a major because it sounds fun or so you can be in classes with your best friend. If you don't know what you want to do with your life, get some counseling. You may need to sit out for a few semesters until you do find out.

Beware of offers for credit cards for students. You will be amazed to find the major credit card companies setting up shop right on your campus. They are going to come after you with a vengeance. They will make you feel mature and responsible; they will offer you huge lines of credit, and they won't require that you have a job or even require your parent to cosign. You will be tempted, believe me—you'll be tempted to accept one or two. They'll try to convince you that you need a credit card just in case of emergency. It will be difficult to say no, but I want to encourage you to do that.

If you accept a credit card with a big line of credit, I can guarantee you will have lots of emergencies. They'll come in the form of pizza and airline tickets, clothes and social events. Before you know it, you will have a huge debt, and then you'll be in big trouble. If you don't have the money to pay for the things you want, do not go into debt to get them. What makes you think you'll have the money next month when the bill arrives? Instead, show a little discipline and maturity: save first and spend later.

The time will come when you will need to get one good, all-purpose credit card. I suggest that time will be in your junior year. By then you'll be a little older and more experienced. You will need to get one credit card at that time to begin establishing credit. Use it responsibly. Never roll the balance from one month to the next and never pay interest or fees.

Any kind of unsecured debt is a negative thing—whether it's credit card debt or student loans. Never think of getting a loan as free money, as beating the system or getting away with something. You won't get away with anything, and just thinking that will set you up for a life riddled by debt.

Your college years are the perfect time to practice frugality—another way of saying "living beneath your means." You don't have a family and young children depending on you. You have a lot of freedom to make your own decisions. It's a great time to practice making the right choices.

Never spend all that you have. No matter how little you have, save something for later. Learn to be content with what you have. Look for ways not to spend money—don't be obnoxious about it, just wise and conservative. The standards you set for yourself during these wonderful years will become the foundation for the rest of your life. When you graduate owing no one, your options will multiply. You'll be free to get a job, serve as a short-term missionary, travel, go on to graduate school, and on and on. The possibilities are endless, and the world will be your oyster.

If, on the other hand, you graduate with huge credit card debt and a mega-student-loan package for which payments will become due (and sooner than you think), you will feel weighed down and defeated. You'll have no choice but to take the first job you can find. The carefree college years of fun and freedom will quickly fade as you face the daily grind of living from paycheck to paycheck in bondage to your creditors.

An education is a privilege, not a right. You are not entitled to attend the college of your choice. It is a privilege you must earn and something you should never take for granted. Because you will have made a huge investment in yourself, your degree will become something that you value highly—not something that your parents made you do.

## Chapter Twenty-Two

Building Wealth on an Ordinary Income

BASICS OF RESPONSIBLE INVESTING

A faithfully kept program of savings and conservative investments can give you more money and a better life than that of your neighbors who spend everything they get. This is probably the oldest financial advice in the world, but there are some things you can't improve on.

Jane Bryant Quinn

Funny isn't it how the very word *investment* has the ability to turn otherwise intelligent people into quivering masses of intimidation? Perhaps you've experienced this phenomenon yourself. I know I have. For that, I believe, we can thank the investment industry. It has gone to great lengths to create an impression that investing is difficult and not something mere amateurs like us should attempt. Investment professionals want us to think they are operating for our own good to protect us from something that could harm us greatly. More than that, investment professionals are all but obsessed with making forecasts. They insist that unless you can time the market (predict when values will rise and fall so you can buy low and sell high) you have no business making investment decisions.

The truth is, nobody knows for sure what's coming next year, next month, next week, or even tomorrow. Nobody. Market forecasts are not only confusing—they can be contradicting, misleading, and potentially expensive to those who allow outsiders to make their investment decisions based on them.

I do not profess to be an investment counselor or adviser. I am not formally trained in the matter of high finance, nor do I hold any Wall Street type certifications. I do possess, however, a basic understanding of investing and the knowledge necessary to develop and manage our personal investment portfolio. I take a very conservative approach to investing and stay away from risky situations. I'm the quintessential buy-and-hold kind of investor. I take the simple route and count on the value of time to build our wealth.

What I know about investing I learned from reading excellent books by those who teach the fundamentals of investing, but mostly from the book *Sound Mind Investing*[1] by Austin Pryor. Even if you are not yet ready to begin building your investment portfolio, I recommend you read that book—just as soon as you finish this one—so you will have your plan in place and be ready to go when the time comes.

Two Kinds of Investors

If investing were a black-and-white issue, investors could be divided into two categories: reactive and proactive. Reactive investors do exactly as their name implies: Their investment decisions are reactions. They do not initiate their moves but rather react to what happens. They wake up in the morning unsure what their next move should be because they've not yet read the financial page or logged on to their favorite stock quote website. They make their investment decisions in reaction to what happens in the news or what their hungry broker recommends that particular day. Reactive investors don't have a specific plan or strategy in place. Reactive investors flunk the pillow test: They have a difficult time sleeping for all their worries about what the market is doing today or might do tomorrow. They are plagued by fear that they might make the wrong move, miss a forecast, or fail to time the market.

Proactive investors in the extreme have a specific plan—an investment road map. They invest according to sound principles and specific investment strategy. They don't pay attention to what the market is doing from day to day. When it comes to the pillow test—it's lights out the minute the head hits the pillow.

Is one approach to investing right and the other wrong? No. But for the beginning investor with limited experience, knowledge, and money to invest, the conservative proactive offers a level of safety and simplicity that makes it possible for even the novice to step into the investing arena. As you gain experience and confidence, you will develop your individual investment style.

A friend of mine, for example, is a very conscientious investor who uses elements from both styles of investing to her decided advantage. She diligently follows the activities of about thirty different stocks she believes could fit into her portfolio under the right conditions. Some of them she owns; others she'd like to own when they reach a price she is willing to pay. She's a bargain hunter and as such is blending her proactive style of investing with calculated and well-reasoned reactions. While her road map might be completely different from mine, that doesn't make one approach more right than the other. Still, my friend didn't start out at this level. Through years of learning, patience, researching, and building a respectable portfolio, she has developed her individual investing style. She knows how much risk she's willing to take and where to go for specific advice.

This chapter is for beginning investors with limited money who lack knowledge and experience but desire to step confidently into the investing arena. You can begin investing with as little as $25. To become a proactive investor you need to:

1. Learn what you need to know about investing to get started. Don't wait until you know everything there is to know or you'll never get started.

2. Build a strategy on how you will invest your surplus funds.

3. Understand your tolerance for risk based on your temperament and personality type and then invest only within your comfort zone.

WHAT INVESTING IS AND WHAT IT'S NOT

Investing is not magic or mystery. It is the deliberate act of putting money to work in a commercial endeavor with an expectation of reasonable gain and with the full understanding that there exists no investment that is without some level of risk.

Speculation is exposing money to high levels of risk with the expectation of a large return in a short period of time. Speculation should be left to highly experienced professionals.

Gambling is not investing at all, but rather putting money at unreasonable risk in an effort to profit from the outcome of a game of chance.

Day-trading, a recent phenomenon, is tantamount to gambling within the stock market. Day-trading is the act of buying and selling stocks for a profit in the same day with no overnight holds. The risks are so high that the chances of winning are miniscule. Day-trading is highly inadvisable.

TYPES OF INVESTMENTS

There are only two ways you can invest money. You can become either an *owner* or a *lender.*

When you invest by *owning,* your intention is that the investment you own will increase in value so that you can at some point sell it for more than you paid for it, realizing a profit. Investments where you own something generally have a higher risk level and also a higher expectation of return. Real estate, stocks, art, and antiques are examples of investing by owning.

When you invest by *lending,* your money experiences a gain in the form of interest paid to you by the individual; corporation; insurance company; or local, state, or federal government that borrowed it from you. When you lend money, your risk is less than when you become an owner, but so is your reward. Investments where you loan historically return less than owned investments. The risks are twofold: the borrower is unable to repay the loan and you lose your principal, or you get locked into a low rate of interest in an economy where interest rates are rising. Savings accounts, Certificates of Deposit, commercial paper, bonds, Treasury bills, notes and bonds, cash-value life insurance, and fixed annuities are examples of investing by lending.

WHEN TO BEGIN INVESTING?

In the same way you need to be physically fit before embarking on a physically challenging activity, you need to be financially fit before you begin investing your surplus funds. Financial fitness means you're prepared for emergencies and you are debt free. Ultimately, *fit* means your mortgage is paid in full as well. If you are living paycheck to paycheck, carrying unsecured debt, and are not adequately prepared for emergencies and unexpected expenses with a Contingency Fund and a Freedom Account, you need to direct every dime of surplus to getting those things in place.

Every investment has some level of risk—there is a chance you will lose all or part of the money you have invested. It is not advisable to put any of your money at risk until you have reached financial fitness.

Let's say you owe $5,000 on a credit card account and you have a surplus of $100 a month. If you put that $100 at risk in an investment, you could lose it but you would still owe $5,000. If, however, you apply the surplus to the debt, you will owe $4,900 regardless of what happens in the stock or real estate markets. It makes sense to invest your money in your debts! Austin Pryor, in his book *Sound Mind Investing,* says, "No investment is as secure as a repaid debt."[2]

Once you have all these things in place—Contingency Fund, Freedom Account, and you are completely debt free— you will have a pile of money to invest each month—your 10-percent savings as well as the money you'll redirect from debt payments into investment. Now, as your investments ebb and flow in value, you won't be financially devastated because you are in a strong financial position.

THINGS TO KNOW BEFORE YOU BEGIN

DIVERSIFICATION

Diversification is the result of not having all of your eggs in one basket. As you assemble and grow your portfolio, you will want to concentrate on two things: high safety and low risk. You want your invested money to be as safe as possible while exposed to manageable risk. Diversification is the way to achieve both without sacrificing your rate of return.

It would be foolish to have all of your investments in the stock of a single corporation. For example, if that company gets into serious trouble, you could lose everything in one mighty blow.

Nor would you want to have all of your investments in a single type of investment. Understand that the stock and bond markets are cyclical. When one is up and prosperous, the other might be flat and lackluster. The most conservative approach to investing says you should have a good mix of investments in your portfolio. Then if one section of your portfolio goes through a downturn, not all of your portfolio will suffer.

The mix of investments you determine is right for your portfolio should be in harmony with your personality type (some people are risk takers while others are naturally more cautious) and season of life. The younger you are, the greater amount of risk you can tolerate; you have time to ride out downturns plus the time to recover. As you approach the second half of life, however, and you are more likely to depend on your investments to cover your cost of living, you will want to move into lower-risk, safer positions.

LONG-TERM INVESTING

Conservative investors look at the long-term rather than the in-and-out-quickly approach to investing. In this philosophy is found safety and minimal risk.

If you were to view a snapshot of the stock market in this country since its inception more than sixty years ago, you would see that even with all the ups and down, any consecutive ten-year segment of that graph shows overall growth. My point is that if you are invested in the stock market and are committed to leaving your money there for a period of time (ten years is good; five years is minimal), you are more likely to experience growth than if you are in and out, reacting to the ups and downs. Generally speaking, as a conservative investor, your approach should be to buy and hold.

Dollar-Cost Averaging

One systematic strategy for long-term investing is called dollar-cost averaging. This requires investing the same amount of money in the same investment at regular time intervals. This approach automatically accomplishes the goal of the wise investor: buy more shares when prices are low and fewer shares when prices are high.

Let's say my strategy requires that I buy $100 worth of stock in the DPL Corporation each month. This month on the day that my purchase is recorded, the per share price is $5, so I add 20 shares to my portfolio. However, next month the price jumps to $7. Now my $100 will buy 14.28 shares—fewer than last month when the price was down. The stock takes a plunge the following month and drops to $4 a share. The price is down, so my $100 buys 25 shares. Over the three months, I invested $300 and purchased 59.28 shares for an average of $5.06 per share. With dollar-cost averaging, I'm happy no matter the state of the market: when the prices are low, I can buy more shares; when the prices are high, I'm making more money. That's a good investment attitude.

Dollar-cost averaging is an excellent way gradually to invest a large sum of money. The reason I like the dollar-cost averaging strategy is that it's a no-brainer. It's practical. It's neither complicated nor time-consuming.

Automatic Purchase Authorization

Automatic purchase authorization plus dollar-cost averaging makes for a winning combination. Many types of investments will allow you to sign up for this kind of automatic purchasing. You fill out the appropriate paperwork authorizing the mutual fund company or corporation in which you are buying shares of stock to withdraw automatically from your checking account on a specific date each month. Now what was a no-brainer (dollar-cost averaging) becomes even simpler. You can truly forget about it and allow your wealth to grow. Of course, you'll want to make sure the automatic withdrawal is covered by sufficient funds in your checking account. I do predict, however, that by the time you reach this place in your debt-proof living journey, bouncing checks will cease to be a problem.

SOME INVESTMENT OPTIONS

BONDS

Bonds are relatively low-risk, high-security, heavy-duty IOUs that offer low returns and little in the way of excitement—the perfect choice for the very cautious investor. Because bonds score high in the reliability department, they can bring stability and strength to an investment portfolio. When you invest in a bond, you know up front what your return will be because the interest rate is stated. Bonds have varying maturity dates. Some might be for three years, ten years—even thirty years. While it might be nice to know for sure that you will receive a set rate of interest for a long time, remember that the chance of that interest rate being woefully under market during the life of the bond is a risk to be considered. The major risk in bond investing is if the bond issuer (the borrower) is not credit worthy and defaults while you are still holding that bond. Losing your principal in this way is the worst-case scenario. The way to neutralize this risk is to buy only highly rated bonds issued by credit-worthy entities and to limit your activity to terms of no longer than three years.

Bonds can be sold prior to maturity in the secondary market. However, if you're locked into a long term at a below-market interest rate, you will likely have to discount the face value in order to find a buyer.

STOCKS

When you purchase shares of stock, you become a part owner of a corporation. As the value of the company increases, so does the par value of the shares. Many companies sell their stock only through stockbrokers; however, more and more companies have gone to direct purchase and reinvestment programs, also called DRIPs. The benefit, of course, is that there are no commissions to be paid when you purchase directly, although most companies charge a small handling fee. Many of the popular personal finance magazines like *Money* and *Kiplinger's Personal Finance* list the names and phone numbers of companies with DRIP programs. These companies are also eager to assist you with automatic monthly purchases.

A great resource for more information on DRIP investments is the Direct Stock Purchase Plan Clearinghouse. This is a toll-free service that provides a one-stop source of enrollment information on a growing number of direct stock purchase plans. This service is free to investors. Call 800-774-4117 for more information.

MUTUAL FUNDS

Wouldn't it be great if we could stop worrying about understanding every little detail and nuance of investing and just hire a professional to take care of it for us? We could write the guy a check every month and forget it. Let him take care of it.

Of course we'd need to find someone we could trust to invest our money in the kinds of companies we like. And it wouldn't hurt if he was educated, reputable, and had enough smarts to make a few excellent investment recommendations now and then.

If this investment manager was really top-notch, he'd spend all of his time working just for us—doing all those Wall-Street-like things investment professionals do.

Naturally, we wouldn't actually want to pay the guy, but I don't think we'd have a problem chipping in for his expenses. Basically we'd want 100 percent of the money we gave him to go straight into the purchase of stocks or bonds—no commissions! And let's not forget the paperwork. We'd want to make sure he did all the paperwork and just sent us a simple report once or twice a year.

Who are we trying to kid? We'd be dreaming if we ever found that kind of situation. Or would we?

What we just dreamed up is a very loose description of a segment of the investment industry that has exploded in recent decades: mutual funds.

A mutual fund is all the money thousands of small investors put together to form a big pool of money that gives the fund as a whole much greater buying power and financial advantages than a small investor would have on his own.

The money in the pool is managed by a hired professional and regulated by the Securities Exchange Commission (SEC). When a mutual fund is first formed, it establishes ground rules that limit the types of investments and protect the investors. Some mutual funds invest in stocks; others, in bonds and any variety or combinations determined by the goals and objectives established by that particular fund.

Advantages of Mutual Funds

Austin Pryor, who is quite a mutual-fund enthusiast, says mutual funds offer twenty major advantages for beginning investors:

1. Mutual funds can reduce the anxiety of investing. It's like trusting a master mechanic to fix your car rather than attempting to do it yourself.

2. Mutual fund shares can be purchased in small amounts that make it easy to get started. Most funds have minimum requirements to open an account which run from $500 to $3,000; however, many funds eliminate the minimum requirements when you agree to make regular monthly deposits to build your account.

3. Many funds will set up an automatic deposit for you. Painless investing.

4. Mutual funds reduce risk through diversification. The typical mutual fund holds as many as two hundred stocks in its portfolio.

5. Mutual funds' price movements are more predictable than those of individual stocks.

6. A mutual fund's past performance is a matter of public record. Most funds post their daily activities in the newspaper the same way stock prices are reported. You can check on how they've faired in the past.

7. Mutual funds provide full-time professional management.

8. Mutual funds allow you to reinvest your dividends efficiently (distribution of profits to shareholders). You can instruct the fund to reinvest your profits automatically so your account will grow even faster.

9. Mutual funds offer automatic withdrawal plans. Pre-planned selling enables the fund to mail you a check for a specified amount at a frequency you specify.

10. Mutual funds provide individual attention. In a mutual fund, the smallest member of the pool gets exactly the same attention as the largest because everybody is in it together.

11. Mutual funds can be used for your Individual Retirement Account (IRAs) and other retirement plans.

12. Mutual funds allow you to sell part or all of your shares at any time and get your money quickly. All of this can be done by phone in a quick and efficient manner.

13. Mutual funds enable you to reduce instantly the risk in your portfolio with just a phone call. You can switch funds.

14. Mutual funds pay minimum commissions when buying and selling for the pool. Individuals get socked with huge commissions.

15. Mutual funds provide a safe place for your investment money. But remember, every investment carries some level of risk.

16. Mutual funds handle your paperwork for you. You get simple reports in the mail.

17. Mutual funds can be borrowed against in case of an emergency. I hope you won't, but the value of your mutual fund holdings can be used as collateral for a loan.

18. Mutual funds involve no personal liability beyond the investment risk in the portfolio.

19. Mutual fund advisory services are available that can greatly ease the research burden. You can check your fund's ratings on the Internet by clicking on "stock quote" on any search engine.

20. Mutual funds are heavily regulated by the Securities Exchange Commission (SEC) and have operated largely scandal free for decades.[3]

Prospectus

A prospectus is a legal document that outlines a mutual fund's objectives, policies, performance, per share data, performance history, a summary of the fund's expenses, and how to buy or redeem one's shares. Typically, an application to open an account is enclosed in the prospectus. Anyone can request a prospectus by calling that mutual fund company's toll-free customer service number. The prospectus will be sent to you in the mail. Most mutual fund companies now have websites where you can request a prospectus as well.

Opening a mutual fund account is similar to opening a bank account. You must give your Social Security number, name, address, and the name of a beneficiary and send it in with a check to establish the account. This application also carries instructions for establishing an automatic purchase program.

CREATING YOUR SPECIFIC INVESTING STRATEGY

It is at this point on the subject of investing that I must defer and refer. I am simply not qualified to advise you on the specifics of the investment portfolio you need to create. What I can tell you again is that everything I know about this topic I learned from my favorite book on the subject, *Sound Mind Investing* by Austin Pryor. I have followed the specifics of his "Just-the-Basics Strategy" because it is simple, understandable, and simple to administrate.

In his book, Pryor provides specific fund recommendations, telephone numbers to get started, plus investing models that I can follow simply and easily—models that address my husband's and my personalities and particular season in life. With great confidence I refer you to Austin Pryor's excellent book as you prepare for the exciting world of investing.

FINANCIAL PLANNERS

While not discounting the fact that I believe you should be able to develop and manage your own investment portfolio, let me say that the time may come when you need to seek more advanced advice from the services of a professional financial planner.

According to the College for Financial Planning, "Financial planning is a process in which coordinated, comprehensive strategies are developed and implemented for the achievement of financial goals."[4] A financial planner is not a stockbroker, money manager, or insurance agent with a single focus, but rather a professional with training and experience to address all aspects of your financial life and provide professional guidance as you develop a coordinated plan. While you may doubt it at this point, let me assure you that if you follow the principles outlined in this book, the day will come (and sooner than you think) when you may need a more sophisticated level of financial advice. That does not mean you've abandoned your resolve to be a proactive investor, throwing all caution to the wind, but that you've moved to a more sophisticated level and are wise enough to acknowledge your areas of weakness.

If at that point in your journey you decide to hire the services of a financial counselor, I suggest you find a fee-only planner. The reason is simple: A commission-based planner will earn a commission on every product that he advises you to purchase and/or sell. That is, in my opinion, a conflict of interest. It is only human nature to direct one's clients to the products and services that will best compensate one's own bank account. Your best interests will not be the commissioned planner's top priority.

A fee-only planner, on the other hand, will charge a flat hourly or session fee that you will agree to ahead of time. The compensation will be the same whether you follow the advice, buy everything that is recommended, or change your mind altogether. Now you can be reasonably confident that this planner's recommendations will be in *your* best interest because the conflict has been removed.

The best way to find reliable services is to get a referral from a friend or relative. If you are unable to find a fee-only financial planner in whom you have confidence, contact the National Association of Personal Financial Advisors, 1-888-FEE-ONLY, or visit their website, www.napfa.org, where you can find planners who practice in your area.

When it comes to the matters of investing and financial planning, never forget who is in charge: you. Don't allow or depend on others to make your financial decisions. Seek outside advice but never outside authority.

⌒

---

1. Austin Pryor, *Sound Mind Investing* (Chicago: Moody, 1996).
2. Ibid, 33.
3. Ibid, 88–93.
4. Don Hardt, "Should You Use a Financial Planner?" *Sound Mind Investing Newsletter* (Louisville, Ky.: Kentucky Financial Group, 1996).

## Chapter Twenty-Three

Moving into the Second Half of Life

PREPARING FOR RETIREMENT

It's darling and challenging to be young and poor, but never to be old and poor. Whatever resources of good health, character and fortitude you bring to retirement, remember, also, to bring money.

Jane Bryant Quinn

If I could use only one word to describe what debt-proof living is all about, it would be *options*. Of all the things you bring to the second half of life, none will be more important than options—the choice to quit working, keep on working, change careers, take up some serious leisure, travel the world, invest your life in your grandchildren, and serve others. These are some of the options you will have as you head into the second half of life, provided you've arrived free from debt, mortgage paid, Contingency Fund in place, and with a strong investment portfolio working for you day and night.

The wonderful news is that, unlike your grandparents and perhaps even your parents, you don't have to retire if you don't want to. Thankfully the days are gone when to retire meant you were all washed up and your days as a useful, productive citizen were over. The notion of a mandate to quit at age 65 is terribly outdated and, in my opinion, horribly misguided.

Stephen M. Pollan, in his thought-provoking book *Die Broke,* says:

> Giving up the pursuit of retirement has a great many practical and psychological advantages. But it also has an added spiritual bonus: By eliminating the finish line, life stops being a race. With all of us on our own path, there's no way your progress can be compared to anyone else's. No one—not your parents, your friends or *Money* magazine—can look at your life and say you're not as far along as you should be. More important, you can stop measuring yourself against an arbitrary standard and feeling inadequate for not meeting the grade. You're on your own unique self-chartered journey. Where it ends only God knows, so until then all you can do is keep rowing.[1]

The Social Security Act became law in 1935. Citizens who reached the ripe old age of 65 were eligible to collect retirement benefits, meager as they were. Back then, the average American died at age 63, so living long enough to collect was something of considerable note.

Nearly 70 years later, and thanks to medical breakthroughs and healthy living, the average American now lives to be 75, an average that is anticipated to reach 81 by the year 2040. Somehow the idea of quitting at the tender age of 65 no longer seems reasonable or practical the way it might have in 1935 when if you reached 65 you knew your life was about over.

Personally, I wouldn't mind if the concept of retirement as conceived in 1935 was itself retired (a shelf in the Museum of

American History would be nice) and the invisible line between age 64 and 65 was forever erased. In its place I believe we should expect a seamless transition into another chapter of life rather than seeing retirement as the epilogue.

Clearly there is no set age for retirement. So, whether you plan to hang it up on your sixty-fifth birthday or continue working until your dying day, one thing is clear: you want the choice. It's one thing to choose to continue to work into your sunset years and quite another to have no choice in the matter.

REASONS NOT TO QUIT AT AGE 65

Age 65 is not old. I am more convinced of this fact with each successive birthday. When 65 was selected as the age to receive retirement benefits, it was way out there. In 1935, work meant backbreaking, physically taxing labor. Bodies wore out sooner. For the typical worker, quitting was not a choice but a physical requirement. Thanks to modern technology, most work today is not so physically challenging. Age 65 is simply getting younger and younger.

Meaningful work is more fulfilling than leisure. There's a lot to be said for leisure, but for the able-bodied, healthy adult, it can get boring. How many rounds of golf can you play in a week anyway? How many hours a day—day after day after day—can you garden, ski, or lie on the deck? Leisure, like a rich dessert, is a wonderful commodity—but in measured portions. The physically able need also to participate in meaningful work that produces personal satisfaction.

Activity staves off the negative effects of aging. While the phrase has been overused perhaps, still it carries a lot of truth: use it or lose it. Minds as well as bodies wear out more quickly when they are not in use. Antiaging experts agree: You need to learn something new every day to keep your mind alert and sharp. You need to be physically active to keep your body in tip-top shape. If you are in good health, you will have the option to be highly productive well into your eighties and beyond.

Recently I had the distinct pleasure of meeting Mrs. Ruth Peale, age 92, wife of the late Dr. Norman Vincent Peale. This encounter did not take place in a nursing home. Mrs. Peale hosted a large dinner at a convention to which I was invited. With great energy and poise she greeted, mingled, and addressed the crowd. Now if that wasn't amazing enough, I learned from the gentleman sitting next to me that this remarkable woman runs a large corporation, goes to the office and puts in a full day every day, travels extensively throughout the world on business and pleasure, and keeps a pace that would exhaust most people thirty years her junior. I am certain that quitting has never entered her mind.

Mature workers make excellent employees. Speaking as an employer, I am convinced that the mature worker brings value to the workplace unequaled by younger, less-experienced coworkers. A senior citizen is in a different stage of life, so there are fewer outside pressures. The mature worker has a wealth of knowledge and wisdom, is less prone to be absent, makes fewer mistakes, and is overall more reliable. The employer benefits greatly by hiring the mature worker, and the employee benefits too. Doing something constructive every day fulfills that inherent need to be needed.

It doesn't make economic sense. Realistically, more and more people simply are not prepared financially to quit working at age 65. Many have loaded themselves with so much debt that they've simply not socked away the kind of money they will need to support themselves for twenty years or more without earned income. Thankfully, at the young age of 65 they have many opportunities to make up for lost time.

SOCIAL SECURITY

Many people believe the Social Security system as we know it will be long gone by the time they are eligible to collect. Perhaps you find yourself in that group. By all indications, even if the system remains intact, it will provide little financial security. It is difficult, if not impossible, for individuals these days to exist on Social Security benefits alone, so just imagine how great the disparity will become between the cost of living, say, ten years from now and a meager Social Security check— if the system makes it. The safest attitude when it comes to Social Security is: Don't count on it!

If you assume you can spend everything you earn during your younger and most productive years because Social Security will be there to take care of you when you can no longer work, forget it. Even if the system remains at its present level, the typical monthly benefit will not be enough to live on. Social Security benefits that you might receive should be thought of as only a supplement, and a small one at that.

So should you just forget about Social Security altogether? No. It's money you've been required by law to contribute, so you need to be the best steward possible.

Here's how it works. Social Security is based on a system of credits, or "quarters," you earn while you're working. To receive retirement benefits, you need to accumulate forty credits if you were born after 1928 (and fewer if you were born before that). In 1998, you earned one credit for each $700 you made. But you can earn only four credits a year, no matter how much you make. For example, a college student who earns $2,800 waiting tables during the summer accumulates four credits—but so does a mortgage broker who earns one hundred times that amount. The minimum dollar amount per

credit is increased every year to reflect changes in the cost of
living, just as the maximum income on which you pay Social
Security taxes is. But once you hit forty credits, you're set.
Working longer may mean your benefit is larger, but you don't
need more credits.

If you have ever been employed (either as an employee or
self-employed), you can be reasonably sure you've paid into
the system. That means you have an account—you and hundreds of millions of others just like you. The chances of there
being an error in your account are high. Just a slip of a digit
or a transposition in a Social Security number could have your
earnings deposited to another's account. It is imperative that
you become your own watchdog.

Let me give you an example. During my high school and
college years, I worked for the Northern Pacific Railway
Company. Railroad employees, like schoolteachers, don't pay
into the Social Security system, but rather into a retirement
fund specifically designed for railway workers. Later, after I
was married, I worked for the U.S. Air Force as a civil service
employee. Guess what? Federal employees don't pay into
Social Security either. That means for at least seven years of
my work life, I was not paying into the Social Security system.

Over the years that followed, I worked here and there,
sometimes as an employee—but mostly as an independent
contractor with self-employed status. I paid Social Security
taxes at the self-employed rate, which is considerably higher
than what I would have paid as an employee.

Several years ago, as I began learning about the importance of managing my own Social Security account, I requested
an earnings statement (more on that to follow) that listed by
year every dollar I had contributed to my Social Security
account. I was in for a huge shock. Up to that time, as far as

the administration was concerned, I had not worked or earned enough credits to be eligible for any kind of benefit. Ever. The report went on to project that at the rate I was going by age 65 I would be eligible for zero benefits. Nothing, nada, zip, zilch. The problem? I simply had not made sufficient contributions even though I paid Social Security taxes on every dollar I earned as a self-employed individual.

When I left my railway and civil service positions, I had the option either to convert my retirement to Social Security or take it out in a lump sum. You can guess which choice I made, and it wasn't a very good one since I spent the money rather than investing it. So I had no credit in my account for all those years of employment.

By the time I got the report, I'd been self-employed for many years, first in real estate and then as a newsletter publisher and author. Year after year as we filed our joint tax return, everything we paid into Social Security was credited to my husband's account because his was the first Social Security number to appear on the return. He had far more than the maximum credits, and future contributions would do him absolutely no good, while I was getting no credit.

If we'd not become aware of this situation, it is likely we would have continued filing the same way every year—right through to age 65. Imagine the shock of reaching benefit age and then learning I'd paid tens—perhaps hundreds—of thousands of dollars into the system but was not entitled to a single penny in benefits because of a simple oversight in the way we filed our taxes. Of course, we switched our Social Security numbers on our subsequent returns, and now I'm more than sufficiently vested in the system for whatever that might be worth someday.

I've heard other horror stories of people checking their accounts only to find a good deal of their earnings have never made it to their account. It happens all the time. Unfortunately, you do not have an unlimited period of time to uncover errors—nor can you hold the system accountable for those errors. When dealing with the government, the burden of proof falls on the individual's shoulders.

CHECKING YOUR ACCOUNT

Now that you are sufficiently worried about your situation, let me tell you how you can become your own auditor.

First, request form SSA-7004—Request for Personal Earnings and Benefit Estimate Statement (PEBES). You can do this online at www.ssa.gov, or call 800-772-1213 anytime, including weekends and holidays. You should receive the statement in four to six weeks. Go over it with a fine-tooth comb. If you discover a discrepancy, report it immediately as outlined on the statement. You will need documentation such as W-2 forms, tax returns, and pay stubs to substantiate correct information and to prove your claim. In addition to incorrect financial information, report any misspellings in your name or errors in your address. Then after sufficient time has passed, request another statement to verify that the corrections have been made as promised. Remember, billions of pieces of information are input every year by fallible humans. Mistakes happen.

I suggest that even if nothing is amiss, like your credit report, you should review your Social Security records at least once a year. If you are not currently employed you should request the form as outlined above. But if you are actively employed, you will automatically receive a Social Security statement about three months before your birthday. You will receive a four-page statement designed to help you with financial planning by providing estimates of your retirement, disability, and survivors' benefits. The statement will also provide you with an easy way to determine whether these earnings are accurately posted on your Social Security records. Keep them from year to year so you have a good paper trail. It will help you spot any problems easily. Each adult member of your household should perform this audit annually whether employed at the time or not. It's your money, your responsibility.

STAY INFORMED

To say that the way the Social Security system works is horribly complicated is to make a gross understatement. Unfortunately, that is not a good reason to avoid dealing with it. You need to learn all you can.

A place to start is the administration's website (www.ssa.gov). It is quite extensive and a place you can begin your quest to learn its restrictions and benefits. Most questions that you might have are answered on the site somewhere. As a word of caution, I find the site biased toward a system that is, shall we say, terribly flawed. Take in the information and then make your own judgments.

As you approach age 65, you'll need to make significant decisions regarding Social Security, and you'll need good information to make those decisions intelligently. For instance, as the system stands right now, if you are eligible, you can begin drawing reduced benefits at age 62. Is that better than waiting until 65 to claim the maximum to which you are entitled? That will depend on your overall situation at the time. You may need the counsel of your tax preparer, accountant, or attorney.

During the years between age 65 and 70, citizens who draw benefits are severely penalized if they have earned income over a certain threshold. If you are earning income, it may not be in your best interest to draw benefits until you've reached age 70.

Just as sure as night follows day, the rules of the game will change. There is pending legislation at this writing that if passed could change considerably the future of Social Security. There's talk of changing the benefit age from 65 to 67 or older. No matter the changes, you need to be informed. Make it your business to know what's going on in your account as well as in the system. As a bonus, you will become an informed voter.

SEAMLESS TRANSITION TO RETIREMENT

The debt-proof living plan not only creates more options and freedom during your younger years; it also creates options galore for retirement. If you head into the second half of your life with a strong Contingency Fund, are totally debt free (meaning even your mortgage is paid in full), and you have a well-rounded investment portfolio, you will have so many options you won't know what to do with all of them. You will transition seamlessly from one life chapter into the next without severe adjustments.

Ideally your income requirement will drop because your fixed expenses will be significantly lower than they were during your career-establishing, equity-building, child-rearing years. Now the fun begins.

You'll have the option to stay with a long-term career or leave that field to pursue something you've only dreamed of doing with your life. Go back to school; take up a hobby that has always piqued your interest; spend a month or two on a mission trip; try something brand new that will shock your system and sharpen your senses.

The debt-proof living plan you've read about in this book is the ideal preparation for this new season of life. The discipline and hard work will pay off handsomely. Here are a few guidelines:

Project your expenses. This should be nothing new—it's what you will have been doing for some time. Your Spending Plan will take on a new look as many of your expenses drop and insurance needs shift. You may decide to eliminate some categories of spending altogether in favor of new ones more tailored to your lifestyle.

Anticipate your income. This will be a combination of any private pension plans, Social Security benefits, income from your investments, and earned income. You will need to consult with your accountant or tax preparer for specific guidance on converting investments to spendable cash.

Be mortgage free. Your goal is to make sure your mortgage is paid in full by this time. With a fully paid mortgage you give yourself the best option of all: rent-free living for the rest of your life. Your sense of security will soar knowing that no one will be able to take your home from you.

Keep building your Contingency Fund. Now more than ever you need a liquid reserve. As your income decreases (either by full retirement or by shifting gears into a lower paying or part-time job), it is very important that your Contingency Fund grow so that it contains enough money to pay all of your living expenses for at least six months. You will have to determine what that amount is, but if it is more than the $10,000 you've been holding, take immediate steps to grow it to the proper level.

Maximize retirement accounts. Rather than slowing down your retirement account contributions (401[k]s, IRAs, Keoghs, SEPs, and so on) as you approach retirement, you should contribute the maximum allowed if at all possible. You will build wealth and at the same time realize incredible tax advantages while sheltering income. Shift your investments from high-risk to low-risk funds and securities.

Rethink life insurance. Now is the time to reassess your need for life insurance. Remember, life insurance is not for you—it's for those you will leave behind. If no one is dependent on your income and you have sufficient liquid reserves to cover your burial and funeral expenses, you may not need life insurance at all. If your spouse is dependent but you have sufficient assets to meet her (or his) needs upon your death, you still may not need life insurance. If you have a child or dependent that will never be able to take care of him- or herself financially, you should consider a new popular life insurance product—second-to-die life insurance. This type of policy covers two individual's lives for the price of one. It pays a benefit only after both have died. In the case of the needy dependent, he or she would become the beneficiary only after both parents have passed on. In determining how much second-to-die coverage you would need, don't ask the insurance professional ready to sell you the policy. Instead, look to a health professional who is familiar with the dependent's special needs to determine how much will be required to supplement government and community care that might be available for that dependent's lifetime.

Beef up disability insurance. While you may not need to insure your life at this stage of the game, you should take a hard look at insuring your income. Disability insurance will become increasingly necessary as you are statistically more likely to become disabled. Take a hard look at your current coverage, and increase it as you feel appropriate.

Concentrate on health insurance. You're going to want the best health insurance you can afford. If you qualify for Medicare benefits, you will get Part A but will need a supplemental policy or "gap" insurance for Part B. As with Social Security, Medicare is utterly confusing. If you are employed, you may opt for the health coverage offered there. If you retire at age 65, you have the option to keep your employer's plan in lieu of Part B coverage. You will need to apply for Medicaid seven months before turning 65. Even if you are not retiring in the traditional sense of the word, you can still apply for Medicare as your primary health insurance. You can find specific information about Medicare at www.ssa.gov. Call AARP (American Association of Retired Persons) at 800-424-3410 and ask them to send you everything they have on Medicare and Medigap. A valuable book on the topic is *Medicare Made Easy* by Charles B. Inlander (People's Medical Society, 1999).

Long-term-care insurance. If you think Social Security and Medicare are confusing subjects, you haven't met this new animal called long-term-care insurance. Basically it's supposed to cover the high cost of living in a nursing home and home health care—items not typically covered by health insurance or Medicare. Even the industry offering these types of policies is confused. And beware of scam artists peddling long-term-care insurance and taking advantage of the confusion and fear surrounding the topic. Remember, a policy is only as good as the company standing behind it when it comes time to pay a claim.

My suggestion is that if you are not yet 65, pass on this kind of coverage. Yes, the premiums are lower the younger you are, but the risks involved don't warrant the potential liabilities. If you are over 65, consider a good policy, but deal only with a very highly rated insurance company. (A. M. Best is a reputable service that rates insurers. You can call 908-439-2200 for more information on how to get automated ratings for each of the insurers you are considering; or log on to www.insure.com.) Get a policy with a long waiting period, one that covers both nursing home and home health care, and one that has inflation protection with coverage limited to one year. Inflation protection ensures that your dollars will buy the same type and amount of care when you put in a claim as they did when you signed the deal, regardless of how the actual costs of care have risen in the interim. It should be a policy you can afford (long-term-care insurance can be very expensive). As this insurance becomes more sought after, the industry will begin regulating itself, and the scam artists that are so prevalent will be flushed out. Hopefully.

A WORD OF ENCOURAGEMENT FOR THE LATE-BLOOMERS

Even if you feel you've done everything wrong and there's no hope to achieve the kind of options you'll need to retire, take heart. Remember, with knowledge comes power. You have enough information in this book to turbocharge your efforts. Take drastic steps now to get your financial house in order. You will be amazed at the progress you can make when your commitment is steadfast and your faith secure.

It's only too late if you don't start now!

⌒

---

1. Stephen M. Pollan, *Die Broke* (New York: Harper Business, 1998), 59–60.

Chapter Twenty-Four

Making This Work
TAKING THOSE FIRST DIFFICULT STEPS

Financial security may still be a long way off,
but as you begin to take control of your financial future,
you'll find that many rewards accompany the
sacrifices along the way.

Jonathan Pond

When everything is said and done, here's the best advice I can offer as you contemplate debt-proof living: Use your common sense.

Take all the information you've read in the preceding twenty-three chapters and plant it in your mind. Ponder it, nurture it, and then trust yourself to make the right moves. Effective personal money management is not difficult. You can make your own decisions—even the difficult ones.

If you don't know exactly what to do to get started, I can help. Get a pen and small notebook. Write today's date on the first page and write down exactly how you spend your money today. Nothing complicated—just what and where. Tomorrow, turn the page and start over with tomorrow's date. Write everything down—the big things, the small things, even the embarrassing things. If you are in any kind of a financial fog, this is going to help clear it.

Every day as you track your spending, something amazing is going to happen—you will start paying attention. You won't be able to keep yourself from focusing on where your money is going. Continue writing everything down for at least thirty days as you contemplate the first half of this book.

During this time, get your head on straight regarding the need to bring balance to your finances. Begin by giving away some part of everything you receive (see chap. 3). Do it thoughtfully, joyfully, and with all the gratitude your heart can muster. Also, find a place to start saving part of everything you receive. Make plans; do some research. Find out where you can open an account for your savings. Make it a top priority in your life.

Next, develop your spending plan (back to chap. 3 again). Just do it! There's no wrong or right way. As long as you are processing your money according to a specific plan you have created, you will begin to move toward success—one step at a time, day after day after day. At first it will feel awkward—you'll think this planning ahead stuff is way too confining. But soon the shackles that bind you will begin to loosen. As you gain control, you'll also experience a new kind of freedom. Managing your money well will become a wonderful new habit in your life.

As you continue to give and save consistently, you'll begin to see your savings develop into your ever-growing Contingency Fund (see chap. 6). Now you're on your way. Take the next step and face your debts head-on. Get to work on your Rapid Debt-Repayment Plan and your Freedom Account.

I know that all of this may seem overwhelming. It is. But you can do it. Don't let those feelings sabotage what you know you must do.

Please know that I am always available to read your letters and messages. I cannot promise I'll always respond, but I do read everything that comes to me by mail or E-mail. It should help you a lot to know you are not alone. There are thousands of us working toward the same goal. We support each other and offer a sense of community.

If you remember only one thing from what you've read, I hope it will be this: Money is not for spending. It is for managing first and then for spending.

Exercise your directing skills well. Persist. You will be richer in the end.

Afterword

It is only right that I disclose my personal debts of gratitude, which are considerable. I've incurred so many over the past years, I'm not sure I'll be able to repay all of them.

First, my heartfelt thanks to the untold numbers of gracious readers who have shared their hearts and their lives with me. You have sent me in search of answers, and by doing that, I've grown, exceeding my perceived limitations.

Cathy Hollenbeck, my manager and friend: Thank you for keeping my office and professional life together against tremendous odds and for holding back the world so I could check myself into book jail to get the work done.

Mary Ann Woirhaye: You've taught me the worth of a friend. Thank you for pushing, prodding, encouraging, praying—and laughing at me when I tell you, "This is it . . . my last book, ever!!"

Vicki Crumpton, Janis Whipple, and Kim Overcash, my editorial team extraordinaire: Thank you for your uncommon patience and gentle ways. I treasure your friendship.

Paul Mikos, Jennifer Willingham, Kenny Holcomb, Mary Beth Trask, David Woodard, Heather Hulse, Robin Patterson, and Gabe Wicks, my marketing and publicity teams: You take such good care of me.

Cheapskate Monthly staff: By taking care of all the technical stuff, you free my life considerably. You have no idea how much I depend on you.

Jeremy and Josh, my sons: You color my life and motivate me to live it well.

Harold, my husband: Thank you for keeping everything balanced (and I don't mean just the checkbook). Our boat would have capsized long ago had it not been for your steady ways, constant support, and unconditional love.

You, my dear reader: Thank you for giving me the reason to write this book . . . and the next one too. Perhaps Mary Ann is right after all.

Glossary of Terms

401(k) savings plan: An employee-provided, salary-deferral plan approved by the Internal Revenue Service that allows qualified persons to save and invest pretax dollars.

acquisition fee: The fee the automobile leasing company charges the customer to acquire the vehicle and set up the lease. Also called the "initiation fee." Sometimes this fee is negotiable. Typical charge: $450.

adjustable-rate loan: Also called variable-rate loan. The interest rate fluctuates, adjusting periodically to the moves of a key rate, such as the prime rate or one-year Treasury bills.

affinity card: A credit card marketed to a group of customers with a common bond, such as membership in an organization.

allocation: The way in which your savings are divided among the different accounts you have selected.

annual fee: The annual charge, from $20 to $400, paid by a credit cardholder to the credit card company for the privilege of owning that particular credit card. Many credit cards do not charge an annual fee. The annual fee is billed directly to the customer's monthly statement.

annual percentage rate: The true cost of borrowing money, expressed as a percentage. Includes interest and fees on some loans such as an auto loan. The interest rate on a mortgage or home equity loan does not include fees however. Also called APR.

appreciating asset: An asset that has a reasonable expectation of increasing in value with time.

appreciation: An increase in value.

appropriate: To set aside funds for a specific use.

APR: See annual percentage rate.

asset: Anything of value that you own.

ATM card: A plastic card that gives the owner access to the automated teller machine when used with one's personal identification number (PIN). An ATM card often doubles as a debit card.

attitude: A way of thinking or behaving.

austerity: A severely simple lifestyle.

automatic deposit: A deposit that is made from one's account or paycheck into an investment or other account every month or at specific intervals directed by account holder. Authorization is made by the employee or account holder and can be retracted or amended at any time. A painless way to get into the habit of saving or investing regularly.

automated teller machine: A convenient way to deposit and withdraw money from your savings or checking account any time of the day or night. Often thought of by children as a place in a wall from which Mommy and Daddy get as much money as they want.

automobile loan: A loan from a bank, credit union, or finance company to purchase an automobile.

balance transfer fee: Fee charged customers for transferring an outstanding balance from one card to another.

bankruptcy: A legal declaration of insolvency. The bankruptcy law contains several types of bankruptcy. Chapter 7 is full discharge of all of one's debts except for student loans and obligations to the IRS. Chapter 11 and Chapter 13 denote reorganization repayment plan set up and administered by the courts.

belief: A feeling of certainty about the meaning of something.

biweekly mortgage: Another form of prepayment. Fine in theory, though often a scam in practice. If you make mortgage payments every two weeks—or the equivalent of thirteen payments a year, rather than twelve—you can reduce the term of a thirty-year mortgage by eight to twelve years. Middlemen who set up such programs at great expense don't always forward payments as promised. You can do your own biweekly equivalent.

biweekly schedule: A method by which a person pays one-half of a monthly payment every two weeks. The net result is twenty-six half-payments each year or the equivalent of thirteen monthly payments. A fairly painless way to pay more than is required and thus reduce the time and fees associated with the indebtedness.

budget: A formula for adjusting expenditures to income.

buying power: Worth determined by how much it will buy. For instance, the buying power of a dollar today is much greater than it will be fifty years from now when we'll be lucky if a dollar is worth a nickel.

canceled checks: Checks that have been paid by the bank as directed by the checking account holder. Canceled checks are sometimes returned to the customer for record keeping, although these days many banks and credit unions retain copies but do not return the actual canceled checks.

cap reduction: Any down payment and/or trade-in that reduces the final cap cost (total amount leased). An increase in this figure should reduce your monthly payment and cut your financing costs.

capitalized cost: The price of the car in a lease deal. This is what the leasing company is paying the dealer to purchase the car so they can turn around and lease it. This cost should be negotiable. The lower this figure is, the lower your payments will be.

card-hopping: The act of transferring your credit card balances to a low-interest card for just the introductory period, then transferring again to another card for its introductory period. Card-hopping can be very detrimental to one's credit report.

cash advance fee: Charge by the bank to the customer using credit cards for cash advances. This fee can be stated in terms of a flat per-transaction fee or a percentage of the amount of the cash advance. For example, the fee may be expressed as 2 percent/$10. This means the cash advance fee will be the greater of 2 percent of the cash advance amount or $10. Banks may limit the amount that can be charged to a specific dollar amount. Depending on the bank issuing the card, the cash advance fee may be deducted directly from the cash advance at the time the money is received or it may be posted to your bill as of the day you received the advance.

cash advance: A very expensive loan taken against a credit card's credit limit.

cash flow: Generally referred to in terms of the money that flows into your possession. If you spend more than you bring in, you have a negative cash flow. Your goal is always to maintain a positive cash flow, where more comes in than goes out.

Certificate of Deposit: An interest-bearing receipt from a bank guaranteeing that upon deposit of a specific amount of money, at a specific point in time, a guaranteed amount of interest will be paid to the bearer along with the original deposit. CDs are available in a variety of denominations and for varying time periods. The longer you agree to leave your money on deposit, the greater the interest rate you will earn.

cheapskates: Those who give generously, save regularly, and never spend more money than they have.

closed-end lease: In this type of automobile lease, the leasing company assumes all risk in the event the vehicle drops in value due to excess depreciation. Customer can just walk away at end of lease. This is the preferred approach of automobile leasing.

cobranded card: A credit card that is issued through a partnership between a bank and another company or organization. For instance, a large department store may co-brand a card with a bank. The card would have both the bank name and the store name on it. Some co-branded cards are also rebate cards that provide the consumer with benefits such as extra service, cash, or merchandise every time the card is used. Also called an affinity card.

coinsurance: Your share of any doctor or hospital bill.

collateral: An asset owned by the borrower that is pledged and held by the lender pending the borrower's faithful repayment of the debt. Something of value such as real estate, stocks, bonds, or other assets offered as security to encourage a lender to make a loan.

commercial paper: Short-term IOUs of large U. S. corporations.

compounding interest: The concept that money makes money, and the money money makes, makes more money. When interest is allowed to remain in the account rather than being paid out, it becomes principal. Now interest is earned on the interest. Compounding interest is what allows investments and savings to grow so well.

consumer credit industry: That segment of the business world that extends credit to consumers on an unsecured basis.

consumer debt: Unsecured loans offered to consumers to buy goods and services.

contentment: Wanting what you have.

Contingency Fund: A pool of money that is readily available within forty-eight hours, held as a hedge against emergencies such as health and safety issues or the loss of one's income.

corporate downsizing: The process by which a corporation pulls in its belt by drastically reducing overhead and expenses. Corporate downsizing is often the catalyst for massive layoffs.

credit card: A small piece of plastic that has the ability to make its bearer do strange things he or she probably wouldn't dream of doing with cash.

credit inquiry: A notation on one's credit report that indicates the person gave a company permission to look into their credit file.

credit insurance: Insurance that pays off all or part of a loan if the borrower dies or becomes disabled or unemployed.

credit report: A report filed by subject's name, birth date, and Social Security number that gives an accounting of that person's credit activities and payment history. This report will help a new lender determine the credit worthiness of the applicant. Many prospective landlords and employers look at a person's credit report to get a true picture of the applicant's character. Major companies providing these credit report services include, Experian (formerly TRW), Trans Union, and Equifax.

credit scoring: A point system lenders and credit bureaus use to assess your credit worthiness. Almost invariably computerized these days.

credit union: A nonprofit financial institution formed for the benefit of its members. Since there are no stockholders, profits are partially paid back to the members in the form of dividends. Offers checking accounts, savings accounts, and makes loans. Generally better interest rates, lower fees, and personal service. Must qualify to join. Not open to the public.

cyberspace: The world accessible via the Internet.

daily spending record: A simple list of where you spent your money today. Should include every single expenditure, even the small ones.

day-trading: A form of investing that involves buying and selling stocks for a profit in the same day with no overnight holds. The chances of losing money are very high.

debit card: A plastic card that gives you electronic access to your checking account. Often doubles as an ATM card.

debt: Something that is owed.

debt trap: That place one finds himself in when overcome by too much debt. A place of bondage.

debt, intelligent: That to which the borrower is obligated in a loan transaction secured by collateral that can be repaid anytime.

debt-proof living formula: Give away 10 percent, save 10 percent, and live on 80 percent.

debt, secured: A loan that is collateralized.

debt, stupid: A debt that is not secured, has no collateral attached to it, and can be incurred with your signature alone.

deductible (auto): The amount of each claim the insured agrees to pay first before the insurance company begins to pay.

deductible (health): With health insurance the deductible is the portion of the medical bill that you pay out of pocket each year, before the insurance coverage kicks in.

dejunk: The act of getting rid of all the clutter in your home, office, and life.

depreciate: To lose value simply because of the passing of time.

depreciation: A loss in value or efficiency resulting from usage and or age; difference between cap cost (the original price of the vehicle) and residual value (the market value of the vehicle at the end of the lease period).

deprivation: The act of withholding.

discontentment: Not being happy with what you have.

discretionary income: That which is left after all the bills are paid; money available for nonessentials.

dislocated worker: Anyone fired or laid off due to downsizing or a self-employed person whose business failed because of a turn in the economy.

displaced homemaker: A woman who has left the workplace to rear children, is single as a result of either divorce or death, and requires training to return to the workplace.

disposition fee: The amount of money charged to the lessee at the end of a lease when turning in the vehicle. Negotiate this before signing the lease. Only agree to pay an acquisition fee or a disposition fee, not both. Typical charge: $200 to $400.

diversification: The practice of spreading investments among a number of different investments to reduce risk. It's the opposite of "putting all your eggs in one basket." A mutual fund is an example of diversification because it invests in many different securities.

dividend: A sum of money to be distributed to stockholders.

dollar-cost averaging: Investing the same amount of money in the same investment at regular time intervals.

down payment: The upfront money required to enter into a loan.

DPLs: People actively engaged in debt-proofing their lives.

durable goods: Things that have a life expectancy exceeding three years.

early termination penalty: The price you'll pay to end your lease early. Ask what this is in advance. It could be thousands of dollars. While you may not think this is important at the commencement of the lease when you love this vehicle, it could become very important if you find you've made a mistake or for any other reason decide you cannot complete your obligation.

entitled: Feeling that is the result of having an available balance on one's credit card account.

equity: The value remaining in excess of liabilities or loans.

excess mileage charge: Additional charge at end of an automobile lease for exceeding the mileage limit. Usually 15 to 25 cents per mile. Watch out for low-mileage leases where miles are limited to say ten thousand per year. This charge can cost thousands of dollars and come as a very big surprise at the end of the lease.

f (fixed): If the letter *f* appears after the annual percentage rate (APR), the interest rate is fixed and not subject to adjustment.

falling payments: Payments that fall in direct proportion to the outstanding balance, such as minimum monthly payments on credit card accounts, as opposed to mortgage payments that remain fixed regardless of the current outstanding balance.

family heritage documents: Those records that include birth, death, military, retirement, adoption, divorce, and financial data, kept in a safe place.

federal tax withholding: Money withheld by one's employer and sent to the IRS in anticipation of payment of federal income taxes and Social Security taxes.

federally insured: Money deposited into a bank or savings and loan that is covered by insurance. In the event the financial institution becomes insolvent, the insurance will reimburse the depositor.

fees-for-cash-advances: Money charged in addition to interest for taking money against one's credit card line of credit.

financial bondage: That uncomfortable situation where one owes so much money to so many creditors he feels like a slave.

financial calculator: A calculator that figures payment schedules and debt payoff periods.

financial freedom: The state or condition of being free from financial pressures brought on when one lives from paycheck to paycheck and under the bondage of heavy debts.

financial security: That point in time when you can live the lifestyle you have chosen, financed from the assets you have accumulated, without the need for additional income.

fiscal year: A company's accounting year, often from July 1 through June 30, as opposed to a calendar year.

for-profit corporations: A corporation that has stockholders and the expectation of making a profit, which is then paid to said stockholders.

Freedom Account: A separate checking account into which you deposit monthly 1/12 of your known irregular expenses.

frugality: That which is necessary to keep your expenses less than your income.

gambling: Putting money at unreasonable risk in an effort to profit from the outcome of a game of chance.

gap insurance: An automobile insurance policy that covers or fills in the gap or difference between balance owed on lease and normal insurance coverage. If you are in an accident and total your leased car, you want to make sure the insurance will pay off whatever remains on the lease. Needed in case of theft or total loss due to accident. Unless you have gap insurance, you will have to pay the difference. If you lease, insist that this coverage be included.

grace period: The period of time the customer is allowed to pay the monthly bill before an issuer begins to accrue interest. Issuers determine grace period based on different stages in the transaction. A grace period can begin based on one of the following: transaction—the actual date you used your card for a purchase or a cash advance; posted—the actual day the issuer received the charge and posted it to your account; billing—the date that your bill is generated for mailing to you.

HEL: Acronym for home equity loan.

hoarding: Saving to an extreme and to the detriment of your joy and ability to do good in the world.

home equity loan: A loan secured by the equity in your home. Also called a second mortgage.

home mortgage: A loan from a bank or other lender that is secured by the value of the home.

income: The money that flows into your life.

index: A published, market-based figure used by lenders to establish a lending rate. Examples of the most common indices are: the One-Year Treasury Constant Maturity Yield, the Federal Home Loan Bank (FHLB) 11th District Cost of Funds, and Prime Rate as it appears in the *Wall Street Journal.*

indexed rate: The sum of the published index plus the margin. Example: if the index is 9 percent and the margin 2.75 percent, the indexed rate is 11.75 percent.

individual retirement account (IRA): A personal savings account specifically designated for your retirement. Anyone who has earned income may contribute up to $2,000 dollars a year to an IRA. The money placed into an IRA may be tax deductible depending on your income and participation in other retirement plans. Even if it is not, all money in your IRA account grows on a tax-deferred basis—taxed only when you begin withdrawing funds.

insurance premiums: Payment for insurance coverage.

intelligent borrowing: Borrowing only when the loan is secured and the proceeds go to buy something that will appreciate.

interest: A fee the borrower pays to the lender for the temporary use of the lender's money.

interest-bearing account: A savings or checking account that earns interest for the account holder.

introductory rate: Also called the "teaser rate," this is the rate charged by a lender for an initial period, often used to attract new card holders. This rate is charged for a short time only and is used to entice borrowers to accept the card terms. After the introductory period is over, the rate charged increases to the indexed rate or the stated interest rate.

investing: The deliberate act of putting money to work in a commercial endeavor with an expectation of a reasonable gain and with the full understanding there exists no investment that is without some level of risk.

investment portfolio: The entire collection of one's investments. A portfolio should represent lots of different types of investments, including stocks, bonds, mutual funds, real estate, security, and cash. A well-diversified portfolio is one that offers the greatest security.

IRA: Individual Retirement Account. A tax shelter into which to place investments. IRAs can contain a wide variety of investments of your choosing. Working persons who qualify—they are not participating in a retirement plan at work and they qualify income-wise—can put away up to $2,000 a year for retirement and deduct it from their federal income tax return.

irregular expenses: Any expenses that do not recur on a monthly basis.

late fee: Charge to customer whose monthly payment has not been received as of the due date or stated deadline for payment as shown on the billing statement. This fee can be stated in terms of a flat per-transaction fee or a percentage of the amount of the cash advance. The fee may be expressed as follows: 3 percent/$25. This means that the late fee you will be charged will be the greater of either 3 percent of the amount of the balance or $25. Late fees are a serious indication of the borrower's lack of financial integrity and show up on one's credit report for future lenders or others assessing one's character to see.

lease rate: Monthly rate charged by automobile leasing company, similar to interest rate. Includes both interest and profit. Lease rate = [final cap cost + residual] x money factor.

leasing: Renting for a specific number of years. Leasing carries a legal obligation on both the part of the lessor (owner) and lessee (renter).

liability: A financial obligation.

lien: A legal right to claim or dispose of property in payment of or as security for a debt.

line of credit: A preapproved loan where you can draw down as much or as little of the line as you want and pay interest only on the amount you actually use. A credit card limit represents a line of credit as does a home equity line of credit where the loan is secured by the equity in the home. If the borrower defaults, the lender can foreclose on the property.

liquid cash: Money that is available right now in spendable cash. An investment in stock is not liquid. It would have to be sold to convert it to cash.

liquidating: Turning assets into cash.

liquidity: The ability of an asset to be turned into cash. Your checking account is very liquid because you can draw out the cash at any time. U.S. Savings Bonds are somewhat liquid, but it takes about three weeks to receive the cash once liquidated. The equity in your home is less liquid because of the time necessary to go through the sale and actually receive cash. Great Uncle Fred's stamp collection would have a low degree of liquidity.

living beneath your means: Spending less than you earn.

long-term investment: An investment you intend to hold for a minimum of five years.

loss-leader: An item priced below the store's cost that is advertised as a way of baiting customers to come into the store and hopefully dump a load of money on other stuff they cannot resist.

lower-rate cards: Credit cards with amazingly low interest rates. Usually the low rates are limited to the first six months or so until the real rate kicks in.

means: Money or other wealth available to provide one's living.

minimum monthly payment: The least amount a creditor will accept as the monthly payment on your debt. Often the minimum payment represents only the creditor's profit and does not reduce the principal.

money factor: Used to determine automobile lease rate. (This is usually negotiable—it should not be greater than the rate on auto loans readily available at the time of leasing.) Money factor = annual interest rate divided by 24.

money leaks: The ways money leaves your life unnoticed and unaccounted for.

money managers: Caretakers of money.

money market account: A savings account offered by a bank that pays better interest than a passbook savings account. Offers check-writing privileges and is guaranteed by FDIC up to $100,000. Not to be confused with money market funds that are not FDIC insured and issued by mutual fund companies.

money market fund accounts: Specialized funds sponsored by mutual fund organizations that take your money and make very short-term loans to big businesses, the U.S. Treasury, and state/local governments. A way of pooling your money with other small investors and getting a better deal on interest rates. A savings account disguised as a mutual fund. It is not insured against loss the way a money market account in a bank is insured by the FDIC.

monthly interest rate: The annual interest rate divided by twelve. Credit card companies use the monthly interest rate times the average daily balance to determine the monthly interest payment on a credit card account.

monthly spending record: Four week's worth of daily spending records blended into categories to reveal the money leaks and a picture of where your money goes.

MSRP: Manufacturer's suggested retail price on a new automobile. This is almost always negotiable (except on Saturn vehicles).

mutual fund company: Corporation chartered by a particular state that pools the money from shareholders and invests in a portfolio of securities. It is "mutual" because the fund is actually owned by its shareholders who pay a pro rata share of fund operating expenses and receive a pro rata share of income earned and capital gains realized.

net asset value (NAV): The current value of a mutual fund share, stock share, or bond share. The net asset value of any mutual fund, stock, or bond changes daily.

net income: Your take home pay reflecting what's left after taxes and other items are deducted.

net worth: The dollar value of your assets (what you own and what is owed to you) minus your liabilities (your financial obligations).

no-load mutual fund: A mutual fund whose shares are sold without sales charges of any kind. Some no-load funds charge a small fee, usually 1 percent, for investments held less than six months.

nonrecurring expense: Any kind of expense that is a one-time charge. An appraisal fee would be an example of a nonrecurring expense of buying a home.

NSF: An abbreviation for "nonsufficient funds," which means the check bounced. It is illegal knowingly to write a check when there are not sufficient funds in your account equal to the amount of the check.

offers of entitlement: Preapproved or preselected credit card applications or offers.

open-end lease: Lessee (the customer) assumes risk for excess depreciation. The leasing company determines ahead of time what the vehicle will be worth at the close of the lease. If they botch it, the customer has to make good on the difference. That means the lessee (customer) might have to buy the vehicle for more than it's worth or sell at a loss and pay the leasing company the difference. Avoid open-end leases.

overdraft protection: A line of credit attached to one's checking account that kicks in $100 at a time to cover checks written in excess of available funds. High interest rate plus significant fee for accessing funds.

over-mileage penalties: Money charged for going over the predetermined number of miles per year on a leased car.

passbook savings: A regular savings account in a bank or credit union the contents of which used to be recorded in a little book called a passbook.

paycheck-to-paycheck: Spending the entire amount of one's paycheck before the next paycheck is earned.

payoff plan: A specific written plan to pay off debt that lists payments, dates, and the date the plan will be complete.

Pell Grant: A gift from the government for one's college education that is not subject to repayment.

personal finance: One's money in one's personal life as opposed to a business.

points: An up-front fee charged by a lender which, in effect, lowers the nominal interest rate on the loan. A point equals 1 percent of the total loan amount.

portfolio: A collection of investments.

poverty: Living on less money than it takes to survive. Always spoken of as a curse in the Bible.

preexisting condition: A problem that was diagnosed or treated—or was obvious—any time from six months to three years before you bought a health insurance policy.

premium: The annual price you pay for an insurance plan as a whole is called a premium.

prime rate: The interest rate a bank charges to its best or "prime" customers. Each bank will quote a prime lending rate. Many institutions quote prime rates established by large money center commercial banks such as Citibank or Chase Manhattan. There is also a prime rate average listed in the *Wall Street Journal* that is an average of the largest commercial banks. You may see this abbreviated as *Wall Street Journal* published prime.

principal: The amount borrowed separate from interest.

private mortgage insurance (PMI): The insurance homebuyers must maintain until the equity in the property reaches at least 20 percent. This insurance protects only the lender in case the borrower defaults on the loan. Sometimes confused with mortgage insurance, which is similar to life insurance.

prospectus: A legal document that describes the objectives of an investment, such as a mutual fund, including risks, limitations, policies, services, and fees. By law a prospectus must be furnished to all prospective investors.

providential provision: Something that comes into your life as the solution to a difficult problem and appears to have no other source but God himself.

purchasing: Acquiring goods and services with a plan and purpose in mind.

purposeful giver: A person who does research and looks for needs so that his or her giving is directed purposefully and not in a haphazard or flippant way.

quitting points: Events or occurrences in our lives that weaken our resolve never to give up and tempt us to quit.

Rapid Debt-Repayment Plan: Also referred to as RDRP. A simple, powerful plan to repay rapidly your unsecured debts.

rebate cards: Cards that allow the customer to accumulate cash, merchandise, or services based on card usage.

rebate: Something given back. In the case of a grocery product, the rebate is the amount of money sent back to the consumer in exchange for a proof-of-purchase or some other qualifier.

repossess: To take back. Lenders repossess cars or homes they've lent money on when the borrower defaults or refuses to make payments as agreed.

resale value: The value of an asset determined by what it could bring if sold.

residual value: What the car is supposed to be worth at the end of the lease; what the leasing company wants you to pay at the end if you buy the car (this is also negotiable). A higher residual should result in lower payments, but don't buy the car at that price—offer less or walk away.

retirement nest egg: That money exposed to interest and growth during your working years that becomes the security of your retirement years.

revolvers: Credit card customers who roll a balance over from month to month, pay interest faithfully, and never quite have enough money to pay the balance in full in any given month.

revolving debt: Debt that continues from month to month, year to year.

saving: Putting money in a safe place where it is not exposed to the risk of loss and pays only a pittance in interest—not enough to keep up with inflation.

savings bond: An IOU from the U.S. government in exchange for a loan. U.S. Savings Bonds are very safe but pay low rates of interest.

second mortgage: A second loan on a house or other real estate that is second in position to the first mortgage holder. If the homeowner gets into financial trouble and cannot pay, the lender in first position has first right to the property.

secured debt: A debt that is secured or guaranteed by something of value. A mortgage debt and automobile loan are examples of secured debt. If the borrower gets into trouble, the home or the car can be sold to satisfy the obligation. Also called a "safe debt."

Securities Exchange Commission: The governmental department that regulates the securities industry—the stock market, bond market, etc.

security deposit: Money given up front to a landlord or car leasing company as a promise of the lessee's faithful performance of the deal. Typically security deposits are returnable or applied to the final month's rent or lease, provided the lessee has kept up his end of the bargain. Security deposits often instigate strife because the parties have differing opinions on whether the property was returned in the same condition it was received, allowing for normal wear and tear.

selective amnesia: That mental "condition" where you conveniently forget that Christmas is coming; then when you finally remember, it's too late to do anything but shop with the credit card.

SEOG: Supplemental Educational Opportunity Grant; $200 to $4,000 a year available to very low-income undergraduate students.

severance package: The money and other benefits, such as health insurance and so on, offered to an employee terminated against his will.

shopping: The activity of cruising through stores and shops with a credit card, checkbook, or cash but no real purpose in mind except to find great stuff.

signature loan: An unsecured loan that can be obtained with your signature alone.

single-cycle billing: A billing method to determine interest owed on a credit card bill by multiplying the monthly interest rate by the average daily balance of the past thirty days.

slippery places: Slippery places are situations, events, or locations where you could easily trip and fall, financially speaking. That might be the mall where you could easily slip into an old habit of shopping mindlessly and running up a lot of debt before you have time to analyze what's going on.

solvency: Having enough money to pay one's bills, debts, and obligations, with some left over.

speculation: Exposing money to high levels of risk with the expectation of a large return in a short period of time. Speculation should be left to highly experienced professionals.

spending limit: A term credit card companies use for your credit limit to soften the idea of a loan or debt being involved.

spending plan: A written strategy for how you plan to spend your money.

spending record: A detailed, written account of where the money was spent.

statement closing date: The date on which the credit card company cuts off the billing cycle. Purchases made after the statement closing date will show up on the next month's statement.

stupid debt: A debt that is not secured, has no collateral attached to it, and can be incurred with your signature alone.

SuperNOW account: A type of checking account that requires you to maintain a higher minimum balance and in return pays you a higher rate of interest. The minimums are usually set at $2,500. If you have that much cash, you want it in a genuine savings or money market account rather than a low-paying checking account.

surplus: That amount of money over and beyond what is needed to pay all of your expenses.

teaser rate: Something to beware of. Common with adjustable-rate mortgages and some home equity loans, this is a rate that tells you things seem better than they really are. The teaser is almost guaranteed to rise whenever its term expires—and that could be after as little as one month.

term: Length of automobile lease. Don't lease longer than three years, or excess wear-and-tear charges could be expensive.

thrift: The economical management of assets and resources.

transaction fee: A fee charged for the privilege of borrowing money through a cash advance.

Treasury bills: Government issued bonds that have very short-term maturities. Also called T-bills.

two-cycle billing: A billing method to determine interest owed on a credit card bill by multiplying the monthly interest rate by the average daily balance of the past sixty days.

U.S. Treasuries: IOUs issued by the U.S. government in the form of Savings Bonds, T-Bills, T-Notes, and T-Bonds.

unclutter: To simplify your life by getting rid of the clutter and unused stuff.

unemployment benefits: Proceeds of unemployment insurance available to someone who is laid off, but only for a short period of time.

uninsured bills: Those bills not covered by one's health insurance. These might include physical exams, well-baby checkups, and routine dental bills.

unsecured loan: A loan not guaranteed by the pledge of any collateral.

upside down: Owing more money than the collateralized asset is worth. Typically used to refer to a car loan or lease where the car has a fair market value of less than the balance due.

v (variable): If this letter appears after the annual percentage rate (APR), the interest rate is variable and subject to change.

values: Specific types of beliefs that are so important and central to your belief system that they act as life guides.

windfall: An unexpected sum of money in any amount.

work-study programs: A federal program that provides on-campus jobs for students. Money earned from job goes to the payment of tuition and is not subject to repayment.

Index

More great *Debt-Proof Living* products from America's Favorite Cheapskate

Mary Hunt